SECOND EDITION

THEORIES OF HUMAN DEVELOPMENT

SECOND EDITION

THEORIES OF HUMAN DEVELOPMENT

NEIL J. SALKIND
University of Kansas

John Wiley & Sons

New York • Chichester • Brisbane • Toronto • Singapore

Library of Congress Cataloging in Publication Data:

Salkind, Neil J.
    Theories of human development.
    Includes index.
    1. Developmental psychology—Philosophy. I. Title.

BF713.S25 1985   155   84-19680
ISBN 0-471-80575-0

Printed in the United States of America

10

For my father, who, through example, taught me to look to the future.

What a piece of work is man! How noble in reason!
How infinite in faculty! in form, in moving, how
express and admirable! in action how like an angel!
in apprehension how like a god!

—*William Shakespeare*

Preface

There have been several changes made to this edition of *Theories of Human Development*. Perhpas the most important is the inclusion of additional theoretical approaches that are becoming increasingly popular in developmental psychology. The original emphasis on Gesell and maturation has been expanded to include a new chapter on sociobiology and ethology. The section on social learning theory is now more historically complete with the addition of the early work on child rearing done by Robert Sears and his colleagues at Stanford University. Finally, Jerome Bruner's influence on the field of cognitive development is reflected in a description of his information processing approach to understanding cognitive development.

As we understand the developmental process better, we also see how the methods that are used to study development are intricately tied to the substance of the different theories. In this edition, the discussion of each new theorist is accompanied by the section "How They Study Development." These boxes summarize empirical studies that use the methods dictated by the theory under discussion and illustrate what kinds of questions the theorist might ask. These boxes have been very useful as a tool for students who have difficulty making the link between theory and human development in practice.

In the previous edition, summary questions were posed and answered at the end of each major section of the book. This new edition also includes such questions, but they have changed. The first edition focused on the issues of heredity and environment, maturation and learning, age, critical periods, continuity, and structure.

In this edition, the issues are broader and better integrated within the actual text and include the nature of development, the process that guides development, the importance of age, the rate of development, the shape of development, individual differences, and how development is studied.

Two types of suggested readings have been included as pedagogical aides to the student and teacher. The first are "Further Readings" about the specific chapter content. Some of these are references to the original work of a theorist featured in that particular chapter. These readings might also be important empirical studies that are cited in a discussion of one of the theories covered in that chapter.

The second set of readings is called "Other Readings of Interest" and are fiction and nonfiction works that are related to the topics discussed in the chapter. For example, there may be a particularly interesting book or popular periodical piece about the philosophy of science or a novel concerning adolescents and egocentrism. Reading these books and articles makes the material more clear and relevant for students.

A revision like this takes the commitment and efforts of many people besides the author. I thank the following reviewers for their comments: Dr. Bernard S. Gorman, Nassau Community College; Dr. David Brodzinsky, Rutgers University; Dr. Kathleen McCluskey, West Virginia University; Professor Robert Fuqua, Iowa State University; Dr. Paul Roodin, SUNY College at Oswego; Professor Patricia T. Ashton, University of Florida, Gainesville; and Dr. Mary Evans Pharis, University of Texas. Michelle Cleveland suffered through one of our colder Kansas winters to finish typing the revision on time with constant attention to detail. Mark Mochary, psychology editor and Carol Luitjens, publisher at Wiley, provided the support and created a working relationship that other authors would envy. Susan Goodall, editorial assistant, took the initiative to see that important editorial tasks were completed when necessary. Through her efforts and good sense of humor, much of the writing of the revision was made easier than would otherwise be. I thank her for this. I would also like to thank Miriam Seda, senior production supervisor for bringing a sometime difficult manuscript to fruition.

Since the last edition, my three-year-old daughter Sara grew into a vibrant and independent eight year old, and we also now have a son Micah. This book is dedicated to their grandfather, Harry Salkind, who gives them the love they so richly deserve.

I would like to thank Shiela Granda for the design of the book and especially for a cover that reflects the contents of the book.

Neil J. Salkind

Contents

CHAPTER 3
Arnold Gesell and the Maturational Model

CHAPTER 4
Other Biological Approaches: Ethology and Sociobiology

CHAPTER 8
Social Learning Views of Development

CHAPTER 9
The Cognitive–Developmental Approach

CHAPTER 11
A Discussion and Comparison of Developmental Theories

SECOND EDITION

THEORIES OF HUMAN DEVELOPMENT

CHAPTER 1

The Study of Human Development

The universe is full of things patiently waiting for our wits to get sharper.

Eden Phillpots

If I have been able to see farther than others, it was because I stood on the shoulders of giants.

Sir Isaac Newton

Science is built up with facts, as a house is with stones. But a collection of facts is no more a science than a heap of stones a house.

Henri Poincare

WHAT IS DEVELOPMENT?

This is a book about human development and some of the different theories that have been proposed to explain how development happens. If you made a list of all the things that you did in the course of a day and all the things you thought about, and then wrote them down, your list would probably involve thousands of events. Such a list of events, recorded over a period of days or months, would be called a description of your developmental repertoire.

On a grand scale, this repertoire of behavior represents the *developmental process*. This book will continuously ask questions about this process. What different theoretical accounts have been proposed to help us understand how this developmental process happens? Why is our behavior as an adult so different from

1

when we were infants? Does behavior change from newborn infant to preschooler, to middle schooler, or to teenager because of biological programming, or because of environmental events such as your parents' influence? Does it change because of the amount and kind of stimulation you received in your school? Are you what your environment made you, or is your behavior an expression of your biological inheritance?

Regardless of the terms that we use to pose these and other questions, we can think of *development* as a progressive series of changes that occur in a predictable pattern as the result of an interaction between biological and environmental factors. But how much do biological and environmental factors contribute? Does one set of factors predominate in certain domains (such as intelligence) while another set of factors predominates in others (such as personality)? Is the percentage of these contributions of biological and environmental influences fixed or is it variable?

Why do most children walk alone somewhere between ten and fifteen months of age? Why and how does one stage of development follow the next? Why do most children acquire language in the first few years of life? Why do some children learn quickly while others learn slowly? Are most aspects of development inevitable in a "normal" child? How are theories of development different from each other? How are they the same?

All of these questions are examples of the problems that characterize the field of developmental psychology and the study of human development. Answers to these and many other questions are likely to come from research efforts by psychologists, educators, pediatricians, linguists, sociologists, and others who use the tools and knowledge from their own disciplines to understand the developmental process. The different theoretical accounts of development you will read about in this book have a significant influence on many of these research efforts. These theoretical perspectives are different and sometimes complex points of view that attempt to account for the factors that control and explain the developmental process.

THEORY AND THE SCIENCE OF DEVELOPMENT

A Definition of Science

Whatever is known today in any given discipline is due largely to the efforts of people who have devoted their lives to seeking out truth, separating fact from fancy, and trying to understand what happens around them. All of these efforts, and more, are what science is about. To quote the mathematician and physicist Jacob Bronowski, "Science is the human activity of finding an order in nature by organizing the scattered meaningless facts under universal concepts" (1977, p. 225). Science is the process through which bits of information become organized. This process lends meaning and significance to otherwise unrelated and obscure particles of knowledge. It is also a process through which ideas are generated and new directions followed.

Science is the way in which facts or knowledge become bonded together to form something different from what was there before the process began. In fact, "doing" science gives the fragmented events that are observed in the world coherence and integrity. It is not sufficient to study an isolated fact (such as "children walk at around nine to twelve months") without pursuing information about how this fact might be related to other events in a child's life. Science is very much like the blueprint that a builder uses to understand how the many different parts of a structure fit together to form something more unique than the sum of the individual parts.

In addition to having *dynamic* qualities (describing *how* things happen) science also has *static* qualities (describing *what* happens). The static and the dynamic qualities of science go hand in hand because, in part, each determines the other. When people do science, they are taking a logical approach to solving some kind of problem as well as producing a product. For example, through intensive research and experimentation (the process), a vaccine (the product) was developed that effectively immunizes children against polio.

Finally, science is also a self-correcting process, where advances and setbacks all contribute and help refine subsequent efforts at answering a certain question, or understanding a certain issue. Through the nature of the process itself, answers provide valuable feedback. In a pure sense, scientists do not set out to prove a certain idea correct or incorrect, because questions are constantly being asked, answered, and reformulated. Instead, they *test* an idea or hypothesis. The scientist reevaluates the outcomes of an experiment and reflects how new information might modify the original question that was asked.

For example, we might observe a series of interactions between a parent and her child and notice their talking to each other and generally "having fun." We can further understand the developmental significance of "having fun" by examining the parent-child interchange in more detail and looking perhaps for a pattern of behavior. We might then look at other parents and their children to see if there are similarities across groups, thereby lending more or less strength to our ideas about how parents and children interact.

The scientific method is important in any field when goals are the organization of knowledge and the generation of new ideas. It is important to remember that the principles involved in doing science are applicable in all disciplines, whether the focus is developmental psychology, history, or biology. What some of these principles are and how they relate to each other is the focus of the next section.

A Model of Scientific Inquiry

The process of science can be seen as a four-step process: (1) asking a question; (2) identifying the factors or elements of that question that need to be examined; (3) testing the question, and finally (4) accepting or rejecting the premise on which the original question was based.

The first step, *asking the question,* recognizes that something of interest or potential value needs further investigation. What might be a source for such a question? The impetus for these "first" questions most often does not originate in the laboratory, around a conference table, or in some other highly controlled environment. These may be places where some important questions are identified or referred, but they are not where the initial reason as to why something might be worthy of systematic study surfaces. Instead, the sources of scientific inquiry are found in everyday experiences and events. These can (and do) include art, music, literature, and, of course, individual experiences. For example, the development of smallpox vaccine was prompted by Edward Jenner's personal observation that everyone was vulnerable to this disease except for the women who tended the cows. In turn, this observation led to the development by Robert Koch of germ theory, a basic and important principle of immunology. Another example is Newton's popularized "discovery" of gravity, when being hit by an apple while sitting under a tree. Even if this latter example is an exaggeration, it still makes the point; personal experience plays a vital and essential role in the development of valuable questions.

Another example—one that is more central to the theme of this book—is that children's cognitive development occurs in a series of different stages. This observation was made informally by many developmental psychologists, and then approached and studied more systematically by themselves and others.

Clearly, not everyone has the skill to identify those aspects of an experience or to ask the kinds of questions that might lead to new knowledge. From what the untrained mind sees as confusion and disarray, the trained mind selects the important and crucial events. As Louis Pasteur noted, chance favors the prepared mind, and the knowledge base from which most scientists operate (as a result of long and intensive training) provides this necessary advantage.

The second step in the process of scientific inquiry is *identifying what factors are important and how they will be examined.* For example, one of the theorists we will discuss later in this book, Robert Sears, examined the wide range of differences in the way that parents raise their children. A psychologist might begin by identifying factors that might be involved in these differences, such as the number of children in the family, the children's sex, the order of their birth, the family's social class, or perhaps the educational status of the parents. In other words, the developmental psychologist identifies the critical factors that are possibly related to the question asked. At this point the investigator no longer speculates ("Isn't this interesting!") but begins to ask more pointed questions about the importance of certain factors and the nature of the relationship between them.

This is also the point at which decisions need to be made as to how the questions will be answered. This part of the process involves the design and completion of the research. For example, if one is interested in the effects of environmental stimulation on intellectual development, an experiment could be designed to compare the intellectual development of children who were reared in an enriched environment (perhaps beginning school at an early age) with those children who have not experienced an enriched environment (perhaps those who have spent time in an institution). This is the step in the model where one asks: "How do I go about answering my question?" At this point the scientist operationally identifies important factors (or "variables"), states the possible relationship between them, and determines the method of doing the actual research. For those readers interested in an examination of different research methods and techniques in developmental psychology see Applebaum and McCall (1983), or Achenbach (1978).

The third step, *testing the question,* is the most "hands on" stage of the four-step process. Here the data necessary to answer the question are actually collected. For example, at this point the chemist tests which of three compounds most effectively acts as a catalyst, or the developmental psychologist surveys the problem-solving skills of children with learning disabilities. The scientist, given the essential information (reading scores, X rays, responses from an interview), applies some kind of a tool (such as a statistical test or an objective criterion) to determine if the outcome of the third step in this four-step process is consistent with what was proposed in the original question.

For example, a teacher may be interested in knowing whether his or her students learned to read with more comprehension using programmed instruction versus a more traditional teaching method. One way to test this question would be to compare scores on a test of comprehension for both groups. Perhaps the tool used in this comparison would come in the form of a statistical test that assigns a probability that the difference results from either chance or the difference in programs.

Finally, the last step in the model is for the scientist to *accept or reject the premise on which the original question was based* (and perhaps to question the accompanying theoretical rationale). Regardless of the outcome, however, the scientific process does not stop here. If the original question that was asked (for example, "Does enrichment influence a child's intellectual development?") is answered "yes," the psychologist continues asking additional questions and pursuing each question through the steps of the model just outlined. On the other hand, perhaps the results do not support the predicted outcome. The process of science dictates that the scientist return to the premise of the original question and reformulate it in line with this outcome. This will not necessarily change the question itself, but it will perhaps have some effect on the scientist's approach to the question and the meaning of the results. For example, the method might not have been appropriate to the question asked. It is the scientist's responsibility to decide what part of the process may have to be reconsidered. This is often why scientific research is so time consuming. Experiments are continually being redesigned to accommodate new information, new technologies, and, of course, new findings!

Table 1-1 summarizes the four steps involved in scientific inquiry we just discussed and provides an example that illustrates the progressive and focusing

Table 1-1 A Model of Scientific Inquiry

Step of the Model	Example
Asking the question	Do children who are raised in different types of homes develop different levels of intelligence?
Determining what factors are important and how they will be examined	The important factors are parent rearing style, home environment, and child's intellectual ability. Groups of children from different homes will be compared to examine differences in intellectual ability.
Testing the original question	A test will be done to determine if any difference between the two groups exists and if such a difference is a result of parenting styles or some other factor (such as chance).
Accepting or rejecting the premise on which the question is based	Depending on the outcome of the previous step, the original question will be reconsidered, and if necessary, more specific questions will be asked.

nature of the scientific process. As you can see, the psychologist begins with some personal observation and works toward a specific test of a clearly defined question that results in a decision as to what the next question should be.

Tools of Science: Theory and Its Elements

The model of scientific inquiry illustrated in Table 1-1 requires a set of tools or concepts to make it work. The different tools or mechanisms of science we will now turn to are theories, hypotheses, constructs, and variables.

Theory: Definition, Function, and Criteria. A *theory* can be defined as a group of logically related statements (for example, formulas, ideas, or rules) that explain events that have happened in the past as well as predict events that will occur in the future. Theories have three general purposes.

First, they provide us with a guide to collect the kind of information we need to describe some aspect of development. For example, a theory of language acquisition might allow us to describe the process of babbling and then the use of one word sentences (or holophrases) in great detail. The second general purpose a theory serves is helping us to integrate a set of facts into general categories. A theory of attachment, for example, might aid us in organizing and also better understanding the otherwise apparently unrelated interactions of parents and their newborns. Finally, a theory helps present material and information in an organized and coherent way so that subsequent efforts at answering the same or a related question are not just random, groundless efforts.

Like any outcome, a theory can be subjected to criteria that evaluate its usefulness. Murray Sidman (1960) has identified inclusiveness, consistency, accuracy, relevance, fruitfulness, and simplicity as six such criteria. Although some criteria overlap with one another, they are all important.

Theories are *inclusive* "according to the number and type of phenomena they encompass" (Sidman, p. 13). For example, Einstein's theory of relativity deals with many different types of events, including the relationship between time and space, the nature of light, and the speed of objects. In the behavioral and social sciences, some theories attempt to explain a great number of different events (such as a theory of development), while others attempt to explain only a relatively small segment of a more general phenomenon (such as a theory of play).

The *consistency* of a theory determines whether it can explain new discoveries without changing the assumptions it is based on. A theory tends to become more consistent the more it is tested because it is constantly being refined. Newton's theory of gravitation is a highly consistent theory because it is applicable to many different situations, all of which deal with the basic principle that all bodies in nature have a mutual degree of attraction to one another.

The *accuracy* of a theory is the degree to which it correctly predicts future events or can explain past ones. One theory may be so accurate in a certain situation that it predicts almost every outcome, while another theory may be so inaccurate as to be almost useless. The accuracy of any theory (including those covered in this book) depends, of course, on the question being asked. In other words, some theories are better suited to address concerns in one area than another and at the same time have a better percentage of correct predictions.

How *relevant* a theory is depends on how close the link is between the theory itself and the information or data collected within that theory. For example, if one were interested in the influence of prenatal nutrition on later intellectual development, one would examine variables such as developmental quotient (DQ), not the weight of the baby at birth.

The *fruitfulness* of a theory focuses on how productive it is in generating new ideas and directions for future research. There are many theorists whose work is known not for its immediate application, but for its generative qualities. Such theories serve as a stimulus for further research. Perhaps the best example of this is Sigmund Freud's lack of success in having his theory of psychosexual development accepted by his peers, but the profound influence of his ideas had on the generation of subsequent ideas about the developmental process. Many people feel that fruitfulness is an extremely important, it not the most important, criterion to use in judging a theory.

Finally, the last criterion is one that addresses a general goal of all science, that of *simplicity*. Simplicity deals with the degree of detail in a theory to make best use of the available information. Ideally, when a theory is simple (or parsimonious), it is prudent and efficient. In science it is generally true that the simpler a theory, the more parsimonious it is . Some theories, such as the theory of relativity, are simple and straightforward in their argument. On the other hand, some theories are so encumbered with assumptions that their usefulness is restricted. In general, these complicated theories are very difficult to apply to anything other than a highly specific situation.

Table 1-2 illustrates these six criteria and the question that each asks. We also include other criteria that might help you in judging the value of some theoretical approaches to development.

It is doubtful however, that any theory meets all of these criteria. It would be surprising to find a theory that is highly inclusive (applicable in many settings) and yet not fruitful, given its wide range of applicability and its generation of new directions for study. Perhaps it is best to view each criterion as a separate goal, something worth striving for but not absolutely necessary for the successful application of a theory to increasing our understanding of development.

Theories can also explain and predict. They not only help organize already established bodies of information but also serve as a roadmap for future inquiries. In many ways the table of contents or index of a book serve a similar purpose to that of a theory—they organize information. Imagine how difficult it would be to locate specific information in a book without a table of contents or index. A theory makes things more intelligible, easier to assimilate, and provides a framework within which questions can be asked.

Although a theory is often the final product of an effort to organize information, a theory can be a responsive and changing tool. According to the model of scientific inquiry presented in Table 1-1, new information stimulates a theory's evolution by either supporting its basic assumptions or by triggering a reconsideration and refinement of the theory. A theory is as much a changing tool used by scientists as an end unto itself.

Table 1-2   Criteria for Judging a Theory

Criterion	Question
Inclusiveness	How many different phenomena does the theory address?
Consistency	How well can the theory explain new things without having its basic assumptions changed?
Accuracy	How well can it predict future outcomes and explain past ones?
Relevance	How closely is the theory related to the information collected within that theory? That is, how well does it reflect the facts?
Fruitfulness	How well does the theory generate new ideas and directions for inquiry?
Simplicity	How simple or unencumbered is the theory? That is, how easy is it to understand?

Elements of a Theory: Variables, Constructs, and Hypotheses

The first two steps in "doing science" are: (1) asking a question, and (2) deciding what factors the focus of the investigation will be. In other words, what "things" must be measured, assessed, or examined to increase the likelihood that the answer reflects the real world? For example, if a psychologist wishes to study the interaction between a mother and her child, the psychologist must decide *what* to study about this interaction. These "whats" that are studied are called *variables*. A variable is anything that can take on more than one label or value, and usually represents a class of things. Examples of variables are College Board test scores (which can range from 200 to 800), biological sex (male or female), or occupation (lawyer, X construction worker, or home economist, and so on). In the example of the psychologist studying mother-child interactions, the number of times the mother or father makes contact with the infant per minute is an operational measure of the variable we might call parent-child interaction.

Another important element of a theory is a *construct*. A construct describes a group of variables that are related to each other. For example, the construct of attachment consists of different behaviors such as eye contact, physical touching, and verbal interaction between the parent and child. All these behaviors share something in common in that they reflect the general construct of attachment. This group of behaviors could be called something else, like affection, for example. What a group of variables or ideas is named, however, determines the usefulness of the construct. This same set of behaviors could, for example, be arbitrarily called "familial interaction" or "visual contact." If the terminology used to define constructs is so narrow that it defines a very limited set of behaviors (such as "visual contact"), the construct may become no more descriptive than a variable and severely limited in its use.

Constructs become important when they deal with a group of variables since their use is more efficient (or parsimonious) than dealing with each of the variables individually. For example, it is more efficient to discuss the construct of intelligence X than to discuss the individual components of intelligence, such as memory, comprehension, and problem solving.

The development of a construct involves the consideration of many different variables, some that may eventually be included, and some that will not. Constructs, then, are made up of variables that are related to one another on some theoretical level. Often there is disagreement among scientists as to which variables should or should not be included as part of a construct and what they should be called.

The last rung up the ladder of theory development is called a *hypothesis*. A hypothesis is an "educated guess" that posits an "If . . . then" relationship between variables or constructs. It is the question scientists ask when they want to better understand the influence that one variable (used perhaps in part to define a broader construct) has on another variable (or another construct). For example, a developmental psychologist might be interested in better understanding the factors that influence moral development in young children. Through some informal contact with children, he or she has noticed that at different developmental levels children approach moral dilemmas in different ways. The following statement might then be presented as a hypothesis: "There is a significant relationship between the developmental level of the child and the method the child uses to solve a moral dilemma." Implicit in this statement is the "if . . . then" supposition that if the developmental level of the child changes, then the way the child approaches moral dilemmas will change as well. The hypothesis becomes more a direct test of a question.

How does the scientist know whether the proposed hypothesis can be accepted as true or rejected as false? Through the application of some external criterion (such as a statistical test), the scientist can assign some level of *confidence* to the outcome. What this indicates is how confident the scientist is that the outcome of the research is a result of those variables that were examined (or manipulated) and not some other, extraneous influence. For example, moral development might be a function of the society in which a person grows up as well as of the level of a child's development. For the psychologist to have confidence in the outcome of an experiment, such factors must not only be taken into account, but often controlled.

The Relationship Between Science and Theory

In Table 1-1 a four-step model was presented that conveys the essence of how the scientific process operates. The development of a theory operates in a parallel way. Although the natural phenomena that theories represent may have been operating for eons (such as gravity or learning), theories in and of themselves are artificial and are developed by means of a series of systematic steps that involve variables, constructs, and hypotheses. Theory development is a microcosm of the scientific process itself, and any progress that developmental psychologists might make in advancing specific theories is progress in the general science of developmental psychology as well.

Theory is the backbone of science without which scientific advancement could not be possible. It provides a framework within which scientists become aware of what questions are important to ask and how they should be answered. Without a theoretical context within which to operate, new information becomes nothing more than a quantitative addition to an already existing body of knowledge. However, when scientists are aware of where new data may or may not fit, the premise under which they operate becomes infinitely more useful and moves closer and closer to that abstract goal of truth, and the relevance of these new findings to applied settings can increase dramatically.

THEORIES OF DEVELOPMENT: AN OVERVIEW

Each of the theories of development that we will discuss in this book has something different to contribute to understanding the developmental process. On some points these theories may be in agreement, while on others they differ. Before these theories are presented in detail, it would be useful to summarize the characteristics that differentiate them from one another.

Five important questions will be asked about each theory:

1. What are the basic assumptions of the theory?
2. What is the philosophical rationale for the theory?
3. What are the variables that are studied?
4. How is development studied?
5. In what areas has the theory had its greatest impact?

The answers to each of these questions should prepare you for the in-depth discussions that begin in Chapter 3 of one theoretical view, as well as provide you with a framework to compare and contrast these different viewpoints. Table 1-3 presents a summary of these important points across the four different theoretical perspectives: maturational, psychoanalytic, behavioral, and cognitive-developmental. Table 1-4 presents a historical overview of these perspectives.

The Maturational Model

Arnold Gesell, the foremost maturationalist in developmental psychology, represents a unique approach to the study of human development. As a physician, Gesell believed that the sequence of development is determined by the biological and evolutionary history of the species. In other words, development of the organism is essentially under the control of biological systems and the process of maturation. Although the environment is of some importance, it acts only in a supportive role and does not provide any impetus for change.

While working with G. Stanley Hall within the tradition of the Darwinian influence that was very popular during the 1920s, Gesell applied the tenets of recapitulation theory to the study of individual development (or ontogenesis). Recapitulation theory states that the development of the species is reflected in the development of the individual. In other words, the child progresses through a series of stages that recount the developmental sequence that characterized the species.

Gesell believed that the most important influences on the growth and development of the human organism were biological directives. He summarized this theory in five distinct principles of development, which he later applied to behavior. All these principles assume that the formation of *structures* is necessary before any event outside the organism can have an influence on development. Interestingly,

Table 1-3 An Overview of the Major Theories of Development

	General Theoretical Perspective			
	Maturational	Psychoanalytic	Behavioral	Cognitive-Developmental
Basic assumptions of the theory	The sequence of development is determined by biological factors and the evolutionary history of the species.	Development consists of dynamic, structural, and sequential components and a continuously reviewed need for satisfaction of instincts.	Development occurs according to the laws of learning and places great importance on events in the environment.	Development consists of the addition and modification of psychological structures. The organism assumes an active role in the process.
Philosophical rationale	Recapitulation theory	Embryology	Tabula rasa	Predeterminism
What variables are studied	Biological systems of growth	Effects of instinctual needs on behavior	Frequency of behavior	Stage-related transformations
How is development studied	Using cinematic records, co-twin studies, baby biographies, normative approach	Through verbal associations and indirect examination of conflicts	Conditioning and modeling paradigms	Problem solving during transitional points in development
Areas of greatest impact	Child rearing and the importance of biological determinants	Personality development and the relationship between culture and behavior	Systematic analysis of behavior, treatment and management of deviant behaviors, educational applications	Understanding of cognitive processes

Table 1-4   Historical Overview of Theories of Development*

Period	Maturational	Psychoanalytic	Behavioral	Organismic
1920s	Arnold L. Gesell (1880–1961)		Ivan P. Pavlov (1849–1936) Edward L. Thorndike (1874–1949) John B. Watson (1878–1958)	
1930s		Sigmund Freud (1856–1939)		
1940s	Konrad Lorenz (1898–)		Neal E. Miller (1909–) John Dollard (1900–1945)	
1950s			B. F. Skinner (1904–) Robert Sears (1908–)	Heinz Werner (1890–1964) Jean Piaget (1896–1980)
1960s		Erik Erikson (1902–)	Donald M. Baer (1931–) Sidney W. Bijou (1908–) Albert Bandura (1925–)	
1970s				Klaus Riegel (1925–1978)

*This table shows when each major model began having a substantial impact on the field of developmental psychology and when each theorist's work became most influential.
Source: Adapted from Morris, E. K. (1979).

the notion that "function follows structure" was pursued not only by Gesell, but designers, architects, and engineers have also found a great deal of truth in these words as well.

Gesell also believed that behavior at different stages of development has different degrees of balance or stability. For example, at two years of age, the child's behavior might be characterized by and groping for some type of stability (the so-called "terrible twos"). Shortly thereafter, however, the child's behavior becomes smooth and consolidated. Gesell believed that development is cyclical in nature, swinging from one extreme to another, and that by means of these swings, the child develops and uses new structures.

Because he placed such a strong emphasis on the importance of biological processes, the majority of Gesell's work and that of his colleagues (most notably Frances Ilg and Louise B. Ames) focused on biological systems as a beginning point to understanding development. Through Gesell's use of cinematic (moving picture) records, stop-action analysis provided the foundation for his extensive descriptions of "normal" development. This technique allowed Gesell to examine the frame-by-frame progression of certain motor tasks from their earliest reflex stage at birth through a system of fully developed and integrated behaviors. For example, his detailed analysis of walking provided the first graphic record of the sequence this complex behavior follows.

Gesell also made significant contributions with the development of the co-twin method for comparing the relative effects of heredity (nature) and environment (nurture) on development. One identical twin would receive specific training in some skill (such as stair climbing), and the other twin would receive no training in the skill. The rationale for this strategy was that because the children had an identical genetic makeup (they were identical twins), any difference in stair-climbing ability must be the result of training. This is the basic paradigm that Gesell used to question some very interesting and controversial statements about the nature of intelligence.

Unquestionably, Gesell's greatest contribution has been to the understanding of the development of the "normal" child. His detailed cinematic records, their analyses, and their translation into books for the popular press have influenced child-rearing patterns in this country as much as that of the famous Dr. Spock (who incorporates many of Gesell's principles into his philosophy).

Gesell's ideas and theoretical approach never entered the mainstream of current thought about developmental psychology. Perhaps this is because much of his work was seen as too biological in nature and not sufficiently theoretical. Both from a historical and applied perspective, however, his contribution was and still is an outstanding one.

Over the last few years, there has been a heightened interest in other maturational approaches, most notably ethology and sociobiology (both the focus of Chapter 4). These views, even more than Gesell's, emphasize the importance of biological and evolutionary principles as determinants of behavior.

The Psychoanalytic Model

The psychoanalytic model, developed initially by Sigmund Freud, presents a view of development that is revolutionary in both its content and its implications for the nature of development. The basic assumption of this model is that development consists of dynamic, structural, and sequential components, each influenced by a continuously renewed need for the gratification of basic instincts. How psychic energy (or the energy of life, as it is sometimes called) is channeled through these different components constitutes the basis of the developmental process and individual differences.

The *dynamic* or *economic component* of Freud's tripartite system characterizes the human mind (or psyche) as a fluid, energized system that can transfer energy from one part to the other where and when needed. The *structural* or *topographical component* of the theory describes the three separate, yet interdependent, psychological structures called the *id*, *ego*, and *superego* and the way in which they regulate behavior. Finally, the *sequential* or *stage component* emphasizes a progression from one stage of development to the next, focusing on different zones of bodily sensitivity (such as the mouth) and accompanying psychological and social conflicts.

It is difficult to identify the philosophical roots of psychoanalytic theory, because most psychoanalytic theorists would consider their roots to be in embryology, the biological study of the embryo from conception until the organism can survive on its own. This identification with a biological model has a great deal to do with Freud's training as a physician, his work in neuroanatomy, and his belief that biological *needs* play a paramount role in development. Some people believe that the philosophical tradition of preformationism (which in its extreme holds that all attitudes and characteristics are formed at birth and only expand in size) is basic to the psychoanalytic model, but this may be untrue. The preformationists stress the lack of malleability of the developing individual, while the psychoanalytic model describes a flexible character for the individual and the potential for change.

Freudian theory places an important emphasis on the resolution of conflicts that have their origin at an unconscious level. It states that the origin of these conflicts are biological and passed on from generation to generation. Development is an ongoing process of resolving these conflicts.

If the roots of behavior are located in the unconscious, how can they be accessible to study? Through a series of historical accidents, Freud was introduced to hypnotism as a method of treatment. This technique, in turn, gave birth to his now famous method called *free association*, in which individuals are encouraged to freely associate anything that comes to mind in response to certain words or phrases. Freud believed that such an exposition of underlying needs and fears was the key to understanding a typical behavior. This method is a highly subjective way to collect information, and a large part of the criticism leveled against Freud and many of his followers was directed at this practice. The theory itself, however, is based on abstract and subjective judgments, and the fact that the behaviors under study are not easily amenable to scientific verification has caused controversy for years. However, the richness and diversity that Freud brought to a previously stagnant conception of development started a tradition that is healthy and strong even today. Perhaps Freud's most significant accomplishment was the first documentation and systematic organization of a theory of development.

The major impact of the psychoanalytic model and the work of such theorists as Freud and Erik Erikson has undoubtedly been in the study of personality and the treatment of emotional and social disorders. Erikson, unlike Freud, focused mainly on the psychosocial rather than the psychosexual dimension of behavior. The impact and significance of both men's contributions cannot be overstated.

The Behavioral Model

The behavioral model characterizes a movement that is peculiar to American psychology and distinct from any other theoretical model. The behavioral perspective views development as a function of learning and one that proceeds according to certain laws or principles of learning. Most important, it places the major impetus for growth and development outside of the individual in the environment, rather than within the organism itself. The importance placed on the environment varies with specific theories within this general model, but, in all cases, the organism is seen as *reactive* instead of active.

Within almost every behavioral theory, the assumption is incorporated that behavior is a function of its consequences. If the consequences of a behavior (such as studying) are good (such as high grades), studying is likely to continue in the future. If they are not good, the behavior will change (perhaps to a new way of studying) or to not studying at all.

The behavioral model makes the laws of learning and the influence of the environment paramount in the developmental process. Through such processes as classical conditioning and imitation, individuals learn what behaviors are most appropriate and lead to adaptive outcomes. Given that this model views development as a learned phenomenon, behaviors can be broken down into their basic elements. This leads people to see the behavioral model as "reductionistic."

The behavioral perspective views the newborn child as naive and unlearned. John Locke's notion of *tabula rasa* best exemplifies the philosophical roots of the behavioral tradition. Literally, tabula rasa means "blank slate." The newborn child is like a blank page waiting to be written on, with only the most fundamental biological reflexes (such as sucking) operative at birth. The organism is malleable, and behavior develops and changes as a result of events or experiences. This is a more open view than the maturationist and psychoanalytic perspectives, because it sees human potential as unlimited by internal factors. Sometimes, however, biological endowment (an internal factor) can limit developmental outcomes, as in the case of genetic diseases or familial retardation. But even in the case of the severely retarded child, a restructuring of the environment can greatly affect basic competencies and caretaking functions such as eating and toilet training.

Given that the emphasis within the behavioral perspective is placed on events that originate in the environment and their effect on the organism, it is no surprise that the variable of primary interest to the behavorist is the frequency or number of times a behavior occurs. For example, if one is interested in studying an aspect of sibling interaction, behaviors are explicitly defined (or *operationalized*) and must be objective enough to be reliably measured. Such constructs as "nice feelings" would not meet such criteria, but "number of times brother touches brother" would.

Using frequency of behavior, the traditional way of studying development is to examine what effect certain environmental events have on behavior. This is most often done by identifying and observing those events in the environment that control behavior and then, if necessary, manipulating these events to see if the behavior under observation changes. In other words, if a child's speech is delayed, the psychologist might want to observe what the events are that surround the child's verbalizations when left to run their course. Some intervention wherein the parents are encouraged to respond more directly might be suggested, and then additional observation might be done to see if there is any change. This type of design is frequently used in the area of behavior analysis. It illustrates the way in which the effects of certain contingencies can be isolated and identified.

Most interesting, however (given the behaviorists' deemphasis of biological age or stages of development), is the viewpoint that the sequence of experience is the critical factor in development. In other words, when discussing developmental status, experience—and not age—is the important factor. Although age and experience are somewhat related, age should not be thought of as a determinant of behavior but only a *correlate* (a simultaneous outcome).

A more recently popular approach to understanding development is through social learning theory and the work of such people as Robert Sears and Albert Bandura. A social learning theory approach is very much based on the same assumptions of the more traditional behavioral approach we have described here. A major difference, however, is that the social learning theory model incorporates such ideas as vicarious (or indirect) reinforcement. Here the child does not need to directly experience something to actually learn it. This approach still reflects the importance of the environment, while at the same time suggests that individual differences contribute something as well.

The most significant impact this model has had is on the systematic analysis of behavior, on the treatment and management of deviant behaviors, and in educational applications such as programmed instruction.

The Cognitive-Developmental Model

The cognitive-developmental model of development stresses the individual's *active* rather than *reactive* role in the developmental process. The basic assumptions of the model are that:

1. Development occurs in a series of qualitatively distinct stages.
2. These stages always follow the same sequence, but do not necessarily occur at the same times for all individuals.
3. These stages are hierarchically organized such that a later stage subsumes the characteristics of an earlier one.

Another characteristic of the cognitive-developmental model that sets it apart from other theoretical models is the presence of psychological structures and the way in which changes in these underlying structures are reflected in overt changes in behavior. The form these changes take, depends on the individual's developmental level. Many people categorize the cognitive-developmental perspective as an "interactionist" model because it encourages one to view development as an interaction between the organism and the environment.

The philosophical roots of this perspective are found in the predeterminist approach, which views development as a "process of qualitative differentiation or evolution of form" (Ausubel & Sullivan, 1970). Jean-Jacques Rousseau, the noted eighteenth century French philosopher, wrote that development consists of a sequence of orderly stages that are internally regulated, and that the individual is transformed from one into the other. Although Rousseau believed that the child is innately good (and most of the early preformationists believed that the environment plays a very limited role), modern cognitive-developmental theorists would not tacitly accept such a broad assumption.

Although the environment is decisive in determining the content of these stages, the important biological or organismic contribution is the development of structures within which this content can operate. for example, all human beings are born with some innate capacity to develop language and to imitate behavior. It is highly unlikely, however, that human beings are born with a capacity to speak a specific language, or even to imitate particular behavior. Children born in the United States of French-speaking parents would certainly not be expected to speak French (or any other language) without exposure to that language. Within the organismic model the capacity for development emerges as part of the developmental process. Although the environment is an important and influential factor, the biological contribution is far more important because it is the impetus for further growth and development. The sequence and process of development are predetermined, but the actual content of behavior within these stages is not.

Of primary interest to the cognitive-developmental psychologist is the sequence of stages and the process of transition from one stage to the next. It is for this reason that the set of stage-related behaviors and their correlates across such dimensions as cognitive or social development have been the focus of study. For example, the psychologist might be interested in examining how children of different ages (and presumably different developmental stages) solve a similar type of problem. After observing many children of different ages, the psychologist can then postulate the existence of different types of underlying structures responsible for the strategies children use. A great deal of Jean Piaget's work has been directed at a better understanding of the thinking process that children at different developmental levels use to solve problems. In fact, much of the Piagetian tradition emphasizes that these different ways of solving problems reflect, in general, different ways of seeing the world.

Considering the cognitive-developmental psychologist's interest in the concept and use of stages, it is not surprising that the primary method used to study behavior is through the presentation of problems that emphasize differences in structural X organization. The infant might depend on purely sensory information (such as touch or smell) to distinguish between different classes of objects, yet the older child might place a group of objects in categories based on more abstract criteria, such as "these are all toys, and these are food." The "how" of development is seen X to be reflected in the strategies that children use at qualitatively different developmental levels to solve certain types of problems. More important, however, the psychologists focus their attention on why these differences are present. Such studies have resulted in a model that hypothesizes that different underlying structures are operative at different stages.

Undoubtedly, the cognitive-developmental theorist has had the greatest impact X in the different areas of education. Since much of the research conducted over the past fifty years by these theorists has focused on the general area of "thinking," this may be no surprise. Basically, the educational philosophy and practices that have resulted from this theoretical perspective have emphasized the unique contribution that children make to their own learning through discovery and experience. The child is allowed to explore within an environment that is challenging enough to facilitate development within the child's current stage of development, and one that is not boring. Much of the open-school concept, which stresses the child's acting on the environment, has its roots in this theoretical tradition.

SUMMARY POINTS

1. Development is the result of a complex interaction between biological and environmental influences.
2. Science is the process through which information and knowledge become organized.
3. "Doing" science consists of asking a question, defining the elements of the question that will be studied, testing the question, and accepting or rejecting the assumptions on which the question is based.
4. A theory is a group of related statements that explain past events as well as predict future events.
5. A theory can be judged on the criteria of inclusiveness, consistency, accuracy, relevance, fruitfulness, and simplicity.
6. A variable is anything that can take on more than one value, such as height, weight, or intelligence.
7. A construct defines and represents a group of variables that are related to one another.
8. An hypothesis is a statement that presumes an "if . . . then" relationship between variables or constructs.

9. In many ways, science and theory follow a parallel course of development and serve the same purpose.
10. The maturational model stresses the importance of biological influences on development and has had its greatest impact on child-rearing practices.
11. The psychoanalytic model assumes that development is the result of a continuing need for the satisfaction of instincts.
12. The behavioral model contends that development is the result of different types of learning as well as imitation and modeling.
13. The cognitive-developmental model focuses on the transition between different stages of development and views the human being as an active participant in the developmental process.

FURTHER READINGS

Bergman, G. *Philosophy of science*. Madison: The University of Wisconsin Press, 1977.
Brim. O. G., & Kagan, J. (Eds.). *Constancy and change in human development*. Cambridge, Mass.: Harvard University Press, 1980.
Brinton, C. *The shaping of modern thought*. Englewood Cliffs, N.J.: Prentice-Hall, 1963.
Bronowski, J. *The origins of knowledge and imagination*. New Haven, Conn.: Yale University Press, 1972.
Cairns, R. B. The emergence of developmental psychology. In P. Mussen (ed.), *Handbook of child psychology* (Vol. 1). New York: Wiley, 1983.
Skinner, B. F. *Science and human behavior*. New York: Macmillan, 1953.

OTHER READINGS OF INTEREST

Calder. N. *The mind of man*. New York: Viking Press, 1970.
Farb, P. *Humankind*. Boston: Houghton-Mifflin, 1978.

2

Trends and Issues in Human Development

It is not true that life is one damn thing after another—it's one damn thing over and over.
Edna St. Vincent Millay

Human action can be modified to some extent, but human nature cannot be changed.
Abraham Lincoln

One of the most interesting things about the process of development is how different people are from each other. Even among newborn babies, some are more active, some less irritable, and some are even more attractive to adults than others. In spite of the adage "all babies look alike," all look distinctly different from each other— ask any new parent!

Yet despite this diversity, similar developmental processes occur in all human beings and are reflected by the different theoretical perspectives we will consider in the following chapters. Although theories may differ in their explanation of how development happens, they all recognize a set of common influences and processes. These similarities represent directions or trends of development that are stable and reliable indicators of the changing nature of the individual.

There are also, however, certain aspects of the developmental process across which theories of development differ. Often, these differences are discussed as extremes along some continuum, such as maturation *or* learning, or heredity *or* environment. When a science as young and complex as developmental psychology is studied, it is not unusual that such seemingly unresolvable issues are raised.

These points of contention, however, serve a very useful purpose: They help to generate new questions and directions for study, far beyond the significance of the original question itself. The discussion here will focus on the conjunctive nature of these extremes—that is, how neither extreme is "correct" or in some way separable from the other.

There are probably other trends in human development and issues among theories besides the ones we will discuss here that can be identified. We believe, however, that these will provide you with a broad base on which you can begin to compare theories to one another and get a feel for what makes them different.

Each of the issues we discuss gives rise to a general question that we might ask about the nature of development. The seven questions listed in Table 2-1 are useful not only for understanding the position that any one theory represents but especially for comparing theories. Before you begin reading each chapter, you might find it useful to review these questions again. Consider them as organizers that may help you in understanding the material.

At the conclusion of selected chapters throughout the book, we will refer again to these questions to better understand the view that each of the theoretical models presents. Finally, the last chapter of the book will discuss these issues to help organize a comparison across the different theories.

COMMON TRENDS IN HUMAN DEVELOPMENT

From Global to Discrete Response Systems

One trend in human development is the transition from a global system to a discrete system of responding. A *global response* is a generalized one, such as the cry of a newborn infant, that can have many different meanings. A *discrete response* is a highly specific behavior that can easily be distinguished from other behaviors in terms of its intent or usefulness. The crying that was once global soon becomes differentiated into sounds that have specific meanings, such as hunger, discomfort, or pain. As development progresses, crying becomes increasingly discrete, eventually leading to the next stages of vocalization and intelligible speech.

Another example of a global response is the way young children begin to learn about their world by grabbing haphazardly at anything and everything. Eventually this grabbing becomes more refined, and children use their hands to explore the environment more effectively. This similarity is true for physical development as well. Young children first propel themselves by using gross pushing movements that eventually become more refined into crawling and then walking.

An Increase in Complexity

As development progresses, the individual becomes more complex. Biologically, the one cell that was present at conception divides and subdivides to form more

Table 2-1 Important Issues in Development

The Issue	The Question We Ask
The nature of development	What is the major force that influences the course of development?
The process that guides development	What is the underlying process primarily responsible for changes in development?
The importance of age	What roles does age play as a general marker of changes in development?
The rate of development	Are there certain sensitive or critical periods during development, and how are they related to the rate of change?
The shape of development	Is development smooth and continuous or do changes occur in abrupt stages?
Individual differences	How does the theory explain differences in development between individuals of the same chronological age?
How is development studied	What methods are used to study development, and how do they affect the content of the theory?

than one million million separate yet interdependent units. Psychologically, there is an increase in complexity as well: The number of emotions, or the different strategies that are available for solving a problem become more sophisticated. Not only does behavior become more quantitatively discrete, but qualitative change occurs as the complexity or multidimensionality of behavior increases. Most theories of development consider both qualitative and quantitative change as increases in complexity and hallmarks of development.

Increase in Integration and Differentiation

For an individual to survive, behaviors can't continue to function alone, but must become part of a coherent organized system. When behaviors become _differentiated,_ they are more articulated, or distinct, from one another. When they are _integrated,_ they are meshed with or incorporated into one another, often to form something that is qualitatively different from what was there before.

The dual processes of differentiation and integration involve a refinement of behaviors and the combination of these behaviors into a unified whole. Within the cognitive-developmental model, both psychological and physical systems become differentiated yet remain in communication and coordination with one another. Although the separation and integration of psychological systems (such as thinking and feeling) is not as apparent as it is for biological systems (such as respiration and circulation), there is a parallel process, in which larger, more inclusive systems are developed. For example, young children use basic sensory information such as seeing or touching to explore the environment. As children develop, they begin to organize these basic strategies into a more efficient and adaptable system that combines both seeing and touching.

A Decrease in Egocentrism

During the early years of development, children tend to believe that their own perspective of the world is the only one possible. This preoccupation with one's own view of the world is called *egocentrism*. Egocentrism assumes different forms as development progresses, but in almost all descriptions of development it tends to become less and less of a major influence as the individual develops. This may occur because of changing social conditions (that is, people tend to become less self-centered when they begin socializing with one another) or even because of biological changes whereby less effort needs to be directed toward self-growth where energy is devoted to reaching out and exploring the world.

Egocentrism is a major element of Jean Piaget's theory and is discussed in detail in Chapter 9. It plays an important part in both the social and cognitive development of the child.

Development of Social Autonomy

The last general trend we will discuss is the development of social autonomy, or children's increasing independence and ability to provide for their own needs. Initially, the infant is dependent on the others for basic care. In contrast, the older child is much more self-sufficient. Some anthropologists (and psychologists as well) believe that the immature status of the newborn human infant relative to other animals reflects the long period of dependency that characterizes our species and allows for intense socialization to take place.

Eventually most children show varying degrees of independence from their primary caretakers. In addition, when children become more autonomous, other things begin to happen as well. One of the most important is that individuals begin to accept the sanctions and standards of society as interpreted from their own viewpoints rather than, for example, that of their parents.

ISSUES AMONG THEORIES

The Nature of Development

Both from a historical and a scientific perspective, no issue has been more pervasive than that of whether development is a function of genetically transmitted codes (heredity or nature) or the result of external influences (environment or nurture). The question has been the focus of heated debate and voluminous research by people who assume that these two factors are independent of one another. Unfortunately, such actions have confused instead of clarified the issue.

The preformationist position fostered the belief that individuals are fully formed in the sperm of the male (referred to as a homunculist) or the ovum of the female (an ovist). Given this premise, only very limited quantitative change can be expected to take place at conception, and the environment was thought to have little effect on the outcomes that development may have. On the other hand, ideas like John Locke's notion of *tabula rasa* assume that the child's mind resembles a blank slate and that environmental influences are responsible for all developmental changes not biologically based. As a philosopher, Locke left the details of studying and analyzing the specific elements of the environment to those who followed in the tradition of American empiricism and the behavioral perspective (the focus of Chapters 7 and 8).

Over the last half-century, however, a great deal of research and thought on this issue has led psychologists to believe that the relationship between environmental influences and hereditary factors is not a question of the importance of either, but rather the way in which they interact (Anastasi, 1958).

One possible way to examine this interaction is to view both hereditary and environmental forces as having potentially positive or negative effects on development. For example, a positive environmental influence might be good prenatal care, while a negative environmental influence might be the unnecessary institutionalization of the child at an early age. It is more difficult to provide examples of positive or negative influences that are the result of heredity, because it is not clear which traits or characteristics, be they good or bad, are inherited. However, genetically transmitted diseases such as Tay-Sachs and sickle cell anemia are clearly negative.

Table 2-2 illustrates the relative weights that can be assigned to environmental or hereditary influences and the possible models that result. The *main-effect model* includes two viewpoints: nativist and nurturist. To a *nativist*, hereditary factors are the primary influence on development, regardless of the effect of the environment. A nativist would believe that children who inherit some undesirable characteristic can receive little benefit from a restructuring of the environment, because regardless of the potential effects the environment can have (either negative or positive), they are preempted by the effects of hereditary influences. To a *nurturist*, however, the environment shapes behavior and is the ultimate influence, regardless of the individual's genetic inheritance. Consequently, where the environmental influence is positive, regardless of the influence of genetic factors, the final outcome will be positive.

Both main-effect models seem extreme from a common-sense perspective as well as in light of research that has been completed in recent years. It is generally accepted, for example, that certain children identified as being high-risk at birth (for example, low-birthweight infants) can be helped by some course of intervention

Table 2-2   Models of Nature-Nurture Interaction (Potential Outcomes Are in the Cells)

The Main Effects Model

		Environmental Influences	
Genetic Influences		Positive	Negative
	Positive	Good/Good	Good/Bad
	Negative	Bad/Good	Bad/Bad

Nativist View

Nurturist View

The Interactional Model

		Environmental Influence	
Genetic Influences		Positive	Negative
	Positive	Good	Medium
	Negative	Medium	Bad

that will dramatically improve their chances for healthy development. Negative environmental influences can likewise affect a potentially normal child in such a way as to prevent the transition necessary for healthy development. Of course, if both environmental and hereditary influences are simultaneously positive or negative, the outcome most probably will be so as well.

Another way of examining the relationship between hereditary and environmental influences is the *interactional model*. The potential outcomes for this model (when both influences are positive or negative) are the same as in the main-effect model. It is the discordant interactions that provide an interesting contrast. Donald Hebb (1949) discussed this interactive relationship by stressing how heredity and environment both operate 100 percent of the time, and that the influence of one is impossible to understand without considering the influence of the other. For example, children who are born with a genetic abnormality (such as certain types of mental retardation) can be taught to function at much higher levels than was once believed possible. If these children were not given an opportunity in a supportive environment, they might always function at subnormal levels.

The interactional model can help us understand the relative effects of genetic and environmental influences on development. As Table 2-2 shows, unless environmental or hereditary influences are clearly dominant, there is a subtle interplay or interaction between the role that heredity and environment play.

An individual's *genotype* (or their genetic inheritance) sets absolute limits for their *phenotype*—the observable, physical characteristics that result from an interaction between the genotype and environmental factors. Innate characteristics, however, define the lower and upper limits of potential change, and these limits cannot be fully actualized unless the surrounding environment is supportive. Through the mechanism of evolution, more adaptive characteristics have been maintained and less adaptive ones have disappeared. It is fascinating to observe the way in which the limits of our genotypic qualities have forced human beings to seek out and construct an environment most suitable to our innate qualities. The environment in turn then influences the potential of the genetic contribution. Anthropologists recognize that the ape descended from the trees and became a tool user before its brain increased in size; this illustrates the complex and circular interplay involved in the heredity-environment or nature-nurture issue.

In general, the relationship between genetic and environmental factors is one of mutual interaction. On one hand, the genotype sets absolute limits of growth that rarely can be exceeded (for example, regardless of how much we eat, we can never grow to be ten feet tall). On the other hand, environmental factors set absolute limits on the degree to which one's genetic potential can be realized. A society should strive to maximize an individual's genetic potential by providing a wide range of environmental settings in which development can take place.

An Ecological Model of Human Development. One theorist has tried to deal with the importance of the environment without ignoring the uniqueness of the individual. Urie Bronfenbrenner (1977) has developed what he calls an *experimental ecology of human development*. Within this model he stresses the importance of the developing person in his or her surrounding environment. He defines the phrase *ecology* of human development as the study of "the progressive, mutual accommodation, throughout the life span, between a growing human organism and the changing immediate environments in which it lives" (1977, p.6).

His basic argument is that traditional studies in human development are very rigorous and tightly controlled. They are however, also very limited in scope because many of these experiments take place in settings that are unfamiliar to the participants and artificial in their construction. In other words, they don't very accurately represent what the real world is about.

Since he is so concerned with the qualities and characteristics of the environment, part of his ecological model defines a series of structures that are all "nested" within one another. There are four of these structures. These structures nest or "fit" within each other beginning with the microsystem.

The *microsystem* reflects the immediate setting that contains the person. Keeping in mind how our immediate setting changes throughout the day, the microsystem that we find ourself in changes as well. Although the library might be the microsystem in which we found ourselves late at night, our office or classroom might be the parallel microsystem during the day.

All microsystems have three different dimensions. The first is the physical space and activities within the microsystem such as the lighting over our desk or the temperature of the classroom during a test. The second is the people and their roles who are part of the microsystem such as our roommate or our classroom teacher. Finally, the third is the interaction between the people in the microsystem and the person. At one time, for example, we might be angry with a roommate who does not do his or her assigned tasks. At another time, we might act like best friends.

The second level is called the *mesosystem*, and focuses on the relationships between the different settings that the person is in during different times in development. The mesosystem focuses on interrelations among microsystems. For example, the mesosystem for college freshmen might consist of the dining hall, the classroom, home, and the intramural softball field.

The third element is the *exosystem*. Bronfenbrenner believes that the exosystem is a set of specific social structures that do not directly contain the individual, but still have an impact on the person's development. These structures ''influence, delimit, or even determine what goes on'' in the microsystem of the developing individual. The individual does not participate in these settings, but they do have a direct impact on his or her behavior. For example, an exosystem might be the doctor's office, the teacher's lounge, or grandma's house. These are all places with an indirect impact on the person's development.

The last element or structure in his model is called the *macrosystem*. It consists of all the elements contained in the micro, meso, and exosystems, plus the general underlying philosophy or cultural orientation within which the person lives. As Bronfenbrenner says, these are the ''overarching institutional patterns of the culture or subculture, such as the economic, social, educational, legal, and political systems of which local micro, meso, and exosystems are the concrete manifestations'' (p. 8).

A good example of a child's macrosystem might be the ethnic group he or she identifies with. As you may know, almost every ethnic group has a set of unspoken standards for the behavior of their children and adults. For example, in most ethnic groups, the family and especially the children are the center of all activities.

One example of an ecological approach to understanding development is illustrated by the research of Larry Kurdek on divorce. As you can see in Table 2-3, he organizes some of the important factors involved in divorce according to their membership in one of the four structures that Bronfenbrenner discusses in his ecological theory.

This ecology of human development helps us in two primary ways as far as understanding human development. First, it places the interaction between nature and nurture in a very clear and easily definable context of one of the four systems discussed above. Second, it encourages us to move away from laboratory-based settings, and begins to examine development in the ''natural stream'' of when and where it occurs. It is a relatively new and unique approach, and one that will probably receive a great deal of attention.

Table 2-3   An Ecological Approach to Post-Divorce Adjustment

Area of Concern	Ecological Structure	Issue
Vulnerability to sources of stress	Ontogenetic	How well can the child deal with the stress associated with divorce? What impact do multiple sources of stress have on the child?
Age of child at divorce	Ontogenetic	What qualitative differences exist in children at different developmental levels as far as perceptions and interpretations of the divorce process?
Availability of noncustodial parent	Exosystem	Does physical distance from the noncustodial parent affect post-divorce adjustment?
Sex differences and post-divorce adjustment	Ontogenetic and microsystem	Does the impact of divorce differ for boys and girls?
Changes in family patterns	Macrosystem and microsystem	How do post-divorce changes such as economic instability affect children? What impact do changing parental breadwinner roles have on the child?
Parent-child relationship	Microsystem	How does the conflict between parents during the divorce process affect the subsequent parent-child relationship?
Absence of one parent	Macrosystem	What is the effect of the absence of models who can demonstrate a wide range of skills?
Pre-divorce/Post-divorce relationship	Microsystem	Does the pre-divorce parent-child relationship have any predictive validity for post-divorce relationships? Does the equality of parent-child interaction change following divorce?
Nonnuclear support systems	Macrosystem and exosystem	Can kinship availability assist the child in post-divorce adjustment?

Table 2-3   (*Continued*)

Area of Concern	Ecological Structure	Issue
Marriage settlement	Macrosystem	Were decisions on child support, alimony, and other issues settled fairly via mediation?
Quality of post-divorce social relationship	Exosystem	To what degree are the divorced parents satisfied with their social and interpersonal relationships?
Economic conditions following divorce	Macrosystem	How does a sharing of income or a decrease in available resources affect the post-divorce adjustment?
Sex role differences	Macrosystem	How does a parent's concept of sex-appropriate behavior affect child-rearing practices?

The Process That Guides Development

Another issue often raised among different theories of development is the role each theory ascribes to the mechanisms of maturation and learning. The maturation-learning controversy parallels the comparison between hereditary and environmental influences discussed in the preceding section. Instead of focusing on the source or location of the influence, we are addressing the mechanism through which changes take place.

Maturation is a biological process where developmental changes are controlled by internal (or endogenous) factors. Events that result from maturation (such as walking or secondary sex changes at puberty) are characteristic of the species and are never the result of specific practice or exercise—that is, they are not learned.

Waber (1976) conducted an interesting study that examines the relationship between maturation and sex differences. Previous research had shown that males tend to score higher than females on tests of spatial abilities, while females tend to score higher on tests of verbal abilities. These differences are often attributed to inheritance or to social and cultural influences (such as learning). Waber asked the following question: Are these differences in performance the result of differences in maturation or differences in sex? She answered it by testing both early and late maturing males and females. She found that early maturers, regardless of sex, performed better on tests of verbal abilities, while the reverse was true of late maturers (thus confirming her hypothesis). Research such as this does not discount the importance of sex as a variable for explaining differences in performance, but it does emphasize that maturational processes have a broader influence than might have been earlier believed.

Learning is a function of direct or indirect experience. The term refers to developmental changes that result from exercise or practice, and the outcomes of learning are highly individualized and specific. For example, greeting foreign visitors in their own tongue or driving a car is an example of a learned behavior that depends on highly specific training. There are many different types of learning, from simple relationships between events in the environment to complex systems of imitation or modeling. This diversity of learning paradigms provides a foundation for the set of developmental theories that are based on principles of learning and discussed in other sections of this book.

The work of Ainsworth (1979) and Bowlby (1969) on attachment behavior between children and caretakers provides an excellent example of the synthesis of learning and maturation. Ainsworth believes that very early in life there is a developmental predisposition to form an attachment to some caretaker. This predisposition is thought to result from genetic programming and is part of the general maturational process. The choice of the person to whom the attachment is formed, however, is highly idiosyncratic, often situationally determined, and the entire process is quite probably the result of learning.

This is perhaps best illustrated by the strong attachments we can see between adopted as well as biological children and their parents, where no biological process needs to be operating. The attachment process per se is biologically determined, but the focus of that attachment is not.

As a result of social forces and expectations within the American culture, the female has been the primary caretaker and the "target" for attachment. Females may make the best "mothers," but there is ample reason to believe that "mothering" (or parenting) is a learned set of very complex behaviors, rather than a set of traits that are genetically transmitted from generation to generation. Our society also seems to assume that simply having children qualifies one as a parent, and endows one with a knowledge bank about how children should be raised. Unfortunately, as we have seen from an increasing incidence of child abuse and abandonment, this is not the case.

The Importance of Age

Chronological age has historically provided the most convenient and readily available guideline for estimating an individual's level of development. Because chronological age is easily and accurately determined, development is often evaluated against criteria based on expected performance at a certain age. The most frequently used criterion for providing *normative* or comparative standards is to determine at what age a certain number or percent of children can perform at a certain level.

For example, seven-year-olds are expected to know what a certain number of words mean on general intelligence tests.

There is a good deal of debate, however, over whether age is a reliable measure for evaluating development. For example, differences that exist between groups of children of different ages may not always be caused only by age. Factors such as sex, social class, and intelligence might indeed explain more (and allow us to understand more) than age alone. One of the problems with using age is that it tends to relate to almost everything (because so many things are related to it), yet it explains very little. We all know that as children get older, they grow taller. Their height, however, is only incidentally related to their age, and is much more a function of diet, quality of healthcare, and heredity. Chronological age is nothing more than an indicator of how much time has passed between two events. It does not help us understand what might cause differences in development. Developmental psychologists must then systematically study the events that occur over time (both internal and external to the developing child) to fully understand all the factors affecting developmental outcomes.

Werner Schaie (1965) identified some of these other factors besides age that can help us explain developmental outcomes. Two factors are *time of testing* (when a behavior is being measured) and *cohort* (a group of people born in the same year). These factors have been shown in some instances to explain more of the reasons in differences in development than age alone can by itself.

In Table 2-4, there are three different cohorts of children (born in 1968, 1969, and 1970) who are tested at three different times (in 1975, 1976, and 1977). What do the three different factors of age, time of testing, and cohort represent? According to Schaie, age differences between groups can represent maturational factors; differences caused by when the group was tested (time of testing) represent environmental effects; and cohort differences represent environmental and/or hereditary effects or an interaction between the two. For example, Baltes and Nesselroade (1974) have shown how adolescents of the same age perform differently on a set of personality tests as a function of the year in which they were born (cohort) as well as when these characteristics were measured (time of testing). We can even look to our own experiences to recognize how college age students of today are so different from those of 10 or 20 years ago.

Table 2-4   Age, Cohort, and Time of Testing

		Time of Testing		
		1975	1976	1977
	1970	5[a]	6	7
Cohort	1969	6	7	8
	1968	7	8	9

[a]Age.

Donald Baer (1970) elaborated on this perspective when he presented the thesis that *age is irrelevant to development*. He believes that a distinction should be made between an *age psychology* that is dependent on products, and a *developmental psychology* that is characterized by processes. Baer argues that age is only a convenience for noting change along some continuum, but it is a poor explanation of why developmental change occurs. What is crucial, Baer argues, is the sequencing of events in the environment and their subsequent effects on behavior. This view is representative of those theories that emphasize learning and other environmental influences as fundamental to the developmental process. It also stresses that age has *descriptive* but not *explanatory* power.

There are, however, other views of development that do incorporate age as an important landmark in development. Besides the use of age as a general indicator of when change should occur, age is also used as an index of development. The use of age alone precludes any method of study besides relative evaluations of a child based on other similarly aged children.

Overlap occurs when a child who is associated with one group on the basis of one variable (such as age) is at one extreme on another variable relative to that group. For example, a tall ten-year-old in the fifth grade may be as tall, or taller, than a child in the seventh grade. The overlap between the distribution of children in the fifth and the seventh grades occurs in the area common to both classes as shown by the shaded section in Figure 2-1. Those children whose height falls in the shaded area are either extremely tall fifth graders or extremely short seventh graders (relative to their peer group). Normative measures, in which some children are short, some tall, and some located in between, describe relative, not absolute levels of development. Outliers (extreme cases) are difficult to evaluate using

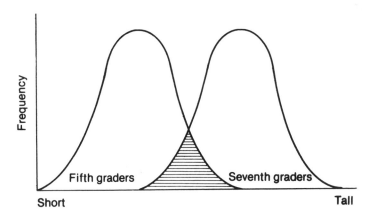

Figure 2-1. An example of overlap.

normative measures, and extreme caution should be taken in attributing characteristics of other members of the group to these individuals. Hence the argument that we need to look at other variables than just age alone when we make judgments.

Rate of Development and Critical Periods

One characteristic of the developmental process—regardless of one's theoretical viewpoint—is that it involves constant change. Some of these changes seem to occur more rapidly during certain periods and less rapidly during others, and developmental psychologists often focus on differences in the rate of change as a major variable of interest. In infancy and adolescence, for example, rapid rates of physical change are accompanied by more subtle psychological changes.

Change often appears as a cyclical phenomenon. For example, two-year-old children are somewhat cooperative and generally pleased with their accomplishments, while the two-and-one-half-year-old might seem uneasy and argumentative (Ilg & Ames, 1955). Similarly, throughout the early years of development, periods of fluctuating extraversion and introversion occur. Although the ages at which these different cycles begin and end differ for different children, this fluctuation, or *periodicity*, is not the result of either genetic or environmental factors alone, but an interaction of the two.

According to Benjamin Bloom, the greatest effects on development take place when these changes are occurring most rapidly. As Bloom states, "Variations in the environment have greatest quantitative effect on a characteristic at its most rapid period of change and least effect on the characteristic during the least rapid period of change" (1964, p. vii). The faster the rate of change, the greater the potential impact we can expect that external and internal events will have on subsequent development. Bloom also stressed (as did Ilg and Ames) that for each dimension of human behavior there is usually a period of rapid change and a period of slow change. This variability in the rate of change over the life span in part forms the basis for the argument that 50 percent of intellectual development is completed by four years of age as a result of the rapid biological and social changes that occur during those early years.

An issue closely related to rate of development is whether critical or sensitive periods exist. A critical period is a span of time during which internal or external events have a maximum impact on development. During this period, the individual is more susceptible to the impact of certain influences than during any other. For example, the research literature on animals (Hebb, 1947; Levine, 1957) and some of the research on humans (Hunt, 1961; Bloom, 1964) suggests that the optimal time to intervene in order to avoid potential problems is during the first three years of life when the rate of change is fastest across many dimensions.

One psychologist (Havighurst, 1952) views critical periods within a framework of what he calls *developmental tasks* that should be completed during a certain stage or time span to ensure the healthy development of the individual. A developmental task is a task that arises "on or about a certain period in the life of the individual, successful achievement of which leads to his happiness and success with later tasks, while failure leads to unhappiness in the individual, disapproval by the society, and difficulty with later tasks" (p. 2).

The completion of developmental tasks lays a foundation on which later developmental progress is based. For example, a developmental task faced by adolescents in American society is an increase in independence or autonomy. Interestingly, successful completion of these tasks is often determined by both maturational and environmental influences. It is interesting to speculate about how these tasks differ from one culture to another and what types of developmental tasks (and changes) may be universal.

In humans, critical periods have been difficult to study due to the ethical and moral concerns that prevent artificial deprivation of needs for stimulation, physical contact, or food during certain hypothetically "critical" periods. On occasion, naturally occurring events provide a situation in which the critical period hypothesis can be tested. An example of such a case is the story of a twelve-year-old boy named Victor, captured in the French countryside during the early nineteenth century. After being declared an incurable idiot and treated as an animal, the boy was placed in the custody of Dr. Jean Marc Itard. Although some progress was made through intensive daily training sessions, Victor consistently failed to learn language. If Victor was not retarded (and Itard believed he was not), then Victor's failure to learn language at the late age of twelve years could support a critical-period hypothesis for language development. According to linguists such as Lenneberg (1967), language development spans a period of time from two years to the onset of puberty. The lack of adequate instruction during those critical years could be responsible for Victor's inability to communicate verbally. An interesting description of Itard's experience can be found in *The Wild Boy of Aveyron* by Harlan Lane (1976) and the film *The Wild Child*.

Another example of a critical period is the timing of sex-role assignment for the young child. John Money has studied children who were reared as the opposite of their genetic sex because of hermaphrodism or some disfigurement (Money & Ehrhardt, 1973). He concluded that, up to the first eighteen months of life, there is a great deal of latitude in the assignment of psychological sex roles. For example, biological males can be socialized to become social females if training is early and intense. This freedom decreases sharply, however, so that by three to four years of age there is little chance of a significant change taking place.

One argument with the idea of a critical period is the basic premise that any developmental component can be so susceptible to change during a relatively narrow span of time. This disagreement is supported strongly by those theoreticians who believe that development is a process controlled by environmental or exogenous forces rather than by biological imperatives.

The use of the term "critical period" can also be misleading, since it implies the existence of a restricted time period and ignores other factors (such as experience) whose effects may be more noticeable at other times in the developmental cycle. A critical period should be thought of as a range or band of time during which an individual is most susceptible to change. Undoubtedly, critical periods for some aspects of development do exist, but to what extent events during these periods result in alterations in future outcomes is still widely open to speculation.

The Shape of Development

Sometimes it's difficult to understand how something that does not have any physical form can have a "shape." But indeed, if we look at changes in behavior over time (which is one way to define development), we can see how the course of development, and its shape, differs depending on one's theoretical orientation.

Development is viewed as a *continuous* process if (1) changes occur in small gradual steps, (2) the outcomes of development are "more of the same" and not qualitatively different from what was present earlier, and (3) the same general laws underlie the process at all points along the developmental continuum.

Theories of development that tend to stress the importance of environmental factors, such as behavioral approaches, view development as continuous.

Development is viewed as *discontinuous* if (1) changes that occur are abrupt and qualitatively different from what existed before, and (2) different general laws characterize developmental change.

Theorists such as Jean Piaget and Jerome Bruner, who believe that development is characterized by a series of independent, qualitatively different stages, view development as a discontinuous process. Figure 2-2 illustrates the difference between continuous and discontinuous change, where one view is smooth and continuous, while the other is stagelike and somewhat variable. In the figure, the continuous line (A at A1) represents continuity, while the segmented line (from A to B) represents discontinuity.

Just as the heredity-environment issue presents a somewhat artificial choice between alternatives, so does the continuity-discontinuity issue. Some environmentalists see development solely as a continuous process, and others consider development to be completely discontinuous. If one examines the actual curves of change over time, however, developmental change can be seen to combine both types.

It is also possible to view continuity and discontinuity as a continuum, and Jerome Kagan (1971) has discussed this in some detail. Table 2-5 presents a continuum ranging from complete continuity to complete discontinuity with gradual changes along the way. For example, a set of behaviors between two points in time (time 1 and time 2) can be identical or different from one another. The underlying process responsible for these behaviors can also be identical, different but related,

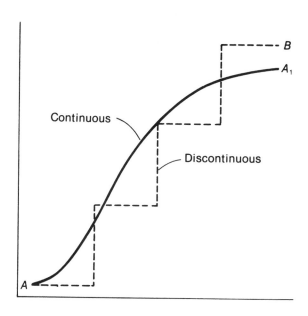

Figure 2-2. Continuous and discontinuous change.

or totally different and unrelated. These are the different relationships possible between a behavior, its cause, and the type of continuity represented by this relationship.

For example, let's take a case of complete continuity. A young child may be very aggressive because he or she has learned this is the most effective way to deal with frustration. As an adult, the same pattern of behavior (for the same reason)

Table 2-5 Different Types of Continuity with Similarity in Behavior Between Time 1 and Time 2

Overt Behavior	Underlying Psychological Process	Type of Continuity/Discontinuity
Identical	Identical	Complete continuity
Different	Identical	
Identical	Related	
Different	Related	
Identical	Different	
Different	Different	Complete discontinuity

operates. In this case, the behaviors at the two points in time are identical, and the underlying psychological process (frustration) is identical as well. On the other hand, a case for discontinuity can be made if the adult's aggressive behavior is at a later date the result of different psychological processes. Perhaps it is frustration at one point, and a reaction to being threatened at another.

From the point of view that is usually adopted by theorists who believe that development is discontinuous, changes in behavior are accompanied by changes in underlying psychological *structures*. We can draw an analogy between the presence of physical structures necessary to walk (sufficient neurological and muscular development) and the presence of psychological structures necessary to solve certain types of problems. These developmentalists would agree that quantitative change occurs (such as an increase in the number of words a child speaks), but these changes in and of themselves do not reflect the true nature of development.

The other point of view would be that behavior is the structure of development itself and that there is no underlying frame or foundation that dictates the sequence of what will occur next. In other words, overt (observable) behavior represents the functional nature of the individual, not the operation of any underlying mechanism. Hence, behavior is continuous in nature. For example, some people believe that certain academic differences between males and females are not the result of structural differences, but instead are due to social learning and people's desire to fulfill expectations that are imposed on them at an early age. This perspective is called *functional* because it stresses the way in which specific behaviors become a function of specific changes in a given setting. This view is characteristic of behavioral approaches we will focus on later in this book.

Individual Differences

Although individuals have a great deal in common, one of the most fascinating things about human behavior is that all individuals are different as well. How different theoretical viewpoints explain these differences can help us better understand differences between theories. For example, even from the very early days of a child's life, individual differences arise. Some babies cry more than others, seem to enjoy physical contact to a greater degree than others, and develop different sleep patterns as well. In fact, Arnold Gesell, the focus of the next chapter, recognized differences in identical twins even at birth.

Six categories of such differences in infants have been summarized by Ausubel and Sullivan (1970) in (1) irritability, (2) activity level, (3) tone, length, and vigorousness of crying, (4) tolerance of frustration or discomfort and reaction to stress, (5) sensitivity to stimulation, and (6) smiling behavior.

There is no question that some developmental psychologists view these early differences as the result of biological processes. On the other hand, as the child grows and differences focus on more complex behaviors such as language development or patterns of attachment, it is much less clear that the process is responsible for any individual differences that we might notice.

Our interest in the discussion of the theories that follow will be the source of differences among developing individuals who are at the same chronological level of development.

How Is Development Studied?

The methods that psychologists use to study development are as varied as the different theoretical viewpoints that they hold about the process itself.

What is most interesting perhaps about the question "How is development studied?" is that the method used usually reflects the question of interest being asked. For example, most behavioral theorists are more interested in the behavior itself, rather than the underlying process responsible for that behavior. Because of this orientation, they are likely to focus on how *frequently* a certain behavior occurs and under what kinds of conditions. It's no surprise that much of the work done in the basic analysis of behavior focuses on frequency, or the number of times a behavior occurs. The method used, basically one of counting, reflects the philosophical orientation that behavior is itself what is important, rather than some other process that cannot be directly observed.

In contrast to this focus on counting observable events, the psychoanalytic framework initiated by Freud stressed the importance of helping the individual reveal unconscious and subconscious thoughts. These thoughts theoretically represent the presence and actions of unobservable processes. The method focuses in a more indirect way (than that discussed above) by making accessible what Freud considered important.

In order to understand how a particular method relates to a particular theory, chapters throughout the book will provide an example ("How They Study Development") that reflects the theoretical orientation discussed in that chapter. We will then be able to see how the assumptions of the study often dictate the questions the theory might ask, and how the answers to these questions depend on the particular method used.

SUMMARY POINTS

1. There are general trends that all humans share as part of the development process.

2. Development progresses from general or global systems of responding to specific or discrete systems of responding.
3. As individuals develop, they become increasingly complex.
4. Biological and psychological systems become increasingly differentiated (or separate) from each other, as well as increasingly integrated (or entwined) with each other.
5. Egocentrism is a preoccupation with one's own perspective. It is characteristic of development at all levels.
6. Most children show increasing degrees of independence and social autonomy with developmental progress.
7. Issues in developmental psychology generate new questions and directions for study.
8. Whether heredity or environmental influences predominate in development is a major focus of developmental psychology.
9. The important question is how heredity and environment interact, not to what degree.
10. Maturation is controlled by biological processes and dictates species-specific behaviors. Learning is a function of experience or exercise and is idiosyncratic.
11. Age can be a misleading index of development because it accounts for only the passage of time, not for events over time.
12. Development is an ongoing process that is characterized by cycles of change; the impact of internal and external influences depends on the rate of change.
13. A critical period is a span of time during which the organism is maximally susceptible to internal or external influences.
14. Development can be continuous (occurring in small gradual steps), or discontinuous (occurring in abrupt and qualitatively distinct stages), but is usually a combination of the two.
15. Individual differences in development can best be explained by examining the basic assumptions of a theory.
16. The method that psychologists use to better understand the process of development is determined by the theoretical framework within which the question is being asked.

FURTHER READINGS

Anastasi, A. Heredity, environment, and the question "how." *Psychological Review*, 1958, 65, 197–208.

Dennis, W. (Ed.). *Historical readings in developmental psychology*. New York: Appleton-Century-Crofts, 1972.

Harlow, H. F. The nature of love. *American Psychologist*, 1958, 13, 673–685.

Kagan, J. *Change and continuity in infancy*. New York: Wiley, 1971.
Mussen, P. H., Larger, J., and Covington, M. (Eds.). *Trends and issues in developmental psychology*. New York: Holt, Rinehart & Winston, 1969.
Wohlwill, J. *The study of behavioral development*. New York: Academic Press, 1973.

OTHER READINGS OF INTEREST

Lane, H. *The wild boy of Aveyron*. Cambridge: Harvard University Press, 1976.
Gardner, M. *Fads and fallacies in the name of science*. New York: Dover Press, 1957.

3

Arnold Gesell and the Maturational Approach

The purpose of learning is growth, and our minds, unlike our bodies, can continue growing as we continue to live.

Mortimer Adler

There is nothing permanent except change.

Heraclitus

As the twig is bent the tree inclines.

Virgil

Arnold Gesell's (pronounced Gēzel) long life of eighty-one years included an enormously productive career that saw him become a psychologist then an educator and a physician and writer. In all these endeavors, he was single-mindedly interested in the development of children and the importance of biological controls. After working in the field of education, he went to Clark University, where he was influenced by G. Stanley Hall's interest in *recapitulation theory*. This theory held that in the development (or ontogenesis) of the child a sequence of stages occurs that recapitulates the evolutionary history of the development of the species. In other words, *ontogeny* (the development of the individual) recapitulates *phylogeny* (the development of the species). Much of recapitulation theory as well as Gesell's early work was influenced by Darwin's theory of evolution as presented in *The Origin of Species* (1859). It is interesting to note how much influence the biological sciences (such as biochemistry and physiology) were having on newer disciplines such as child development.

At Yale University, Gesell studied for his medical degree and, with his training in education, psychology, and medicine, he devoted his life to the scientific and practical concerns of the field of child development, especially child rearing. In 1911 he became the director of the Clinic of Child Development, and when he retired in 1948 his work and the work of his students comprised an impressive contribution to the field of developmental psychology. Although these contributions can be reviewed both in terms of their theoretical orientation and innovations in methods used to study children (such as the use of motion pictures), the most lasting effect of the work has been its impact on child-rearing practices. Since Gesell was well versed in many different fields, he could speak knowledgeably to different constituencies. In addition, because he wrote for scientific, professional, and popular audiences, his impact was widespread. Even though this impact is still apparent today, many practitioners who reflect his influence are not directly familiar with Gesell's contribution.

THE THEORETICAL OUTLOOK

Gesell's theory was not a formal set of hypotheses or postulates that was to be successively tested as part of the process of theory development we discussed earlier. Instead, his theory places heavy emphasis on biological forces that provide both the impetus and the direction for development. As we mentioned earlier, Darwin's theory of evolution had a significant impact on Gesell's developmental work. He also was influenced by the work of Coghill (1929) and the role that structure plays in relationship to function. Coghill believed that structure determined function. This is still a very popular thesis, especially within the theoretical view that hypothesizes how the operation of underlying structures account for behavior. Simply put, physical structure must be present and developed before function can occur, and behavior is simply not possible if the necessary structures have not yet developed. For example, children cannot walk until they have the structural equipment to do so (including the maturational development of certain muscles as well as neural organization).

Based on the huge body of information he collected, Gesell and his colleagues maintained that development progresses through an orderly *sequence* and that the sequence is determined by the biological and evolutionary history of the species. The *rate* at which any child progresses through the sequence, however, is individually determined by the child's own genotype (the child's heredity background received from his or her ancestors). Although the rate of development can by artificially altered, it cannot be fundamentally changed. Thus, a child who is developing more slowly than average cannot be deflected from his or her course, just as the faster-developing child is similarly set on a course. On the other hand, the environment can temporarily affect the rate at which the child develops. For example, malnutrition or illness may affect the rate of development, but biological factors are ultimately in control. This occurs in the same manner that biological characteristics of the species control the sequence of development.

The essence of this position was effectively summarized by two of Gesell's colleagues in the following statement from one of their many popular books: "A favorable environment (home or otherwise) can, it appears, permit each individual to develop his most positive assets for living. An unfavorable environment may inhibit and depress his natural potentials. But no environment, good or bad, can so far as we know change him from one kind of individual to another" (Ilg & Ames, 1955, p. 64).

BASIC PRINCIPLES OF DEVELOPMENT

Gesell made his most comprehensive statement about development several years after he retired. In a chapter entitled "The Ontogenesis of Infant Behavior" (1954) he detailed the principles of development that described and supported his views of the developmental process. Gesell sought to unite the basic principles of morphological (or underlying structural) growth with behavioral growth in showing how "psychological growth, like somatic growth, is a morphogenetic process" (Gesell, 1954, p. 338). He described five basic principles of development that he thought had "psychomorphological" implications because they represent developmental principles that occur on a psychological level as well as on a structural one. Also, many of these principles are based on the biological functions that Gesell observed in the large sample of normal infants he studied.

1. The Principle of Developmental Direction

This principle assumes that development is not random but proceeds in an ordered fashion. The fact that development systematically proceeds from the head to the toes is a good example of how at any point a developmental trend will be more advanced in the head area than in the foot area. Thus, at birth, the newborn infant is relatively more mature in neuromotor organization in the head region than in the leg region, and coordination of the arms precedes coordination of the legs. This trend is described as the *cephalocaudal* (head to tail) *trend*.

Another example, is how development is more advanced at the center of the body compared to its periphery. The movements of the shoulders show considerably more organization early in life than the movement of the wrists and fingers. This *proximoldistal* (near to far) trend can also be seen in the child's grasping behavior, which at twenty weeks is quite crude and dominated by upper arm movements. By twenty-eight weeks, however, with the increasingly sophisticated use of the thumb, the grasping is dominated by increasingly finer motor characteristics.

Both the cephalocaudal and proximal distal trends illustrate Gesell's contention that development (and behavior) have direction, and that this direction is basically a function of preprogrammed genetic mechanisms.

2. The Principle of Reciprocal Interweaving

Gesell derived this principle of behavior from a complementary principle of physiology called *reciprocal innervation*, proposed by Sir Charles Scott Sherrington, winner of the 1932 Nobel Prize for medicine. This second general principle is modeled after the physiological principle that inhibition and excitation of different muscles operate in a complementary fashion to produce efficient movement.

Gesell asserted that a parallel phenomenon in behavioral patterning, requiring complementary structural growth, operated as part of the developmental process. Thus Gesell described the developmental sequence that results in walking as a series of alternations between flexor (bending) dominance and extensor (extending) dominance involving the arms and legs in a kind of neuromuscular coordination and integration that takes place over an extended period of time. He employed this principle in describing the development of walking, and the development of the dominance of one hand over the other. He summarized this principle as follows:

> The organization of reciprocal relationships between two counteracting functions or neuromotor systems is ontogenetically manifested by somewhat periodic shifting of ascendancy of the component functions or systems, with progressive modulation and integration of the resultant behavior patterns (Gesell, 1954, p. 349).

Through such a complementary process, opposing sets of forces have their ascendancy (or dominance) at different times during the developmental cycle. These forces, which are contradictory to one another, result in an integration and progression toward a higher level of developmental maturity. This idea of oppositional forces operating simultaneously to facilitate the move toward more sophisticated development comes up again and again as a common characteristic of many models of development that place a high degree of emphasis on the role that biological as well as cultural factors play.

3. The Principle of Functional Asymmetry

Not all aspects of development can be described as a balancing of opposing tendencies constantly being reorganized as in the principle of reciprocal interweaving. There is a special case of reciprocal interweaving that is really an exception to the rule. This principle is known as the *principle of functional asymmetry* wherein a behavior goes through a period of asymmetric or unbalanced development to enable the organism to achieve a measure of maturity at a later stage. The primary example that Gesell offers of this complex principle is a basic reflex, called the tonic neck reflex.

This reflex is present when infants assume a position like a fencer with their head turned to one side, one arm extended to the side, the leg on that side drawn straight, and the other arm folded across the chest and the other leg bent at the knee. This asymmetrical behavior is the precursor for the later development of symmetrical reaching, in which the child's two arms come together to grasp a suspended object. This is an important step in the child's efforts to master and understand the environment.

Gesell also believed that the principle of functional asymmetry has a great deal to do with the development of handedness and other forms of psychomotor dominance. It also helps to prevent the infant from suffocation (by turning the head) and is part of the reserve of reflexes that contributes to certain acts such as throwing a ball, for example, and even aggression.

4. The Principle of Individuating Maturation

Within Gesell's theoretical framework, development is viewed as a process of sequential patterning wherein the patterning is predetermined and revealed as the organism matures. Maturation is a process that is controlled by endogenous or internal factors, and cannot be influenced in its basic aspects by exogenous or external factors such as teaching. In other words, the results of maturational processes cannot be learned. The principle of individuating maturation stresses the importance of a *growth matrix* as an internal mechanism that establishes the direction and pattern of development of the individual.

Gesell summed up his feelings about the relationship between maturation and the environment as follows: "Environmental factors support, inflect, and specify; but they do not engender the basic forms and sequences of ontogenesis" (Gesell, 1954, p. 354). Consequently, learning can occur only when structures have developed that permit behavioral adaptation, and no amount of specific training prior to the development of structure will be effective. Gesell places heavy emphasis on the role of biological factors. It is important to note that he did not discount the influence of the environment, but pointed out that its effects on the final outcomes of development are probably quite limited.

5. The Principle of Self-Regulatory Fluctuation

The principle of self-regulatory fluctuation proposed that developmental progress is like a see-saw that fluctuates between periods of stability and instability, active growth and consolidation. These progressive fluctuations, as part of a give-and-take much like the principle of reciprocal interweaving, culminate in a set of stable responses. These fluctuations are not undesirable or irregular, but instead are definite efforts on the part of the individual to maintain the integrity of the system, while assuring that continued growth occurs.

In fact, Gesell believed that a distinct sequence of stages occurs repeatedly as the child matures, and that a stage of disequilibrium or unbalance is always followed by a stage of equilibrium. Figure 3-1 shows the level of balance across the second through sixteenth year of development. The figure illustrates the way in which development occurs in cycles that range from relative equilibrium to relative disequilibrium. The line in this figure represents a hypothetical trend characteristic of behavior in general, and not the behavior of any one child.

THE IMPORTANCE OF INDIVIDUAL DIFFERENCES

Each of these five principles is considered to be characteristic of every child's growth pattern, yet Gesell emphasizes the importance of wide and stable individual differences as well. One of Gesell's unique contributions to the field of developmental psychology was the development of a new method of studying development using moving pictures. Gesell and his colleagues first studied five infants during the first year of life using these "cinema records," and then studied these same five children five years later.

During the first year, each child was rated on fifteen behavior traits, such as energy output, social responsiveness, and self-dependence, and then each child was rank-ordered within the group of five on each trait. The same process was repeated

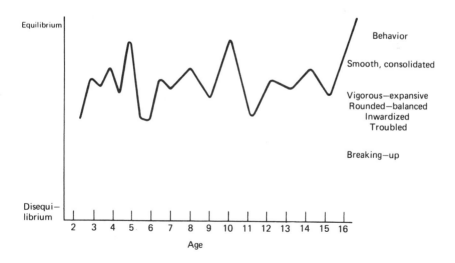

Figure 3-1. The cycles of development (adapted from Ilg and Ames, 1955).

five years later. A comparison of ranks between the first year and at five years showed a remarkable similarity between the two observations on traits such as laterality (handedness), self-dependence, sense of humor, and emotional maladjustment. These findings indicate a certain degree of stability in the development of individual differences, a characteristic that Gesell believed has its source in some kind of biological mechanism.

In another study of thirty-three infants from infancy through the teenage years, a remarkable degree of stability was also found in what Gesell refers to as *trends in mental development*. Infants whose mental development was found to be below normal continued to show the same trend as teenagers. Similarly, children who were superior as infants were also superior as adolescents.

Gesell described individual differences in behavioral development in four different areas: motor behavior, adaptive behavior, language behavior, and personal-social behavior. *Motor behavior* refers to locomotion, coordination, and specific motor skills. *Adaptive behavior* includes alertness, intelligence, and different forms of exploration. *Language behavior* includes all forms of communication, and *personal-social behavior* encompasses reactions to persons and to the environment. Indeed, in the popular books that Gesell and his colleagues wrote for parents, the behavior the parent should expect to see at each age is described in terms of these domains. In addition, these four domains formed the basis for a widely used and well-known screening test for developmental delay.

In each of these four domains the five general principles of development described earlier continue to function, with individual differences in the rate of development dominating. The child is an integral whole within which the four domains interact with one another while under the control of biological forces expressed through the five principles of development discussed earlier. To summarize Gesell's theoretical outlook, the development of the child is controlled entirely by biologically determined principles of development that produce an invariant sequence of maturation. In turn, this maturational process makes behavioral expression possible. Although individual children progress at their own rate (and the rate is not amenable to environmental manipulation), the sequence of development is the same for every child.

Gesell was a tireless empiricist who collected a great deal of information about children, particularly during infancy. He continually sought new and better ways of measuring and recording behavior, and methodologically he made several contributions. As mentioned earlier, he was among the first to use moving pictures for both recording the growth of behavior patterns and for examining the film frame by frame to trace for postural development in infants. These films are currently being prepared for permanent placement in an archival laboratory in Akron, Ohio, under the auspices of the Society for Research in Child Development.

Gesell was also actively involved with children in other ways as well. One of the earliest educational documentaries in the field of child development, a two-reel film entitled *Life Begins*, features Gesell presenting his point of view and encouraging the viewer to believe that science has a contribution to make in safeguarding the successful development of the child. Gesell also showed concern for such issues as standardizing the materials used in research and the reliability or consistency of measurements. Although most of the children who served as subjects in his studies were from white, middle-class families in New Haven, Connecticut, the data base he amassed represents one of the earliest and best-collected normative reference groups. He was able to organize all this information into a description of growth and development and from it he devised a series of tasks to be used in evaluating an individual child's development relative to that child's age group. The result was the Gesell Development Schedule, from which a Developmental Quotient (DQ) could be derived. This schedule became the prototype of most infant assessment techniques used since then.

This *normative* approach relied on repeated testing of the same children over a long period of time (a longitudinal strategy) to obtain characteristic age descriptions and to test the stability or continuity of individual differences. A stable individual difference is one where an individual maintains the same relative position on some measure in comparison to his or her peers at an earlier and later time. Gesell and his colleagues introduced the now classic *co-twin control* method, in which genetically identical twins were used to elucidate the controversy of whether biological forces (maturation) or experience (learning) represented the major force in development (Gesell & Thompson, 1929; 1941). The use of identical twins (two children who developed from the same fertilized egg) allows such a comparison, because both children have identical genotypes or genetic histories.

In this method (illustrated in Figure 3-2), one twin is given specific training and the other twin is left to the natural opportunities of the environment (or acts as the control). Some criterion behavior such as walking is then measured. For example, the twins would be observed for their baseline or initial performance in a behavior such as stair climbing. Then, one twin (#1) would be given specific training in stair climbing, but the other (#2) would not. Each twin was later tested. The twin receiving the training would show slow increments in the behavior, while the control twin showed no increments. Then, when the control twin reached the age where maturationally he or she would be expected to begin learning to climb stairs, intensive training would begin. The results indicated that with a short amount of training, the control twin achieved the same level of mastery as the trained twin. Furthermore, at the end of the experimental period there would be no difference in competence between the two children. Based on such studies, it was concluded that early training before the child was physically mature was of little consequence to the ultimate outcome. Since maturation is such a predominant factor in development, learning is possible only where the maturational, or structural apparatus, is functioning.

The effects of training (or learning) however, need to be looked at for their

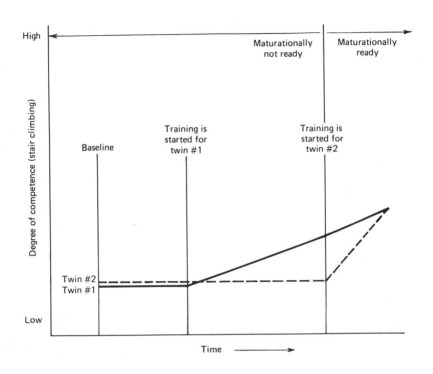

Figure 3-2. Results of the training and twin studies.

immediate *and* long-term impact. Myrtle McGraw, who conducted some of the early studies using the co-twin control paradigm (1935), made a series of films in which the trained twin (who received training in a variety of motor skills) was shown to have developed into a lean, athletic, graceful individual. The control twin, however (who did not receive the training program), was not lean, decidedly not athletic, and quite ungraceful. Gesell believed that training could not modify biologically set characteristics, but he did not seriously consider the cumulative effects of environmental variables as a major part of his research program. Yet in considering the impact of early training, cumulative as well as sleeper effects (those effects that show up much later on) may be very important when immediate effects are not shown to be strong or durable. In fact, this sleeper effect was operating in the Head Start programs initiated during the 1960s, since many benefits of participation in the program are only now beginning to surface.

Given Gesell's strong emphasis on the biological basis of many characteristics, it's not surprising that the Gesellian orientation stresses a fixed level of intelligence.

In opposition to this point of view, Skeels and Dye (1939) set out to demonstrate that environmental enrichment could significantly raise IQ levels. An orphanage in Davenport, Iowa, was chosen for the experiment. One group of children in the orphanage would be given a specially enriched preschool experience, while the other group would not be given any special experiences. In preparation for the experiment, each child was given an IQ test, and two little girls were found to be severely retarded. At thirteen and sixteen months of age they were functioning at the level of seven and eight months. Skeels and his colleagues recommended that the children be placed in an institution for the retarded. Six months later, Skeels (who happened to serve as a consultant to the institution where the girls were placed), visited the institution. He saw the two little girls, now nineteen and twenty-one months of age, running around and acting quite normal for their age. A formal test of the children's developmental level confirmed this impression. Because the investigators did not believe that such a dramatic change (that is, bringing a retarded infant into the ''normal'' range) could occur, the children were left in the institution and retested several months later. Again the result was the same. These two little girls were functioning at a normal level of intelligence and were no longer considered retarded.

Further investigation revealed that when the ''retarded'' infants were originally brought to the institution there had been no place to put them, so they were placed on a ward with retarded older women who would care for them. Indeed these women had! Besides playing with the children and treating them in special ways, the women bombarded them with affection. The nurses had also taken a liking to the children and would often take them on outings. As a result of a high degree of stimulation, a remarkable change had occurred.

Not leaving any of this to chance, a more formal experiment was begun whereby a group of low-normal children from the orphanage was placed on the ward with the retarded women. At the same time, a control group (who tested initially some-what higher in intelligence) remained in the orphanage. The children in the exper-imental group remained in the institution for varying amounts of time, and, like the original two girls, they showed some dramatic increases in their intelligence levels over the course of their stay. Many of them returned to the orphanage only briefly when the experiment was concluded and were either adopted or returned to their biological parents who had not been able to care for them. A follow-up testing two-and-one-half years after the conclusion of the experiment showed that (1) some of the dramatic gains were maintained for the experimental children, and (2) some of the control children who had remained in the orphanage had shown dramatic declines in tested intelligence.

It appears then that a brief and somewhat unsystematic intervention produced remarkable changes in intelligence. These results might be seen as strong support for the environmentalist position regarding the manipulability of intelligence and as evidence against Gesell's claim that mental development is biologically and not environmentally determined. For a number of reasons, however, these data did not have an effect on the controversy.

One of the reasons had to do with the way the research was done. For example, the amount of time in the experiment and the initial levels of tested intelligence varied widely for each child. Further, the persons administering the intelligence tests were aware whether the child was in the experimental or control group, and this perhaps affected their objectivity.

Finally, during the period intervening between the end of the experiment and the follow-up testing, the maintenance of the increase in IQ could not be attributed solely to the experimental conditions because many of the children in the experimental group had not remained in the orphanage. In other words, there were many uncontrolled factors that prevented attributing the changes in the children to any specific cause. Finally, Gesell's contention that development is controlled primarily by biological factors assumes a normal environment. Gesell did not address the issue of a seriously deprived environment, perhaps because his subject population came primarily from average, middle-class homes. If the orphanage is thought of as a seriously nonnormal environment, it is not even clear that Gesell would have interpreted the data as being counter to his position.

When the last of the data from Skeels and his colleagues was published in the early 1940s, the nature-nurture controversy had effectively been defused. Not only had the advent of a world war diverted attention from the argument, but the fury had largely ceased. The heredity-environment controversy was thought to have reached an impasse because of the admitted inability to clearly separate environmental and biological factors in assessing human traits such as intelligence.

In the early 1960s when Harold Skeels was on the verge of retirement from his position at the National Institutes of Health, he set out to see what had happened to the children who had participated in the experiment almost thirty years earlier. The story of that search and a review of all of the earlier data were published in a 1966 monograph. The thirty-year follow-up revealed a remarkably different set of life histories of the two groups of children, who were by then adults.

The experimental group of children (who had initially scored lower in intelligence than the original control group) went on to lead relatively normal, productive lives. The children in the control group, however, either remained in institutions or were employed in menial jobs. Although the original experimental group tested lower, the control group's life outcomes were much lower. Skeels is cautious in interpreting his findings, urging care in concluding that the experimental treatment was responsible for the differences in outcomes. Nevertheless, if one looks at the initial performance of the two groups, and if one takes the Gesellian position on the stability of mental growth, the prediction would be quite different from what is seen in the actual data.

Whether or not one supports Gesell's position depends on how one interprets the data. Gesell and his colleagues firmly believed that their data supported the maturationalists' basic position. On the matter of growth patterns for all children, Gesell's data in the area of motor development have stood the test of time and have seen frequent replication (a hallmark of scientific credibility). Gesell was also among the first to document individual differences in rate of growth and these data have also been repeatedly verified. Gesell stressed individual differences in personality patterns and presented numerous case histories to support his point of view. More recent studies in individual differences from birth onward (Escalona, 1968; Chess & Thomas, 1977; Murphy & Moriatry, 1976) echo some of Gesell's major themes in this area.

Application of Gesell's Theory to Human Development

Gesell and his colleagues wrote three books for the general public: *The First Five Years of Life* (1940), *The Child from Five to Ten* (1946), and *Youth* (1956, covering ages ten to sixteen). In these books Gesell details year by year the expected behaviors in the four domains of motor, personal-social, adaptive, and language performance. Throughout these books he also stresses the principle that growing children are true to their biological nature and that pushing or trying to force development is doomed to failure. Maturational forces, in their own good time, will always win out. When a child does not seem to be doing what other children are doing, given sufficient time for maturational development, the behavior will develop. Children who are not learning are not ready, and when they are, learning will happen. Intervention before the child is ready will be fruitless and frustrating and can create disharmony between the parent, the teacher, and the child.

Thousands of pediatricians, teachers, and parents have been influenced by Gesell's philosophy that time (or the process of maturation) takes care of most problems in behavioral development. Middle-class parents, who are anxious to see their children achieve early in life, are advised not to push their children. In fact, readiness has become the key to explanations for learning or not learning, rather than other factors in the child's world such as instruction or nutritional needs. If one leaves the child alone, most things will happen by themselves as the necessary physical structures come into being and enable the necessary behavioral development to take place.

For most normal children, behavioral development comes along without any special treatment. Unfortunately, the advice that grows out of Gesell's theory lulls one into thinking that because no treatment is necessary, none is happening. We should however, consider the normal environment as an influential treatment in itself. When changes in behavior occur without any obvious intervention, this does not mean that the natural environment was not important in fostering developmental outcomes. In fact, the normal environment itself is a stimulating and active factor, encompassing many different events. It is only recently that developmental psychologist have looked to the ecology of child development to better understand the role of the environment in "normal" development (see Bronfenbrenner & Crouter, 1982, for more on this).

Although Gesell's advice to an overanxious middle-class parent of a normal child may be good advice that is helpful in removing unnecessary and sometimes harmful pressures, such advice may well be relevant only for certain children in certain kinds of settings. The problem is that Gesell's theory leads to a mind set that ignores the process of exactly how the normal environment operates to provide the proper setting in which normal development can occur.

Gesell's theory stresses how maturational forces control development, and it places the normal environment in a supportive but not causative role. One problem with this is not knowing what "normal environment" really means, or how to alter nonnormal environments to make them normal. Probably, in many instances when development is not progressing as expected, parents adopt some intervention strategy without even knowing it. For example, take the instance of a healthy two-year-old girl who does not talk but communicates her desires by pointing. The concerned mother consults the pediatrician, who examines the child, finds nothing wrong, and says to the mother, "Don't worry, she'll talk when she's ready." The mother asks if there is some special treatment that might help, and wonders if the child should be taken to see a speech pathologist. Confident that time will take care of the problem, the doctor dissuades the mother from any special treatment. Six months later the mother reports, and the doctor can see, that the child is now talking: she uses words and has a respectable vocabulary for a two-and-one-half-year-old. The doctor might believe that the advice given to the mother was valid, that no special treatment was necessary, and that time resulted in (or caused) the changes in language behavior. The mother may even agree and be glad that she did not subject the child to needless further examination. Yet probably the mother provided some sort of subtle and effective treatment without even realizing it. Concerned about the child not talking, she might have done a number of things: slowed her speech, repeated words and phrases more frequently, made her speech more distinctive, and made events more clearly contingent upon the child's use of words. In other words, the mother may have altered her own behavior and in doing so inadvertently altered some dimension of what is seen as a normal environment.

In this example, the doctor's advice and the subsequent events were not harmful to the child's development. In an instance in which the reassured mother did not provide a subtle treatment, it is possible that in six months there would have been no appreciable change in the child's language and the doctor would then perhaps begin to entertain the hypothesis that this child's language development is somewhat below normal. If the doctor believes that behavioral development is controlled by maturational factors, the doctor may see his or her proper role as helping the parent accept the fact that this child is developmentally delayed. The real danger here, however, is that should development be significantly delayed or retarded, recourse to the maturational-organismic explanation becomes a self-fulfilling prophecy.

In the realm of popular belief, and in the area of advice to parents, Gesell has had and continues to have an enormous impact. Gesell's colleagues Frances Ilg and Louise Ames still write the daily newspaper column *Know Your Child*, which stresses the powerful natural impetus to growth and change that is contained in the biological system of the developing child. Gesell never said that seriously adverse environments foster normal development, and he was a great advocate of providing healthy environments for children's growth and development, believing fervently that such positive environments lead to good mental health. Yet he was not concerned with a detailed analysis of the environment, perhaps because he trusted so much that most environments were appropriate for fostering good development.

Arnold Gesell's legacy has been significant and large. His basic contributions in the area of how to study development (methodology) and accumulated information (data) will always stand as a significant advance in the area of developmental psychology.

Understanding the Maturational Approach

1. *What is the major force that influences the course of development?*

Unquestionably, the major emphasis in Gesell's theory of development was on the biological basis of behavior, in which genetic or hereditary factors play a commanding role. Throughout his career, he shared this belief with teachers and parents, stressing that these innate qualities formed the basis for the wide and varied differences we see in individuals. While Gesell supported well-designed and child-centered environments that foster the child's development, he always maintained that although influences originating in the environment are of some importance, they are only as critical as the genetic contribution of the individual allows.

Perhaps Gesell's most important conceptual contributions are the idea of a growth matrix that demonstrates the power of internal regulatory mechanisms and the self-righting ability of the child to survive and often prosper in spite of unfortunate circumstances early in life (such as physical or psychological abuse). Both of these contributions illustrate the impact that genetically determined processes can have on development.

2. *What is the underlying process primarily responsible for changes in development?*

Gesell's heavy emphasis on the biological or genetic forces underlying behavior parallels his belief that maturational forces, and not learning, are the mechanisms through which development takes place. Thus, his strong interest in the concept of readiness and his belief that, regardless of the learning opportunities that are presented, without sufficient maturational growth little actual development can occur. Gesell's idea of waiting for the child to reach a level at which he or she is receptive to further learning had a great impact on the pediatricians and educators who formed much of Gesell's professional audience. He believed strongly that the course of development cannot be appreciably changed by altering the environment, and criticisms of his work are based on modern views of the plasticity of behavior.

Furthermore, a strict adherence to this readiness doctrine can lead to unfortunate results. Loving parents, taking the professionals' advice, may reject the possibility that their slow child might catch up or stay at the same level if an enriching setting were provided. On the other hand, Gesell's focus on maturation as an important process led to the development of age-related norms that still serve as valuable guidelines for assessing development.

3. *What role does age play as a general marker of changes in development?*

If maturation is the mechanism underlying development and age is a fairly accurate indicator of biological change, then age as a marker of development is crucial within Gesell's theory.

Interestingly, one of Gesell's important contributions was to establish (through cinematic records as well as his own personal observation) how qualitative change can parallel biological aging. This sounds like mere common sense today, but when Gesell started disseminating his work forty years ago, people were still grasping for some taxonomy or organizational scheme to help them better understand the changes they saw in children. One of the consequences, however, of using age as a marker, is a possible dependence on chronological guidelines as expectations for what the child should or should not be doing (see ''How They Study Development''). Since children are so different from one another, such expectations can bias the parent or teacher and limit the child's true options.

4. *Are there certain sensitive or critical periods during development, and how are they related to the rate of change?*

The notion that maturation plays an important role as a mechanism in development suggests the susceptibility of the individual to certain critical periods of development. Although Gesell did not discuss the nature of critical periods in great detail, we can surmise that his combination of genetic influences and maturation stresses the value of timing in development. Again, the issue of readiness arises. When Gesell stressed the cyclical nature of growth (cycles of ascendancy and descendancy), he was illustrating how the individual is more sensitive or receptive to change during certain periods of growth than others. Although we could probably teach a nonreading ten-year-old to read, the fact that the child can be taught in less time and with more lasting results at an earlier age attests to the increased sensitivity of the child in certain areas at particular times.

5. *Is development smooth and continuous, or does change occur in abrupt stages?*
The maturational view of development is characterized by abrupt transitions from one level of development to the next. This is best illustrated by Gesell's belief that there are swings in development from one extreme to the next, during which the child goes from one end of the continuum to the other during a relatively short period of time. When Gesell presented his principle of self-regulatory fluctuation, he stressed how the shape of behavior over time fluctuates for each individual.

More important is Gesell's emphasis on the discontinuous nature of behavior. Different underlying structures operate at different times to produce the behavior we see. Gesell's concept of the form or shape of development is that it tends to be cyclically erratic but not random. The peaks and valleys are influenced by the operation of different maturational mechanisms at different times, and the quiet composure of the three-year-old is not a systematic outgrowth of the cantankerous, negative attitude of the two-year-old.

These changes are structural in nature, because they reflect alterations in the underlying fabric of behavior. Let us consider an analogy: As infants mature, their stomachs change in both the quantity of food they can hold as well as in their facility for digesting different types of food. Underlying structural changes (in the stomach) take place regulated by biological influences (such as maturation). When Gesell discussed *psychomorphological* changes, he was addressing the structural alterations that occur on a psychological level that are manifested behaviorally. In other words, although we see differences in overt behavior, the actual changes occur in the underlying mechanisms that biologically regulate these outcomes.

6. *How does the theory explain differences in development among individuals of the same chronological age?*
If there were an absolutely perfect relationship between a child's age, the process of maturation, and the child's behavior, we would not expect any differences to occur between individuals of the same age. This, however, is not the case.

To begin with, one's genetic endownment sets the limit to what degree of influence environmental factors can have. For example, two five-year-old girls who have been treated quite similarly may indeed be different in their basic abilities because of initial differences in their genotypes.

In addition, even children who may be strongly related (as in the case of twins) might be different from one another, because their respective biological systems (for example, metabolism or energy level) might function at different levels, leading to differences in behavior.

Finally, remember that although Gesell did not place the environment in a causative role, he would not deny its importance. In more than one instance he commented that the environment can either amplify or reduce the final outcome of some biological force.

HOW THEY STUDY DEVELOPMENT

A great deal of Gesell's work, along with that of his colleagues Louise Bates Ames and Frances L. Ilg, focused on the application of knowledge about child development to the educational process. In their 1964 study, the question they asked is whether results from Gesell's developmental tests are better than the child's chronological age as a criterion for selecting children for school admission.

In this study, the two authors hypothesized that the time children begin school should be determined by the child's developmental or behavior age, rather than chronological age alone. Their thesis is that children should behave at an age level consistent with their years.

To answer this question, they looked at the relationship between test data for 52 boys and girls, tested when they first entered kindergarten, and tested again when they were in sixth grade. Each child's readiness for kindergarten was evaluated using three sets of tests: a behavior examination, two personality tests, and a vision examination. Each child was then judged by three experts whether he or she was ready. All children were of the correct chronological age for admission into kindergarten.

The results show that children who were judged to be ready for kindergarten (by two of the three judges) performed in the top two groups as far as their academic performance in the sixth grade was concerned. Likewise, those children who were judged not to be ready for kindergarten did not perform as well, scoring in the lower half of the class in school performance. Finally, the relationship between school performance and the prediction of how ready the children were for school was fairly strong, indicating that these criteria for selecting children were quite reliable.

Here we have a classic test of Gesell's hypothesis concerning the importance of biological forces and their influence on development. Since chronological age reflects a variety of things other than just maturation (see our earlier discussion on this), one might expect it to be a less reliable predictor of educational success than more direct measures of maturational development. Gesell's behavior tests are a more direct measure and, indeed, did a better job of predicting school success.

SUMMARY POINTS

1. Because Gesell studied education, medicine, and psychology and wrote for scientific, professional, and popular audiences, his impact was widespread.

2. Gesell's theory places heavy emphasis on biological variables as providing the impetus to and the guidelines for development.

3. Structure must be present and developed before function can occur.

4. Development progresses through an invariable sequence in each individual, determined by the biological and evolutionary history of the species.
5. The rate at which individual children progress through the developmental sequence is determined by each child's own hereditary background.
6. The environment may temporarily affect the rate at which the child develops, but individual biological factors ultimately control development.
7. Gesell proposed that development has direction, and that this direction is basically a function of preprogrammed genetic mechanisms.
8. Through a complementary process, opposing sets of forces are dominant at different times during the developmental cycle.
9. The principle of functional asymmetry asserts that a behavior goes through a period of asymmetric development in order to enable the organism to achieve a measure of maturity at a later stage.
10. Development can be viewed as sequential patterning that is predetermined and revealed as the organism matures.
11. Gesell believed that a stage of disequilibrium or imbalance is followed by a stage of equilibrium.
12. Gesell's five principles are considered characteristic of every child's growth pattern.
13. Gesell described behavioral development as occurring in four areas: motor behavior, adaptive behavior, language behavior, and personal-social behavior.
14. Development makes learning possible; learning does not foster basic development.
15. Gesell showed early concern for such methodological issues as reliability of measurements, and the importance of the repetition of observations.
16. Gesell and his colleagues were responsible for introducing the co-twin control strategy in which identical twins were used to illuminate the maturation-versus-learning controversy.
17. Gesell's contention that development is controlled primarily to biological factors assumes a normal environment.
18. Thousands of pediatricians, teachers, and parents have been influenced by Gesell's philosophy that time takes care of most "problems" in development.

FURTHER READINGS

Ames, L. B., and Ilg, F. L. Gesell behavior tests as predictive of later grade placement. *Perceptual and Motor Skills*, 1964, 19, 719–722.
Ilg, F., and Ames, L. *School Readiness*. New York: Harper & Row, 1964.

Gesell, A., and Amatuda, C. S. *Developmental Diagnosis.* New York: Hoeber, 1947.

Gesell, A. *The embryology of behavior.* New York: Harper & Row, 1945.

Simon, M. Body configuration and school readiness. *Child Development,* 1959, *30,* 493–512.

Tanner, J. M. Physical growth. In P. Mussen (Ed.), *Manual of child psychology.* New York: Wiley, 1970.

OTHER READINGS OF INTEREST

Gould, J. S. Size and shape. In *Ever Since Darwin.* New York: Norton, 1977.

Eckstein, G. *The body has a head.* New York: Harper & Row, 1969.

CHAPTER

4

Other Biological Approaches: Ethology and Sociobiology

The general theory of evolution . . . assumes that in nature there is a great, initial, continuous and everlasting process of development, and that all natural phenomena without an exception, from the motion of the celestial bodies and the fall of the rolling stone up to the growth of the plant and the consciousness of man, are subject to the same great law of causation.

Ernst Haeckl

Evolution is not a force but a process; not a cause but a law.

Viscount Morley of Blackburn

Man with all his noble qualities . . . with his godlike intellect which has penetrated into the movements and constitution of the solar system . . . still bears in his bodily frame with indelible stamp of his lowly origin.

Charles Darwin

In the last chapter we discussed how Arnold Gesell's training and interest in the biological sciences led him to emphasize the role of biological processes in development. This was best illustrated by his belief that there were certain fundamental forces at work that encourage development to proceed in a specific direction. The way in which neurological development results in a cephalocaudal or head-to-toe trend is only one example of this force.

There are other scientific theories, however, that also stress the role of biological processes in the development of the individual and his or her culture. Both *ethology* and *sociobiology* are relatively new fields in what they have to say about human development. Since our understanding of the biological basis of behavior is increasing, such theoretical perspectives as these become increasingly relevant to our study and understanding of human development in general.

ETHOLOGY: UNDERSTANDING OUR BIOLOGICAL ROOTS

Ethology can most simply be defined as *the study of those behaviors that are rooted in our evolutionary and biological backgrounds*. This definition suggests that we inherit from earlier generations a set of tendencies to behave in a certain way. Within this framework, the transmission of behaviors and traits through genetics plays a significant role in the development of even complex behaviors such as emotion or thinking. Another implication of this definition is that learning tends to assume a somewhat less important position than biological and "evolutionary" influences.

The application of the basic principles of ethology to human development has not really been fully explored up to this time. We can, however, talk about the relative effects that genetics and our "evolutionary" history might have on the process of development. In effect, what we will be looking at is how patterns of behavior in both humans and animals often serve the same functional purpose.

The Theoretical Outlook

One of the most interesting aspects about the ethological approach to understanding behavior is that it may be one of the oldest (or earliest documented) efforts at systematically studying behavior.

Although most popular theories of human development had their beginnings in the early to middle twentieth century, the work of the early evolutionists such as Charles Darwin and Andrew Wallace began around 1830 in their explorations to distant parts of the world.

In that year, the then 22-year-old Darwin set out on a scientific expedition to South America aboard the ship *Beagle*. It's not really clear to what extent, but perhaps his father's 1794 poem *Zoonomia* (which discussed the concept of evolution) had some impact on his later work.

Through his extensive observations on the Galapagos Islands, Darwin realized that all living creatures must compete with one another in their natural habitat for sustenance, and that it is the "natural order" of things that those who cannot compete will eventually die. Likewise, these who do survive will adapt to changes around them, and eventually "pass" these new sets of characteristics and behaviors on to the next generation. Interestingly, these ideas came to Darwin when he was reviewing the famous thesis on population growth by Thomas Malthus written in

1798. Darwin would not, however, express these ideas on paper until almost two years after his return.

Like most great discoveries in any field of science, Darwin was not alone in his speculations regarding how new species of animals might have originated, and how they might survive through various changes demanded by their hostile environments. Around the same time, Andrew Wallace (working in an entirely different part of the world) developed a theory of evolution as well. In addition, Robert Chambers in 1843 also anticipated some of Darwin's thoughts about the role of evolution.

It was not until 1857 that Darwin and Russell formally presented their thoughts about evolution to the London Lineage Society. In 1858, Darwin published his now famous book on *The Origin of Species*, which then confronted many fundamental religionists who believed that humans did not evolve from their animal ancestors, but instead were created in a moment of cataclysmic glory without biological ancestors!

You may recognize that this debate is alive and well today in many classrooms and courts as the evolution versus creationism issue.

The Meaning and Role of Evolution. Evolution is the complex process through which organisms change in response to the pressures that are placed on them by a changing environment. Those that cannot change and adapt die. Those that change become stronger and more adaptable.

One simple example of this is the way in which the physical posture of human beings has become more erect over millions of years to better suit the needs of the species to walk upright, defend itself, and free its hands to develop and use tools.

But at the heart of the process of evolution are two necessary factors. One is that the combination of genes that takes place in parents to produce offspring occurs in a random fashion. The second is that without change, survival is impossible.

As for the first, you may remember from your basic course in psychology that the genetic makeup of any organism (or the *geneotype*) is passed from the parent (or parents) to the offspring through reproduction. When this occurs, however, the genetic makeup of the new organism is highly dependent on the chance alignment of different genes with one other. There are all kinds of possibilities for eye color, yet an offspring will have an eye color depending on the chance combination of certain genes.

All of the genes (and chromosomes) that control the expression of certain traits, behaviors, and appearance are contributed by previous generation of parents. We do not, however, have any way of knowing which combination will occur. Sometimes these combinations produce blue eyes or tallness. Other times these combinations produce a mutation that is not adaptable such as a tragic birth defect, which may eventually result in death. One way nature controls the transmission of undesirable traits is by making it impossible for defective organisms to survive long enough to pass the traits on to subsequent generations.

It was Darwin's contention that when chance is allowed to operate, and when there is a need for change, the process of *natural selection* (later termed evolution) can operate. He based his theory of natural selection on three assumptions, all of which relate to the factors of chance and necessity we just mentioned.

The first assumption is that through reproduction, organisms vary and that this variation is inherited over time. With each successive generation, a new combination of genetic material results.

The second is that organisms always produce more offspring than can survive. This tends to be less true for humans and other more "advanced" species, but we must remember that we are among a small minority as far as numbers and types of animals that exist on the earth. It is also true since certain species of organisms such as humans have developed sophisticated and complex systems for caring for their young. In other words, the per birth rate is low since the likelihood is very high that the offspring will reach maturity and reproduce itself.

Finally, Darwin believed that offspring that vary in favor with the demands of the environment will live to reproduce. In addition, the selection of traits and behaviors that are favorable (or favor the survival of the species) will tend to accumulate in these groups.

It is important to stress that all these assumptions give the organism a survival advantage over others—an advantage that can result in the organism's passing on these traits to its offspring, who in turn will modify their behaviors and traits so that new more adaptive changes can again be passed on.

This process, which Darwin called "descent with modification," is at the heart of evolution and classical ethology. Darwin emphasized the use of the phrase "descent with modification" instead of the term "evolution" for a very good reason. He believed that an organism's place along the phylogenetic ladder does not necessarily imply that it is more or less advanced than an organism at some other place along the same ladder.

We might like to think of ourselves as being more "advanced" than other animals, and perhaps in some ways we are. Darwin's point, however, was that evolution and social progress cannot be equated with one another.

As you may know, many people have been resistant to the idea that the human being is an extension in evolutionary terms of earlier animals. Most of this objection is based on religious beliefs, where it is difficult, if not impossible, to believe that "man" is not something special, unique and separate from other animals. These two beliefs are not necessarily contradictory. Human behavior might very well be strongly influenced by past events, but human beings themselves can maintain a spiritual and moral position above that of other organisms.

Interestingly, scientists in other disciplines have incorporated the notion that humans (and human behavior) are continuous with nature. One of these advocates was Sigmund Freud (who we will discuss later in Chapter 5), who believed that humanity had to endure two "insults" brought on by scientists. The first was when it was realized that the earth (and therefore humans) was no longer at the center of the universe. The second was when "biological research robbed man of his particular privilege of having been specially created, and relegated him to a descent from the animal world" (Gould, 1977).

Basic Assumptions of Ethology

The most fundamental tenet of ethology as it applies to our understanding of human development is that human behaviors are like biological organs—they are structural parts of a living and developing organism. Just as the structure of the body is passed on through the genetic code, so are certain classes of behaviors and tendencies to act in certain ways.

In other words, certain sets or classes of behaviors are biologically based, and do not have to be formally learned in order to accomplish their intent. Ethologists refer to these classes of behaviors as *innate behaviors*, of which there are several types, including *reflexes*, *taxes*, and *fixed action patterns*.

Before we discuss each of these types of innate behaviors, let's first see if we can better understand what an innate behavior is and what role it might play in development.

Innate Behaviors: Definition and Function. Ekhard Hess, an ethologist who has extended the work of others with animals to humans, believes that innate responses are of ultimate importance in the course of development.

The primary reason for this belief is the survival value of these responses, which for the new organism of any species, is the highest order of business. If an organism can't survive as an individual, it cannot pass on its "good" qualities and will, of course, vanish.

In its simple form, *innate behaviors are behaviors that occur without learning.* If you remember from our discussion in Chapter 2, we defined learning as a change in behavior that occurs as the result of exercise or practice. In general, learning is not the result of any biological process and is highly specific to the individual. Although learned behaviors are specific to the individual (such as memorizing a list of words), innate behaviors are specific to the species. For example, mammals have among their many innate behaviors a sucking reflex that has the obvious survival advantage of providing nutrition. This is not a learned behavior. Often babies not more than minutes old exhibit this response when placed at their mother's breast.

In many young birds, an innate response of following the mother (or whatever figure is present) is *imprinted* into the genetic code, thereby ensuring that the young will follow the adult. Again, this early innate behavior allows the young offspring to receive adequate nutrition, as well as protection from predators.

Different Kinds of Innate Responses. The most basic innate response is the *reflex*, which is a simple response to a stimulus. These are most characteristic of the newborn infant and tend to account for a great deal of early behavior.

Some 25 basic reflexes have been identified in the neonate, from simple sucking or grasping to a walking type of reflex when the infant is held up and the feet are allowed to make contact with a table or some other flat surface. An ethologist could contend that many of these early (and sometimes primitive) reflexes are carried on from our early ancestors and once served a very useful and important function. The strong and intense grasp of the newborn child might be a carryover from the newborn who *must* cling to his or her mother for survival. Likewise, the newborn aversion to having his or her face covered helps to ensure a free and uninterrupted flow of air to the lungs. The presence of these reflexes, and others, have clear implications for the survival of the species.

Many of these newborn reflexes do not last for very long. Instead, they are replaced and supplemented by more sophisticated learned behaviors. Why do they disappear? Probably because after a certain point, they no longer serve any kind of survival or evolutionary function. In fact, the presence of some of these reflexes later in early development can be a sign of some kind of neurological imbalance or a developmental delay.

Another kind of innate behavior that has been identified by ethologists is called a *taxes*, or an orienting or locomotory response to some stimulus. An example of one in the animal kingdom would be the postural stance that dogs assume when they smell another animal, or the humped back of a cat when it is threatened.

Certain events in the environment prompt these animals to assume a certain position, whether it be for seeking food or defending against some threat. Both of these functions, however, clearly have survival value. Another locomotory response in infants is the way they tend to "cuddle" or fold into the arms of the adult who is holding them. The baby might be seeking shelter, or anticipating a feeding, but in either case, unlearned behavior is occurring.

Again, it is important to stress how each of these orienting responses are unlearned and transmitted from one generation to the next through the transmission of genetic material via reproduction. It's also important to remember that taxes partially consist of one or more innate reflexes. In some ways, a taxes is almost like a more complex reflex.

The last of these three classes of innate responses is called a *fixed action pattern*. A fixed action pattern is by far the most complex of the three as well as the most significant in terms of our understanding the application of ethological principles to human behavior.

A fixed action pattern can be thought of as a genetically programmed sequence of coordinated motor actions. And as we might expect, since this sequence is genetically programmed, it simply does not vary within a species. One example of a fixed action pattern in dogs would be the fact that even after they have just eaten, they will continue to hunt if given the opportunity. Fixed action patterns in human behavior can be represented as a very complex sequence of actions, such as nurturing a small child's growth.

Because fixed action patterns are more complex in nature than either reflexes or taxes, there are several components to any pattern that need further discussion.

Figure 4-1 illustrates the relationship between the resulting fixed action pattern and the other components: the *innate releasing mechanism* (or IRM) and the *signed stimulus*.

In any organism's environment, a host of stimuli are present. Some of these can have a direct impact on the behavior, while others will not, and are generally ignored. For example, we stop our car at a red light, yet probably ignore the color of the cars passing by us. An infant may ignore other children in the room yet may become quite agitated when his or her mother leaves for even a moment.

Such a stimulus as the parent's withdrawal could elicit a response of despair or anxiety in the infant. Stimuli that have such "power" or significance are called *signed stimuli*, so named because they have a valence attached to them giving them a value to the organism that other stimuli do not have. There are also stimuli that have such power, not as a result of learning, but to some biological or evolutionary perspective. Signed stimuli in turn stimulate an *innate releasing mechanism* (IRM) that initiates the fixed action pattern. In Figure 4-1, you can see that only one of the four stimuli has this "power" to set off an IRM, which in turn stimulates some fixed action pattern.

Konrad Lorenz, one of the most famous of all ethologists believed one such innate releaser or "trigger" is common across a wide range of animals. This similarly illustrates the commonality that many species share in their form and function.

We might know this releaser as the degree of "babyishness" that characterizes many animals during early development. From our own personal experience, we have observed how many people find the young of any species much more attractive and "cuter" than the adult of the same species. Have you ever noticed how hard it is to pass a new puppy without stopping to pet it?

Lorenz (1965) took this idea a step further and speculated that the toy industry tries to attract adults rather than children to the product based on the characteristics of the dolls. After all, the parent makes the purchase, not the child.

What are some of these characteristics that the toy and doll makers would try to incorporate into their designs? Lorenz believes they are "a relatively large head, predominance of brain capsule, large and low lying eyes, bulging cheek region,

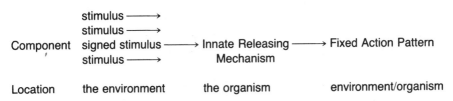

Figure 4-1. The components of a fixed action pattern.

short thick extremities, a springy elastic consistency, and clumsy movements'' (from Gould, 1980). One creature that fits this description is the human baby, and this should not be much of a surprise. Babies exhibit these features, and in turn attract adults, since they need such attention and care to survive.

A humorous, but accurate application of this idea was completed by Harvard scientist Jay Stephan Gould. He shows how over the years, one of this country's favorite cartoon characters, Mickey Mouse, has become increasingly more juvenile. Gould measured the characteristics we described above on drawings of Mickey over a thirty year period. In all cases, head size, eye size, and the size of the cranium became larger, and in effect Mickey came more and more to resemble a younger and younger child. This "progressive juvenilzation," as described by Gould, is called *neoteny*. Gould applies this argument to human development as well. Through our own evolution, we have retained juvenile characteristics as evidenced by our ancestors having the more adult features of protruding jaws and small craniums. The Hollywood look of future races (such as in *Close Encounters of the Third Kind*) are large, bald-headed members of advanced civilizations, much physically like the newborns of our species.

We must remember that the innate releasing mechanism is internal to the organism, and acts almost as a switch that is activated by the presence of a signed stimulus. If the signed stimulus is not there, the IRM will not be activated and the fixed action pattern will not take place. Ethologists would say the signed stimulus was probably not necessary anyway.

Let's extend our example about the infant being separated from the parent a bit further. Any fixed action pattern does not occur at the slightest provocation or presence of a signed stimulus. For example, if the mother simply leaves the room, but the baby can hear her voice, her absence alone might not be sufficient. In addition, innate releasing mechanisms become operative only under certain conditions with a combination of several factors.

Ethologists believe that one of these conditions is the presence of a sufficient amount of *action specific energy* much like the notion of "readiness" we discussed in earlier chapters. Action specific energy reflects the ease with which a given signed stimulus elicits or releases the corresponding fixed action pattern through the IRM. What ethologists have found is that the longer the time since the last response, the greater the amount of action specific energy to activate the IRM and in turn the fixed action pattern.

Another example of such a fixed action pattern is a parent's response to a distressed child. In the everyday course of parent-child interactions, there are many stimuli that are unattended to because they hold no inherent value. For example, what the baby might be doing in the playpen might be pleasant to watch, but mom or dad might feel perfectly comfortable attending to a letter or paying the bills. In this case, the child's playing alone and amusing him or herself holds no value as a stimulus. The child's behavior is only one of many stimuli, all of which may have a similar level of meaning at that moment in time.

Let's assume, however, that the child gets a sharp pain from an earache and begins to scream in pain. Parents respond quickly, dropping the letter, and rushing over to try and find out what the problem is. In this example, the signed stimulus is the scream from the child, which "sets off" whatever innate releasing mechanism operates for that kind of parental behavior. This in turn eventually results in a pattern of behavior that we might call "caring," where the parent begins a routine of aspirin, calling the pediatrician, and so on. The complex set of behaviors that began with the shrill of pain is very much a fixed action pattern. It is not evolution or biology that fixes the content of the pattern, but it is these factors that determine when and how the pattern will be activated.

We can see how such fixed action patterns are species specific by looking at another example. At parks and playgrounds adults will frequently come to the aid of *any* child when that child needs some help. As with other animals, the young who need help are "adopted." Also, you might have seen how young children in a crowd seeking security often attach themselves quite securely to the wrong leg or hand in their search!

Not all signed stimuli and fixed action patterns, however, necessarily result from the child or parent being under some kind of stress. The origin of many other parenting behaviors might be found in an ethological perspective. For example, the young child smiles and attracts the attention of adults, who in turn provide that child with attention and nurturance. Similarly, the parent who encourages the "almost talker" to continue by telling the child how nice it sounds might also be playing out the role of encouraging the kinds of behaviors that are necessary for later adaptation and essential for survival.

How Ethologists Study Behavior

Scientists who study development always try to use a method to answer their questions that reflects some of the basic assumptions of that perspective.

For ethologists, one of their basic goals is to study the influence of environmental factors on genetically based behaviors. In order to do this, most ethologists are interested in observing behavior in its "natural" setting.

This means that if ethologists are interested in how families adapt to stress, they are more likely to observe a family under an actual stressful situation, rather than studying them in some laboratory setting within some hypothetical situation. What ethologists try to do in using natural settings to study behavior is to establish the *ecological validity* of the behavior. In other words, they want to observe the behavior as it occurs in its natural setting and understand the flow of natural events that surround the adjustments that need to be made.

To further understand this, we have to return to one of the basic assumptions we discussed earlier. Although behavior is genetically based, it takes place within a certain environmental context. This context or setting is essential to understand if we are to appreciate the significance of the behavior. Remember, the selective pressures of the environment result in changes in behavior, not the status of one's genetic makeup. Without pressure for change, no modification of internal or external structures is possible, and theoretically the species would perish.

To study behavior, ethologists use what they call an *ethogram*, which is an inventory of the organism's behavior. The rationale for using such an inventory speaks to the very heart of what ethology really is. If we agree that the environment does exert selective pressures that help to shape behavior, the place we would look first to understand the origin and modification of these behaviors is in the organism's natural surroundings.

The inventory itself consists of several categories of behaviors. Table 4-1 illustrates what an ethogram might look like for a rabbit or a human being before the ethogram is actually completed. We can see that both organisms participate in at least five different functions: feeding, resting, defense, reproduction, and elimination. In looking at these five areas, we are making the assumption that they are, to different extents, necessary for survival.

If we were to take the time and observe these two different kinds of animals in their respective settings, we would get a thorough and probably very different picture of what constitutes part of the *ethnography* of being a rabbit or a human being.

For example, we might observe that both newborn humans and rabbits tend to suckle for nourishment, yet defend themselves in very different ways. While the rabbit might adopt a strategy of camouflage, the human moves in a direction of a parent or familiar elder when threatened.

One important point is that all of these functions (and of course others) are necessary but are performed in different ways according to the species of the animal. Interestingly, the discipline of comparative psychology has a great deal of its historical and substantive roots in the study and principles of ethology.

Ethograms are a valuable tool, especially when the ethologist is studying more than one kind of animal from different species, but who are theoretically related

Table 4-1   An Ethogram

Function	Rabbit	Human Being
Feeding		
Resting		
Defending	The entries here would be concise descriptions of both the behavior and	
Reproducing	the environmental context within which the behavior took place.	
Eliminating		

to one another. Using such a strategy, ethologists can often define "links" between and across species based on their behavior, and the assumption that at least some of the behaviors serve the same function and share some (no matter how little) genetic similarity.

Applying Ethology to Human Development

There is no question that the application of the various principles of ethology to the understanding of human development is just beginning. There is, however, at least one area that has a major part of its conceptual and empirical work grounded in some of the ideas and methods we have discussed. This is the study of attachment between human infants and their caretakers.

The person who is most responsible for this accomplishment is John Bowlby, who, in his paper "The Nature of a Child's Tie to His Mother" (1958), discussed contemporary attachment theory within an ethological framework.

In this paper, and in later extensive writings, he placed great emphasis on the biological functions of behavior and contended that these behaviors are present because they offer a definite survival advantage. For Bowlby, the primary function of the complex system of behaviors we call attachment is to protect the infant from harm, while nurturing it toward adulthood (where it can then be responsible for the next generation).

When discussing attachment within an ethological framework, it is important to understand that Bowlby does not believe that human infants are genetically predisposed to becoming attached to a particular person. Rather, it is the process of learning and experiences shortly after birth that determine to whom the attachment will be formed.

This is not unlike the type of imprinting that Lorenz observed, where baby ducklings would follow him rather than their mother if he was the first to be seen during some critical or sensitive period. In much the same way, human babies might imprint by following with their eyes the movement of a caretaker, since they are not yet equipped to follow by walking.

The Phases of Attachment. Over the years, Bowlby has developed a model of attachment that includes four separate phases.

The first of these phases, called *pre-attachment* takes place during the first few weeks of life and is characterized by the infant's readiness to respond quickly and easily to stimuli produced by other members of the species. Notice how at this stage the infant is ready to react to any "friendly" or inviting stimulus, regardless of its origins. It appears that there is some inborn mechanism that helps to orient the infant to where and how he or she should react in the presence of a potential caregiver.

In effect, the eye following, noises, and even early precursors of smiling are all efforts on the infant's part to encourage and increase proximity and contact between the child and his or her caregiver, usually the mother. These behaviors are somewhat gross in nature, and not directed toward any one person in particular.

With time, the infant's behavior becomes more discriminative, and the second phase called *attachment in the making* begins. During this phase, which starts after the first month of life and lasts well into the second six months, the infant forms an attachment to some specific figure. The specificity of responses in this phase is demonstrated by the infant's smiling more in the presence of the "target" of attachment (for example, the mother) while smiling to others decreases significantly.

The next phase described by Bowlby is that of *clear-cut attachment*, when the infant has greatly increased mobility and can walk. This increased mobility allows the child to further distance him or herself when necessary from the goal of attachment, yet still maintain a mental image of the caretaker when not in the caretaker's presence. This ability to form an image is characteristic of the changes in cognitive skills that will be discussed later in our coverage of cognitive-developmental theory.

The infant has now developed a wide diversity of attachment behaviors, and attachment has become a pattern of well-integrated and directed behaviors.

The last phase of attachment during the second year is the *goal corrected partnership*, when the infant begins to better understand the mother's (or father's) behaviors, and consequently will adjust to them and initiate attempts to influence what she or he does. From an ethological standpoint, the infant, with increased physical and cognitive competence, tries to anticipate the caregiver's behavior to maximize contact and nurturance.

By definition, ethology examines a multitude of factors and—perhaps better than any other theoretical approach—combines the influences of hereditary and environmental factors. Like many other approaches, it does not place these forces at opposite ends of one extreme, but rather speaks for their mutual impact on the development of the organism.

For this reason some of the most exciting discoveries yet to be made about human behavior will perhaps be completed within this theoretical framework.

SOCIOBIOLOGY: GENES AND DEVELOPMENT

In the first section of this chapter, our discussion of ethology stressed how behavior is seen within a gene-environment interaction with an emphasis on the influence of ecological factors on genetically based behaviors. Although one's genetic endowment takes precedence, environmental factors and selective pressure to change are critical components as well.

Now we are about to discuss a more recent extension of some of these ethological principles into a relatively new discipline called *sociobiology*. A major difference between ethology and sociobiology is that sociobiologists view *all* aspects of development as being controlled and caused by specific genes and they give very little importance to factors that originate outside the organism.

Little if any actual research has been done applying sociobiological principles to human behavior. It's primarily for this reason that we need to keep in mind the limitations of such a new approach, but at the same time appreciate its suggestions for different and, perhaps, better ways of understanding development.

The Theoretical Outlook

As we saw in the last chapter, one of the ongoing arguments as far as human development is whether we are distinct and separate from our primate ancestors (such as great apes), or are simply a continuation or an extension of them, only at a more "advanced" level.

Most ethologists would agree that our ancestors contribute a great deal to our current repertoire of *biological and psychological potentialities*. Sociobiologists would agree with this as well, but would take this argument one step further and discuss *biological and psychological determinism*.

They contend that the continuity between an individual's current evolutionary status and that of the immediate and past genetic ancestry is almost unbroken. What this means is that, first, the actions of genetic endowment as the cause of behavior are paramount. Second, it means that humans are not as morally and spiritually unique as some people would like to think. In fact, most sociobiologists believe that even our most prized attribute—that of altruism or sacrifice—has a genetic basis.

Sociobiology has been popularly defined as "the systematic study of the biological basis of all social behavior" (Wilson, 1975, p. 4), with social behavior defined as the interaction between organisms. The ardent sociobiologist has no qualms about considering even the most complex of human behaviors, such as the selection of a spouse or the rearing of children, as having a biological basis in nature. These complex behaviors are the outcome of millions of years of evolutionary "progress," do not result from learning, and are highly similar to the same category of behaviors in other animals in form and function.

The task of the sociobiologist is to study the social acts of animals and demonstrate how the animal's actions assist the developing organism adapt to its environment. More specifically, the "prime directive" or the organism becomes the development of such patterns that contribute to the successful reproduction of the species, often at any and all costs to the parent generation.

For example, it is not uncommon in the animal world for parents to sacrifice their food, shelter, and at times their very lives for their young. All of these sacrifices represent an effort to increase the chances of the young to prosper and reproduce. In terms of human behaviors, we can look to the Eskimos for such an example of the ultimate sacrifice within this sociobiological model.

In the Eskimo culture, grandparents retain a position of honor and respect. This deference comes from the real and legendary sacrifices they have made for their young when it was time to find a new home, yet the amount of supplies were not sufficient to carry all the family members through to the journey's end. Instead of eating their share of food at the expense of the other (younger) people in the tribe or family (and the breeders of the next generation), they would forgo their share, stay behind, and quietly die.

A sociobiological interpretation of this would be that the grandparents, who have lived a full and rewarding life, made the only choice they could. This was a sacrifice, on an individual level for the good of the entire tribe, to ensure that the species (and the gene pool) continued to survive. Further, the motivation for such sacrifice comes not from the recognition these people will receive as honored and revered members of the society, but theoretically from one's genetic inheritance.

The major problem with this argument, however, is that it is certainly impossible to adequately test, let alone prove. The notion that people sacrifice certain things, and even their lives under specific conditions, can either be the result of some genetic predisposition or in fact a learned or culturally acquired phenomenon. The only way to settle the question would be to manipulate one's genetic potential and observe the outcomes in future generations. We might be able to do this with fruitflies in the laboratory, but certainly not humans. We have neither the technical capability to accomplish this, nor the ethical and social mechanisms to deal with such experimentation.

For now, however, let's assume that we can accept the argument that behavior is under the control of genetic mechanisms and continue our discussion by expanding on the idea of how behavior begins or what causes it.

The Causes of Behavior

Sociobiologists believe that there are two general categories of causes that we can look to for an understanding of what precipitates animal (including of course human) behavior. These are called *first level* and *second level causes*.

Figure 4-2 shows the relationship between these two causes and the eventual expression of a social behavior. Second level causes, which are further removed from the actual behavior (or less directly influential), consist of *phylogenetic inertia* and *ecological pressure* (more about these in a moment). These in turn influence what are called first level causes, identified as *demographic variables, the rate of gene flow*, and the *coefficient of relationship* (more about these as well to follow). All of these result in what we generally know as social behaviors, leading up to, of course, the reproduction of the species and the sharing of the most adaptive genes.

Both these categories of causes are somewhat "removed" as direct influences on behavior. First level causes are, however, more immediate and more traceable

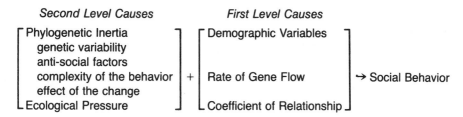

Figure 4-2. First and second level causes of behavior.

as influences. That is, they are more closely related, and perhaps more clearly a cause of the specific behavior or pattern of behavior under consideration.

Since the process begins with second level behaviors, that's where we will begin our discussion.

Second Level Causes of Behavior. The first second level cause is *phylogenetic inertia*, which emphasizes the strongly nature orientation of sociobiology. You may remember from your studies in physical science that inertia is defined as resistance to change. In the sociobiological sense, phylogenetic inertia can be defined as the tendancy to remain genetically unchanged or the tendency to continue as formulated. It's the ease with which an organism's genetic endowment and tendencies might be alterable. In some cases this inertia may be high, and change is difficult to accomplish, while in others the opposite may be the case. What are some factors that might be involved?

Four factors determine the degree of phylogenetic inertia that is associated with any pattern of behavior. The first of these is the degree of *genetic variability* that exists in the species. The higher the degree of variability (and the accompanying increased opportunity for new combinations of genes to take place), the lower the inertia or the resistance to change on the part of the organism. This also means that there is an increased likelihood of generating new and more adaptive behaviors, a very important function for all animals to be able to perform. On the other hand, if there is very little variability available, then the level of inertia will probably be quite high. In sum, an opportunity to increase the gene pool decreases phylogenetic inertia since more new material is being introduced, and the likelihood of a change increases.

Antisocial factors are the second determinant, or anything that encourages the species (as represented by the individual) to isolate itself. In doing so, the likelihood of increased genetic variability goes down (because of fewer potential partners to chose from), phylogenetic inertia increases, and there are reduced chances for adaptive changes. This is clearly an argument against inbreeding of species. Not only does it exaggerate the recessive and often nonadaptive traits and characteristics, but also minimizes the chances for genetic variability. A sociobiologist would argue that the social taboos we have against incest have their origin at this level of isolation from other sources of potential variation.

The third factor is the *complexity of the behavior*. The more elaborate the behavior is, the more component parts there are likely to be to the behavior. The more component parts, the higher the inertia needs to be keep these parts together and functioning, hence the more difficult the behavior may be to change. We can see this if we look at such a complex human behavior as parenting, which consists of a great number of highly interrelated and complex behaviors. The very reason why it may be so difficult to change one's parenting practices (as any parent will tell you), is because the phylogenetic inertia associated with these complex practices is so high.

Finally, the last factor is the *effect of the change* in behavior on other traits and characteristics. If a behavior is complex (and, as we have just argued, the phylogenetic inertia is high) it takes a major effort to alter the behavior. When one part of a complex system is altered, it probably results in the alteration of other parts as well. In others, the degree to which a change in one part of the system affects a change in another part of the system helps to determine the degree of phylogenetic inertia.

The next of these two kinds of second level causes is called *ecological pressure*, most simply defined as aspects of environment that encourage the organism to change. For the sociobiologist, ecological pressure represents the nurture side of the nature-nurture debate.

As one might expect, certain ecological or environmental events have no impact on the social evolution of animals, while others are very important. For example, one of the most significant forms of ecological pressure is the presence of predators. This is because predators are probably the primary threat to the animal's existence, and therefore to the passing on of that animal's most adaptive genes.

Given this pressure, what has evolved among all animals are very sophisticated and well-designed means for defending oneself against predators. For example, a primary predator of the brown sparrow is the hawk, which will attack these small birds in flight. When a hawk is flying below the sparrows, and they are not threatened, the sparrows usually fly in a loose grouping. When the hawk is above the sparrows, however, and in position to strike, the sparrows bind together in a closely knit flying group. The hawk is much less likely to try and penetrate the group and risk injuring a vulnerable part of its body. Consequently, the likelihood of survival for the sparrows increases, and the opportunity for them to pass on their genetic endowment to a subsequent generation is increased as well.

Another major source of ecological pressure is the availibility of food. Most directly, when food is not available, it is impossible for a species to survive. In such a situation, animals are forced to move on to a new location where nourishment might be more available. For example, many African animals are nomadic in that they move seasonally from location to location following the growth of certain types of plants to feed on. Even today, in some less technologically advanced cultures, tribes follow herds of animals for food and other necessities such as hides for clothing, and so on. It is only relatively recently that humans have learned how to make food grow in spite of hostile environmental conditions.

Probably the most applicable example of a change due to ecological pressure in the human species is when we made the transistion from being a tree-based animal to one that was land based. We began to walk on all fours at first, then later used our hind legs to eventually assume an upright posture. Some sociobiologists believe there was pressure for us to leave our loftier heights to have better access to food. One of the consequences of a more upright posture is a larger and stronger pelvis to help support the viscera and upper body.

A larger pelvis also allows for another change in human evolution, the easier delivery of the newborn with less potential for damage from coming through a too small birth canal. As our heads became larger, more adaptive changes occurred in the structure of the female's body to compensate.

Finally, as E. O. Wilson, a prominent sociobiologist concludes, "manipulation of the physical environment is the ultimate adaption," since it is not until animals manipulate their environment that they seek to control it. And, as Wilson notes, once animals control their environment, the indefinite survival of the species can almost be assured. Humans have made tremendous gains in controlling their environment in a very "short" period of time on the evolutionary clock. Once we discovered the use of tools such as bones to beat animal skins, we in a sense were on our way.

The control we have of our environment has increased dramatically through the design and use of tools including everything from the wheel and plow to the space shuttle. The past half century of human progress has seen incredible increases in human ingenuity and tool usage, but less than comparable progress in adapting to the social impact of these advances. The implications of manipulating genes, maintaining life when there is no mental activity, and going beyond our own solar system (as radio waves are about to do) leave an opening in our evolutionary progress. This opening suggests that the ecological pressures associated with these "advances" are so great that the adaptation process is slow and almost, at times, unnoticeable.

The Relationship Between Phylogenetic Inertia and Ecological Pressure. Both phylogenetic inertia or ecological pressure can be either high or low. If we look at Figure 4-3 we can see the impact that these different combinations might have on the development of later social behaviors.

When ecological pressure is low, it is unlikely that the organism will change. There is simply no pressure or incentive to do so. If phylogenetic inertia is high, there is increased resistance to any kind of genetic alteration. For example, let's examine how parents provide nourishment for their young. Given an abundance of

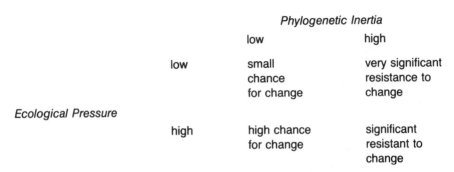

Figure 4-3. The relationship between phylogenetic inertia and ecological pressure.

food in the local environment and isolation from related species (low ecological pressure and no phylogenetic inertia), there is not much "biological" incentive to change.

On the other hand, if phylogenetic inertia is low (for example, there is opportunity for mating with other animals and increasing the diversity of the gene pool) and ecological pressure is high (the stores of food have been eliminated through some natural accident such as an increase in predators), then change in feeding behavior is much more likely to occur.

It's difficult to predict what would occur if both ecological pressure and phylogenetic inertia are both high. This combination of circumstances would probably result in no change, given the strong biological directive to resist genetic alteration.

First Level Causes. First level causes are no more less important than second level causes, but they are less removed from the actual behavior. That is, if we looked for a cause of behavior that was more traceable to the behavior itself, we would first look to one of the following three categories as a likely candidate (see Figure 4-2).

One first level cause has to do with the *demographic variables* (or characteristics) of a certain population. Among these are birth rates, death rates, and the population size. In combination, these three factors directly reflect "quality" of life.

For example, a good deal of research with animals has been done that examines the effects of overcrowding. In one set of experiments conducted at the National Institutes for Mental Health, white mice lived in their own "city" where they were allowed to reproduce and socialize. As the population increased, there was also an increase in aberrant social behaviors. Death rates increased as well, and less genetically well-equipped mice were being born. That is, they were more susceptible to disease and stress, and hence passed on less adaptive traits when they reached adulthood.

Such conditions are highly conducive to some kind of change in social behavior, for otherwise the animals have no direction in which to grow but toward their own extinction (in that limited society anyway).

Another first level cause is *gene flow*, or the introduction and sharing of genes from genetically different individuals who are introduced into a new population. The rate of this flow has a great deal to do with how quickly an animal's behavior can adapt to a change in the environment. For example, when the rate of the introduction of new genes is slow, change is much less likely than when the rate is high. Gene flow is one of the most direct ways that a behavior becomes adaptive since it can take place within relatively few generations. It is almost an artificial way of speeding along the natural process of selection that can take many generations, and often, thousands of years.

Finally, the third cause is the degree of *genetic similarity* that exists within species as a function of relatedness. The more genetically similar groups are to one another, the higher this coefficient is. The higher the coefficient, the more likely the social behavior directed by a set of genes is to be stable within that species. Finally, the more stable the behavior is, the less likely it is to change as a function of other factors.

This stability might be encouraged since it ensures the continuity of presumably adaptive behaviors. However, species that share their own genes (hence a high coefficient of relationship) must be careful of the consequences of inbreeding we discussed earlier. On one hand, it does help to ensure stability. On the other hand, however, it also emphasizes the expression of maladaptive traits.

It's important to remember that none of these first level causes operates in isolation. They all operate in conjunction with one another, as do the groups of first and second level causes discussed earlier.

Applying Sociobiology to Human Development

For the sociobiologist, human behavior is a reflection of first and second level causes. In effect, human beings are an extension of the animal kingdom governed by the same rules and principles.

Yet the application of these principles to human behavior has been difficult and controversial. It has been controversial since many people feel that their uniqueness from other animals is not only spiritual and intellectual, but also biological. Many of them are also taken aback by thoughts of sophisticated behaviors being reduced to simple biological acts. For example, is moving to a new city for a better job in any way like the predator who follows a group of animals waiting for the kill? Many people would argue against this analogy, but others would argue that they are both attempts at improving chances for "survival."

The primary argument that sociobiologists use to substantiate such claims is that of *universality*. That is, since the same behaviors are found among humans as are found among other primates, these behaviors must be genetically related. The problem with this logic is that the same outcome does not always result from the same cause. Others reason that just because we are animals does not mean we are nothing but animals.

Most of what we have discussed in these past two sections points to the same conclusion. That is, everything an animal does, whether it be fighting off a predator or foraging for food, is aimed at the goal of reproducing itself.

One of the major functions within this reproductive purpose is that of parenting. David Barash (1977) discusses parenting within a sociobiological framework. He defines parental investment as behaviors that increase the likelihood of survival and reproduction by offspring at the cost of investment in other offspring. Therefore, parents who have their first child later in life (say, age 40) rather than earlier (say, age 20) should invest more in their offspring, since they have fewer years they will be biologically suited for reproduction.

Although the presence of other offspring takes away resources from the new offspring, to this one "hope for the future." Perhaps this in part accounts for the strong religious and emotional attachments made to the first born child. It also may relate to significant differences between children as a function of birth order, where first borns are usually higher achievers and more successful later in life.

Another application is in the area of parent-child interaction and conflict. Children, like their parents, seek to maximize the child's level of fitness and potential to reproduce. Given such a goal, children would demand that the parents maximize their level of investment to children, and hence increase the competition for resources. We might expect that children would not be easily weaned from their mothers, or accept parental encouragement for independence. In addition, we might predict that sibling rivalry serves the function of competition for available resources.

Sociobiology, like ethology, is a new and relatively untried discipline as it applies to human behavior. There are many people, however, who believe that the next advances in understanding the development of human behavior will be preceded by an increased understanding of biological and psychobiological processes. Sociobiology provides a great deal of room for future research and fascinating speculation about the nature of development.

HOW THEY STUDY DEVELOPMENT

One of the most useful tools for the ethologist is the ethogram, a running description of behavior in as "natural" or uncontrived a setting as possible.

In this chapter, we pointed out how the most widely applied use of ethological principles has been in the study of attachment based on the works of John Bowlby (1969) and Mary D. S. Ainsworth (1973). One technique that has been used to study attachment (and the effects of separation) within an ethological framework is called the Strange-Situation Procedure, where the baby, a parent (traditionally the mother), and a stranger (a confederate or colleague of the psychologist studying attachment) all interact in a highly structured setting.

This procedure is divided into eight episodes over a 22 minute time period and can be described as follows. All the episodes except the first last for three minutes.

Episode 1 lasts for about one minute with the baby and mother present. They are shown the experimental room filled with toys; there is a place for the mother to sit and the baby to play.

In Episode 2 the baby and the mother are together, and the mother responds to the baby's requests for interaction, but does not initiate any on her own.

Episode 3 lasts for three minutes and includes the introduction of the stranger into the room with the baby and mother. The stranger enters the room, sits quietly for one minute, talks to the mother for one minute, then interacts with the baby for one minute.

Episode 4 begins with the mother leaving the room. The stranger watches the baby playing alone and interacts if the baby indicates an interest. If the baby is crying the stranger tries to comfort the baby. This episode is stopped if the baby cries hard for one minute, or if the mother requests that it be stopped.

Episode 5 finds the mother calling the baby from outside the room and then coming in. The mother comforts the baby if necessary, and then sits in the room responsive to the baby, but again does not initiate anything.

Episode 6 again finds the mother leaving the room and the baby is alone. If the baby is very distressed, or if the mother requests it, this episode is ended.

Episode 7 includes the baby and the stranger who returns and sits in the room. Again, the stanger will interact with the baby, but only if te baby initiates some king of interaction. If the baby is very upset, the session can be ended.

The last episode repeats episode 5 where the mother comes back in the room and is responsive to the baby's interests, but does not initiate any interactions.

What can a series of episodes like this tell us about attachment and separation? Most directly, it allows us to view the child under a set of conditions, when the degree of security of attachment varies a great deal. By observing the child's behavior, we can get some idea of what kinds of attachment behaviors on the part of the child accompany what kinds of environmental conditions. In turn, this can give us some idea about the nature of attachment as it relates to familiar and unfamiliar surroundings.

SUMMARY POINTS

1. Ethology is the study of those behaviors that are rooted in our evolutionary and biological backgrounds.
2. Ethology examines patterns of behavior across all species that seem to serve the same purpose.
3. The process of natural selection, which underlies the study of ethology, focuses on the adaptation of certain characteristics that will foster an increased chance for survival.

4. Certain classes of behavior are biologically based, and are not susceptible to the influences of learning such as reflexes, taxes, and fixed action patterns that are all innate responses.
5. A signed stimulus precedes an innate releasing mechanism and acts to trigger it to action.
6. An innate releasing mechanism initiates a fixed action pattern, or a biologically based set of behaviors that are social in nature.
7. A certain level of action specific is necessary before a stimulus becomes powerful enough to trigger an innate releasing mechanism that in turn leads to a fixed action pattern.
8. Ethologists use ethograms to study behavior, which are records of behavior as it occurs in the natural stream of events.
9. The study of sociobiology focuses on the direct control that genes have on human behavior.
10. Sociobiology can be defined as the systematic study of the biological basis of social behavior.
11. Two general categories of events, first and second level causes, underlie all of behavior.
12. Second level causes are phylogenetic inertia and ecological pressure, and first level causes are demographic variables, rate of gene flow, and coefficient or relationship.
13. Phylogenetic inertia is determined by genetic variability, anti-social factors, complexity of the behavior, and the effect of change on other behaviors.
14. The relationship between phylogenetic inertia and ecological pressure determines the ease with which behavior will change.

FURTHER READINGS

Ainsworth, M. D. The development of mother-infant attachment. In B. Caldwell and N. Riccuiti (Eds.), *Review of child development research.* (Vol. 3). Chicago: University of Chicago Press, 1973.
Barish, D. D. *Sociobiology and behavior.* New York: Elsevier, 1977.
Bowlby, J. *Attachment and loss.* Volumes 1, 2, and 3. London: Hogarth Press, 1969, 1973, and 1980.
Freedman, D. *Human sociobiology: A holistic approach.* New York: Free Press, 1979.
Sameroff, A. J. Developmental systems: Contexts and evolution. In P. Mussen (Ed.), *Handbook of child psychology* (Vol. 1). New York: Wiley, 1983.
Wilson, E. O. *Sociobiology: The new synthesis.* Harvard University Press, 1975.

OTHER READINGS OF INTEREST

Ardrey, R. *The territorial imperative.* New York: Delta, 1968.
Dawkins, R. *The selfish gene.* Oxford: Oxford University Press, 1976.

CHAPTER 5

Sigmund Freud and the Psychoanalytic Model

Everyone is a child of his past.

Edna G. Roston

The child is the father of man.

Wordsworth

Give me the children until they are seven and anyone may have them afterwards.

Saint Frances Xavier

When making a decision of minor importance, I have always found it advantageous to consider all the pros and cons. In vital matters, however, such as the choice of a mate or a profession, the decisions should come from the unconscious, from somewhere within ourselves. In the important decisions of our personal lives we should be governed by the deep inner needs of our nature.

Sigmund Freud

HISTORICAL PERSPECTIVES AND BASIC ASSUMPTIONS

Few psychologists have been responsible for formulating an entirely new perspective on human behavior. What Mendel was to the study of genetics and Einstein to physics, Sigmund Freud was to the study of the underlying forces that influence development. His main emphasis was on the study of unconscious psychological processes as the primary source for understanding mental illness. His theories were thus clearly separate from those of others who maintained that there was an organic basis for all mental disorders (Munroe, 1955). More important, Freud's accomplishments represent the first attempt at developing a systematic and global theory of human development.

Freud's training and experience in his chosen profession of medicine proved invaluable and were to have a profound effect on the development of *psychoanalytic theory*. For this reason, a brief review of Freud's life and times is especially important to a full appreciation of his contributions.

Born in 1856 in Moravia (now part of Czechoslovakia), Freud received his early education in Vienna and began his scientific training as a medical student at the University of Vienna in the fall of 1873. During his first year as a medical student he enrolled in a basic physiology course taught by Ernst Brucke, the German physiologist, a man who was to have a significant influence on Freud's professional and personal life. Because of this relationship and Freud's interest in research, he decided to pursue a career as a neurologist and became an investigator in the Institute of Cerebral Anatomy. Even in the early days of his formal education, Freud expressed an interest in helping people and was especially intrigued by emotional and "nervous" disorders.

During this same period, he became interested in the properties of cocaine as a treatment for anxiety and depression (Byck, 1974). On Freud's suggestion, Carl Koller, a colleague, amplified Freud's basic experimental work and received recognition for the discovery of cocaine as an eye anesthetic. Although Freud felt that Koller deserved the credit, he remained disturbed by this incident and reference to it frequently appeared in his later writings. He felt that making an important contribution early in his career would gain him recognition from his peers and a secure financial future, making possible an early marriage to his fiancée. In spite of the magnitude of his contribution, Freud was never to realize either financial security or unqualified support from his peers.

While at the Brucke Institute, Freud became intrigued with what was becoming the most important theoretical discovery in quantum physics, the principle of *conversion of energy*. The principle states that energy is a quantity, like any other physical substance, and that it can neither be created nor destroyed but only transformed from one state to another. Freud's realization that this principle is applicable to human beings represented the first and most important step in the development of his theory. This same principle was to be applied throughout psychoanalytic theory. It provided a perspective on human development that was new and fascinating yet unconvincing to many.

The publication of Ernst Brucke's Lectures on Physiology in 1874 influenced Freud strongly. Brucke proposed the radical view that the living organism is characterized by a *dynamism*, (a continual state of flux). Freud would soon apply such a notion to the levels and structures of the unconscious mind and the role this dynamism plays in human development.

Because of the close personal relationship between the two men, it was difficult for Brucke to advise Freud to abandon a theoretical career since Freud's need for money could never by realized if he remained in his present position. It was clear that he could no longer expect to receive money from home, because his father, who was not a wealthy man, had other children to support. Disappointed and confused, Freud left his work at the Institute and his career as a researcher and entered the General Hospital in Vienna for further training in clinical work.

This unfortunate turn of events for Freud turned out to be psychology's good fortune. It was through this later experience as a practicing physician and analyst that much of his productive work in psychoanalysis was completed. In retrospect, however, this time (1882) was in Freud's opinion his most professionally unsuccessful. Since he was in financial need (above what his family or his research fellowship with Brucke could provide), he was forced to enter private practice, something he had tried to avoid.

The beginning of his clinical career focused on nervous diseases, a relatively new and uncharted domain. Through his reading of the professional literature, he learned of the impressive accomplishments of Jean Charcot, the Parisian physician. Charcot had been concentrating on the use of hypnosis as a technique for dealing with hysterical behaviors such as the loss of feeling in a limb. There was, however, little understanding of why this technique worked so well and it was Freud's genius that would later provide an answer to this question. From October 1885 through February 1886 Freud worked closely with Charcot at the Salpetriere in Paris, then a home for aged women (Jones, 1953).

Freud's experiences in Paris strongly influenced his later thought and his abrupt but logical change from neurology to psychopathology, the study of psychological disorders. While in Paris with Charcot, Freud's primary task was to detail the distinction between hysterical and organic paralysis. These efforts led Freud to believe that there are disorders, such as hysteria, caused by something other than anatomical dysfunction. Some of the problems brought to his attention were not caused by any organic damage, but might be the result of some imbalance in underlying psychological structures. Up to this time, the general feeling among members of the medical community was that every behavior not considered normal had as its basis some biological irregularity. Freud believed that this perspective was unproductive, and certainly not true in all cases.

His time with Charcot was extremely important to the development of psychoanalysis, because Freud's experiences with patients suffering from hysteria convinced him that other, unseen forces were operating. It was a short step to the hypothesis that certain types of behavior might be the result of something other than observable influences, an assumption that was later in his career to become a cornerstone of psychoanalytic theory.

Freud returned to Vienna in 1886 for more training in the first Public Institute for Children's Diseases. Freud was becoming increasingly dissatisfied with hypnosis as a method of studying unobservable or unconscious influences on behavior. Although hypnosis is highly effective under certain conditions, it produces a temporary state during which the therapist must take certain precautions as well as direct the content of the sessions. In addition, it left many basic questions unanswered since the patient was not readily conscious and could not volunteer any information (Fisher & Greenberg, 1977).

At this point, Freud established contact with someone who influenced Freud's professional and personal development and in many ways the future of psychoanalysis. Joseph Breuer was a Viennese physician who also worked with hysterical patients using an elegant technique that emphasized the "talking out" or overt expression of any thoughts that entered the patient's mind. The immediate advantage of this technique over hypnosis was that the patient could contribute directly to the content of the session. Through the use of this technique, which was later to be popularized by Freud as *free association*, Freud developed an extensive body of knowledge about the way abnormally behaving individuals view their world and themselves. This new technique opened a previously locked passageway to the unconscious, a part of the mind that Freud thought held the answers to understanding more of behavior than was earlier acknowledged.

Unfortunately, during the later years of Freud's association with Breuer, Freud's concentration on sexual instincts as a fundamental component of his theory resulted in a permanent division between the two. In addition, puritanical nineteenth century Vienna also could not accept Freud's hypothesis that the development of an abnormal personality resulted from some conflict present early in life that was as yet unresolved (especially when the source of the conflict was rooted in one's sexuality). The difficulty with accepting such an interpretation was Freud's primary belief that at the seat of all these conflicts were *psychosexual instincts*. These were the early days of the ongoing struggle that left Freud discouraged yet more persistent in his beliefs. During the years prior to the division between himself and Breuer, Freud managed to train a host of highly skilled students such as Carl Jung and Wilhelm Reich, all of whom eventually would also leave Freud's theoretical camp and initiate their own schools of psychoanalytic thought. Their reasons for leaving and the bitterness of these separations proved to be a constant source of discouragement for Freud. Experiences such as these, however, seemed to strengthen his desire to develop psychoanalysis via his model, which was established according to strict dogma and procedures, and this is how training of his students took place.

Throughout his professional life, Freud received little recognition from his peers. His invitation in 1909 at the request of G. Stanley Hall to visit Clark University was the first time in his career that he received an honorary degree. The five lectures that Freud presented were delivered in his own style, with little reference to notes and hardly any preparation (Jones, 1953). As always, he was a lucid and articulate speaker, qualities that were to remain with him throughout his professional career. Through his association with other psychologists at Clark University, the American Psychoanalytic Society had its beginnings. The American Psychological Association began at Clark University as well, with G. Stanley Hall as president.

Only recently have volumes of Freud's personal and professional letters and other writing been released to science historians and others. There is probably a great deal more we will learn about the man and his theory when these materials become widely available.

The following years of Freud's life were filled with a mixture of personal tragedy and professional progress. The deaths of close friends and colleagues, coupled with the untimely death of his young daughter in 1920, left Freud distressed and beside himself. Shortly after, he was granted a full professorship at the University of Vienna. Freud considered this award an empty honor, because it was only after international recognition that the University acknowledged his contributions.

With the onset of aging, a heart condition and cancer placed him in constant discomfort for the remainder of his life. He underwent more than thirty cancer operations, some of them lasting upwards of four hours with nothing more than a local anesthetic. Almost no one remembers him ever to complain of his discomfort, and his courage seemed to increase as his condition worsened. He lived with his affliction, and by providing himself as a model, be brought compassion and encouragement to others who were similarly ill.

Although his fame reached a new high during the early and middle 1920s, he would never realize the extent of his influence. The pre-World War II economic and political atmosphere became more oppressive as the years passed, especially for a Jew. He had experienced anti-Semitism as an adult through his exclusion from many learned societies.

Eventually, Vienna became intolerable as the Nazis indiscriminantly looted homes, burned books, and undermined professional groups such as those affiliated with psychoanalysis. After the Nazi invasion of Austria, there was little choice for most members of the psychoanalytic society but to flee. Freud, however, refused. Finally, after great efforts at persuasion by his family, Freud agreed to leave. In May 1938, after intervention on the part of the American and German ambassadors, Freud fled to London, where he was received with great honor. With the Nazis slowly decimating the Jewish population of Eastern Europe, Freud left with anxious feelings over the safety and well-being of his family. Freud mistakenly took solace in the notion that Austrian Nazis were to provide special laws for minorities, and he never learned of the murder of his four sisters in concentration camps. These last years of his life were spent receiving the acknowledgments due him all along and completing some but not all of his final writings. After countless years of suffering, his personal physician gave him the first dosage of pain killer he received throughout his illness. He died shortly thereafter, on September 23, 1939, with his family and friends close by. Even today, followers of his theories and beliefs meet to honor him on the anniversary of his death.

THE THEORETICAL OUTLOOK

The basic psychoanalytic model of development, which was continually modified by Freud over the last fifty years of his life, consists of three major components: a *dynamic* or economic component characterizing the human mind as a fluid energized system; a *structural* or topographical system that describes three separate yet interdependent psychological structures modulating behavior; and a *sequential* or stage component that stresses the progression from one stage of development to another, focusing on different sensitive bodily zones, developmental tasks, and psychological conflicts. All three of these components overlap (Figure 5-1), yet each must be considered separately to fully understand the developmental thrust of psychoanalytic theory.

The Dynamic Component

Psychic Energy. In keeping with the Zeitgeist (or thrust) of late nineteenth century intellectual and scientific developments, Freud took up the concept of energy and applied it to human behavior. He identified this energy as *psychic energy*, or the energy that operates the different components of the psychological system. According to Freud, (1) psychic energy is biologically based and always available in some form, (2) the total amount of energy within the system does not change since it is a closed system, and (3) the distribution of energy throughout the system depends on many factors, such as biological needs, the individual's stage of development, experiential history, and current environment.

Freud postulated that the primary source of energy is *instincts*, or unlearned psychological drives. Instincts have their origin in the biological needs and metabolic processes of the organism, and Freud believed that the most powerful class of instincts are those that deal with the creation and sustenance of life called *Eros*. Within his theory, this sexual instinct became a major life instinct and differed from other instincts (such as hunger and elimination), because gratification of the sexual instinct is necessary for the survival of the species, while gratification of the other instincts is necessary for the survival of the individual. He also identified another powerful class of instincts called *Thanatos*, representing death and aggression. The special form of energy that is used by these life instincts to maintain and continue development is called *libido*.

In Freud's system, instincts act as a stimulus to the mind, impelling the individual to satisfy certain needs. Instincts can also be seen as a psychological

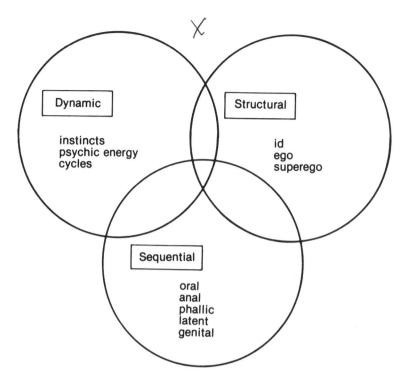

Figure 5-1. The component of Freud's psychoanalytic theory.

representation of a biological process. The majority of psychic energy in the infant, for example, is largely invested in fulfilling biological needs such as eating, elimination of wastes, and bodily stimulation.

The fundamental goal of early instinctual behavior is the reduction of tension (or discomfort) obtained through what Freud called *organ pleasure* (Freud, 1950). For example, a reduction in tension would be associated with filling an empty stomach with food or emptying a full bladder. For the very young infant instinctual gratification is easily and directly achieved. Gradually, however, the great reservoir of initial instinctual energy becomes transformed into energies that represent other more complex experiences of life. A certain amount of energy, however, is always id energy and, according to Freud, other available psychic energy can always be transformed back into id energy.

The Unconscious. One of the significant characteristics of psychic energy is that it is part of the *unconscious*. The unconscious is one of the most important elements in how Freud conceptualized human behavior. The unconscious is initially in control of most early behavior and remains in control of some portion of behavior throughout the life span. According to Freud, the bulk of psychic energy in the unconscious influences behavior, but not at a level that the individual is aware of or can think about. In order to understand how the unconscious operates and functions, Freud's notions about the different levels of the mind and the development of the structure of the mind must first be considered.

We have already mentioned how infants are controlled almost entirely by instinctual energy seeking pleasure and gratification without constraints. They sleep at will, eliminate automatically any place and any time, and, when hungry, eat on demand. The first interplay of how id energy is shaped by reality can be seen by examining the instinctual drive of hunger. The gratification of hunger in the human infant, unlike the gratification of elimination and other instincts, requires interaction with another human being. In the normal course of early events the infant's hunger will not be automatically gratified but will result in tension, most often expressed in crying and increased motor activity. Such infant behaviors serve as signals to the infant's caretaker that the infant is in need of food. With the presentation of the bottle or breast, the infant eats, the hunger drive is satisfied, tension decreases, and the infant becomes content. Through the repetition of this sequence of events the infant gradually learns that instinctual satisfaction requires external events, and the awareness of these external events becomes associated with some portion of id energy. As the infant becomes aware that his or her own behavior results in the activation of these external events, some portion of id energy becomes transformed into energy associated with the conscious associations of the infant's self. This transformed psychic energy is the *ego*.

Once infants develop this awareness that their behavior can bring about or cause events to occur, the elements of the ego have begun to be formed. (Hall, 1954). Some psychic energy is now associated with the infant's development of a sense of self. That sense of self undergoes further development so that eventually a later structure evolves, the *superego*. The superego represents the principles and mores of the society in which the individual lives. Although the two are not entirely identical, some people use the term "conscience" to describe this structure.

The superego can be described by means of the following hypothetical example: A young child is hungry, and knowing that there is a cookie jar in the kitchen cabinet, she realizes that the hunger can be satisfied by going to the cookie jar and taking a cookie. However, on one or more occasions her mother has told her that such behavior is not acceptable, and the child thus becomes aware that there is another set of factors to take into consideration in satisfying hunger—parental expectations, or social reality, both forces more powerful than the child. The mother may tell the child, "No, you may not take a cookie," or otherwise scold or punish her. Gradually, the child, who wants to take the cookie and satisfy her hunger, will begin to weigh the ego factors (the sense of her own self-willed behavior of going and getting the cookie) with superego factors (social disapproval and punishment). When the child wants a cookie and knows she can get it but decides not to, then that child's behavior is being controlled by psychic energy that has been transformed into ego and superego energy.

The fate of psychic energy is to be distributed between the id, the ego, and the superego. During development, the distribution is unequal and in constant flux depending on the individual's stage of development and whatever needs may be present.

The Structural Component

The three parts of the structural component, the id, the ego, and the superego, all serve a well-defined purpose: the attainment of goal objects and the eventual reduction of tension. Although these structures lack any physical reality, they form the basis for the different psychological forces that represent the interaction of biological impulses (the id), adaptive and mediating behaviors (the ego), and moral and ethical standards of control (the superego).

The Id. The id (Latin for "that thing") is present at birth and developmentally is the oldest of the three psychological structures. According to Freud, neither the ego nor the superego is active or even formed so early in the individual's development, when the id serves as the storehouse for all the instincts. Initially, all the psychic energy available in the system is invested in the id, which uses this energy to satisfy basic needs through reflexive or reflexive-like behaviors. These needs must first be satisfied if (1) the organism is to survive, and (2) the organism is to move on to higher, less biologically more socially based needs.

In its most basic form, the id is an inborn biological structure that has as its purpose immediate gratification and reduction of tension. As the initial reservoir of psychic energy, it accomplishes this primary goal of tension reduction through the *pleasure principle* (also referred to as the principle of lust, the pleasure-pain principle, or the lust-unlust principle) (Jones, 1953). The pleasure principle states that the primary goal in mental operations is the achievement of pleasure through gratification (Freud, 1920).

Controlled entirely by the pleasure principle, id energy is under no constraints and makes no distinction between fantasy and reality. Thought that does not distinguish what is real from what is not real is called *primary process thinking*. For example, in the older child or adult, a need can become temporarily satisfied by means of remote representation of the drive object (or that which satisfies a need), perhaps in the form of an image. Daydreaming is thought to exemplify this type of thinking. For example, thinking about a favorite food when one is hungry may relieve hunger pangs for a short period of time. Although daydreaming or primary process thinking satisfies only temporarily, it is an effective way of discharging stored energy and reducing tension so that the tension does not dominate one's thinking.

The psychic energy associated with the id is unconscious in that the individual is unaware of it and cannot talk or think about it. All of the psychic energy associated with the id is unlabeled, or without any verbal associations. It is not available to higher mental processes, and the emotions and feelings associated with it cannot be considered on a rational basis. For this reason some Freudian psychologists believe that events that occur when the child is preverbal cannot be remembered.

The unconscious urges of the id remain active throughout life, but, as healthy development proceeds, a smaller and smaller proportion of psychic energy becomes associated with the id, and more and more psychic energy becomes associated with the more socially adaptive ego and superego.

The Ego. The formation of the ego results from the interaction between the organism and the environment and the continued reduction of the tension associated with certain needs. Freudian theory postulates that the ego begins to develop because of the id's inability, acting alone, to satisfy all the individual's needs (Hall, 1954). The course through which the organism begins to employ ego processes to achieve gratification is called *identification*. The beginning of identification signifies the organism's awareness that goal-directed behavior, as distinct from affective irrational discharges, can result in tension reduction and satisfaction. The organism can now distinguish between reality and fantasy. Ego processes facilitate gratification by distinguishing between ''self'' and ''not-self,'' and then planning with this in mind. This planning is described as *secondary process thinking*. Before the onset of secondary thinking processes, the primary method of obtaining need satisfaction was through some affective or emotional discharge. In itself, these discharges can be an act or sign alerting potential environmental influences (such as a parent), that help or assistance is needed. These affective discharges release tension, but the relief is only temporary. For example, a child's temper tantrum acts as an outlet for a short period of time but does not address the basic need.

In contrast to the relative helplessness of the newborn infant dominated by the id, early ego development permits the child to act on the surrounding world with intention and thus directly reduce tension. For example, the hungry id dominated infant cries; the hungry toddler in the early stages of ego development may smile, try to open the refrigerator, or ask for something to eat. The effectiveness of this behavior helps to further reinforce ego development.

The ego progresses from a *pleasure ego* in its initial stages of functioning to a *rational ego* controlled by the *reality principle*, where ego pleasure is realized through adherence to external realities. Here the subjective expression of needs through emotions is separated from the objective state of the real world. The ego receives the energy to perform such functions from the id, which has been channeled into this reality-oriented structure. Thus energy is redistributed. What was previously invested in id functions is now invested in the ego, which mediates all intellectual decision making.

Although the ego does not employ the pleasure principle of the id, pleasure (tension reduction or the removal of pain) is obtained by means of this reality principle. External realities are represented in reason and thought rather than in emotion.

In addition to the realistic assessment of the environment, the ego also serves another important function. It acts as an organizer of mental processes, mediating at times between the id and the superego (a structure that develops later), and controls the level and direction of energy invested in the outside world. Freud believed that the ego, more than any other structural component, is affected by sensory perceptions, and that these sensorimotor experiences are as important to the function and content of the ego as instincts are to the id. The ego functions as the decision-making mechanism that acts in accordance with the id's unconscious wishes. As the executive branch of the three part structural system, the ego is the arbitrator that takes into account the available energy and balances the expenditure of energy within the entire system to ensure need satisfaction, yet ensures as well the reservation of substantial amounts of energy for future growth.

The Superego. The id directs the organism toward gratification, while the ego strives for gratification through constructive interaction with the environment.

Freud believed that a third structural component, called the *superego*, develops in later childhood. The superego is psychic energy acting as the force that opposes the unbound gratification sought by the id. As a structure, it represents first the internalization and the assimilation of parental authority and second the social and ethical standards of the culture (Freud, 1933). The purposes of the superego are (1) to inhibit or prevent the id from expressing impulses that are inappropriate from society's perspective; and (2) to strive for the ideal (not necessarily the real).

In superego, Freud invested the traditional values and ideals of society. Consequently, the superego is the representative of the internalized standard to which well-socialized people are supposed to aspire. The development of the superego results from (1) the resolution of certain conflicts with parents; (2) the demands that the environment places on the ego, but that cannot always be met by the overly rational ego alone; and (3) the experiences children have during the long period of time spent with parents.

Freud described the psychic energy associated with the superego as consisting of the *ego ideal*, and the *conscience* (Freud, 1923). The ego ideal represents those judgments that the child thinks of as morally good, while the conscience represents those things the child thinks the parents feel are morally bad. In his early writings, Freud (1923) felt that the notion of ego ideal was sufficient to represent this authoritative force. Through extensive clinical work, however, he came to believe there existed another element—what parents think—representing social and moral restraints.

Defense Mechanisms

The dynamic aspect of Freudian theory involves the distribution and transformation of psychic energy. During the formative first five or six years of life, psychic energy is distributed from the id into the underlying structures of the ego and superego. Dynamic and structural components continually interact via a set of mechanisms that helps the individual remain comfortable and minimizes anxiety. The most prominent mechanisms, which begin functioning with the emergence of the ego, are *defense mechanisms*. A defense mechanism is a technique the ego uses to distort reality in the face of dangers that might interrupt healthy psychological development.

There are many examples of defense mechanisms and the way in which they help protect from too much tension or anxiety. Perhaps the best example—repression—occurs when the incestuous feelings for the mother on the part of the son (or for the father on part of the daughter) are not allowed to surface from an unconscious to a conscious level. This conflict, which will be discussed in greater detail later in this chapter, exemplifies how a potentially high level of anxiety can be controlled through use of a very specialized defense mechanism. All defense mechanisms help the individual moderate and tolerate discomfort. They can be used temporarily, or, for some, they become stable and durable modes of operation. When they become stable and durable modes of operation for an adult, they become personality characteristics. For the developing child, they serve as an experimental way of handling unpleasant circumstances.

Defense mechanisms help to restructure the personality—move or transform psychic energy—and during development they keep the structure of personality fluid as the child experiments. Defense mechanisms, however, serve a more important purpose. They ensure that all the available psychic energy does not get invested as anxiety and that some remains to be directed toward growth. In other words, defense mechanisms protect us from recklessly discharging the energy that is necessary for later growth. We are unaware of their functioning (that is, they occur on an unconscious level), but we need them to ensure that a sufficient level of energy can be directed toward future development.

As a child develops, there are changes in the relationship between the id, ego, and superego and the distribution of psychic energy. There is a decreasing amount of energy invested directly into the functioning of the id, while more and more is transformed into energy that will be used in the creation and maintenance of the ego. The ego develops later than the id (which is present at birth) and the superego develops even later. Later structures develop from the energy (and in some cases the surplus) that is invested in earlier ones.

Eventually the ego has more psychic energy invested in it than any other structural component, since it is the ego that for the most part acts as a mediator between the biological needs of the organism represented by the id and the demands of society and those social constraints represented by the superego.

The Sequential or Stage Component

The dynamic component of Freudian theory deals with the source, distribution, and utilization of psychic energy, while the structural component addresses the interdependency of underlying psychological structures and their effect on development. The third and final component, the *sequential or stage component*, has as its central emphasis the pattern or progression of the organism through different and increasingly adaptive developmental stages. Before the five qualitatively different stages of the Freudian theory of development are discussed in detail, it is important to list some of the general assumptions Freud made about this component of development.

As his training dictated, Freud began his thinking about development from a biological perspective. He proposed that development consisted of a series of stages. Each stage is characterized by the focusing of psychic energy on different areas of the body, called *erogenous zones*, and each stage corresponds to sequential changes in the dominance of biological and psychological needs. For example, the earliest stage of development involves sensitivity to stimulation in and around the oral area. It also involves the concentration of psychic energy on the basic need of hunger and the behavior of eating. Similarly, the second stage is focused on an increased or dominant sensitivity in the anal and urinary areas with psychic energy thus concentrated on the basic need for elimination. Interestingly, this second stage occurs around the same time that Western society feels it is necessary to begin formal toilet training.

The importance of the concept of erogenous zones in Freud's theory cannot be overemphasized. Freud believed that infants are born with the ability to experience excitation from skin contact and that surface skin tension builds up and needs reduction by direct skin contact. This excitation was likened to sexual stimulation but was considered qualitatively different from the type of sexual stimulation experienced by adults by being more generalized and undifferentiated. Freud called this capacity for excitation and the need for such excitation to be reduced *infantile sexuality*, as distinguished from *adult sexuality* (Freud, 1950).

This attribution of sexuality to infants and young children created the extensive popular outcry against Freud in the last days of the Victorian era and the early part of the twentieth century. But, based on their clinical experiences, Freud and his adherents stuck to their claims that the psychological-experiential components intermingled with the biologically shifting dominance of the erogenous zones in a sequential manner. Hence, the stages of development were called *psychosexual stages*. Freud assumed that these psychosexual stages occurred universally for all children everywhere. Although the stages were not age bound per se, they occurred in an invariant sequence at approximately the same time for most children. The successful progression through these stages, however, is not guaranteed. Just as a child might experience some type of developmental delay in physical growth, a parallel occurrence can happen psychologically as well. An individual can become fixated at a certain stage when the normal progression from stage to stage is interrupted. Based on some apprehension or fear, the person (or at least certain characteristics of his or her personality) can remain rooted at an earlier level of functioning. The fixations that occur during the five sequential stages that Freud described have direct effects on the formation of later adult personality. Freud classified fixation as a defense mechanism since it protects the individual from potentially debilitating anxiety.

Freud proposed that the onset of each psychosexual stage and some of the forms of the behavior occurring in each stage were controlled by genetic or maturational factors, while the content of each stage would vary depending on the culture in which development is taking place. Here is another clear example of how heredity and environment interact as important forces in the developmental process.

Freud's proposal of developmental stages was significant for many reasons. It was the first theoretical attempt to describe developmental change as an orderly and predictable process resulting from a combination of maturational and environmental influences. Freud's notion of stages also led to a distinction between quantitative differences within stages versus qualitative distinctions between stages. Development was not seen as a continuous uninterrupted process of more and more, but as a process involving differences, reorganization, and sequential restructuring of behavior. This formulation has become the prototype for stage theories of development. Other major theoretical perspectives, such as the cognitive-developmental model, also adopted many of the basic characteristics of this part of Freud's work. Perhaps the most significant aspect of Freud's theory of development was his assumption that the early stages provided the foundation for adult behavior, and that adult behavior and personality structure can only be understood in the light of early developmental experience.

The Oral Stage. The first psychosexual stage is the *oral stage* of development, occurring during the first year of life. The primary focus of stimulation during this stage is the mouth and oral cavity, and the primary source of gratification results from eating. The oral stage dominates the first year of life, and all experience is assumed to be mediated by eating-related activities. It is important to understand that the oral stage is largely dominated by id energy, although with the onset of language and motor competence the beginning of ego development becomes apparent. However, much of the experience during the oral period is without any verbal labels and is, therefore, likely to remain permanently in the unconscious. For this reason, Freudians are very concerned that experiences in the oral stage be positive and that oral conflicts be resolved with a minimum of residual tension.

From a developmental perspective, it is the mother (or primary caretaker) who often satisfies the basic and fundamental needs of the oral period. The sense of satisfaction that can occur during the oral period can be a source of gratification throughout life. The child learns to associate satisfaction with the image of the mother. Subsequently, objects that are associated with the mother, or objects that represent that image, also come to provide a sense of satisfaction and security. In most Western societies the mother is still the figure most likely to gratify the infant's hunger. This occurs through repeated pairings of the mother (and her image) with a reduction in tension (from hunger, for example). These repeated pairings, or *memory traces*, will, in the future, help the child to identify the appropriate goal object and eventually pursue it.

Besides the biological necessity of eating, oral activities also provide pleasurable sensations. In addition to the stimulation received through feeding, oral stimulation is received through sucking, mouthing, and biting.

Freud came to distinguish two separate phases of the oral stage of psychosexual development. The *oral passive/oral dependent* phase and the *oral aggressive/oral sadistic* phase. The infant's first behaviors of sucking are characteristic of the oral passive phase of satisfying needs, and the oral aggressive phase coincides with the onset of teething (around six to eight months). It is characterized by biting and chewing. The oral passive phase precedes the oral aggressive phase, and both are considered as ending early during the second year of life.

The Anal Stage. The second psychosexual stage of development is the *anal stage*, lasting roughly from the second to the fourth year of life. It is accompanied by a heightened sensitivity of stimulation of the mucous membranes surrounding the anal area of the body. As during all stages of development, tension exists that is generated as a result of an interaction between some basic biological need and a heightened physiological sensitivity. The expulsion or elimination of fecal material is a thoroughly pleasurable sensation for the child that reduces tension and discomfort. The young child initially has little control over bowel or bladder functioning. However, society requires more voluntary control of elimination. In Western societies toilet training tends to occur sometime during the second or third year of life. The imposition of the training, in Freudian theory, provides a setting for the child to experience the conflict between immediate gratification (and its pleasures) and delaying gratification (and its discomfort), but with the eventual pleasure of social approval when training is accomplished. The child must learn to delay or postpone necessary elimination functions until the appropriate time and place are available. Just as the elimination process can be viewed as pleasurable, so can the retention or holding on of fecal material, because it provides for heightened satisfaction when released, and also leads to increased social approval.

Just as there are two phases of the oral stage of development, there are two phases of the anal stage. During the *anal expulsive* phase, which occurs first, the child derives pleasure from the expulsion of feces. The second phase, called *anal retentive*, is when the child receives gratification through the retention or holding on of feces. The child is thought to do this because of the feeling that, as a possession, excrement has great power. Children are viewed as thinking that in elimination they are literally giving away a part of their body. Another reason for doing this is that the greater the tension, the greater the pleasure on its release.

The anal period has some very important psychosocial implications. During this stage, according to Freud, the child begins to deal seriously with separation from the surrounding external reality (Freud, 1908). This awareness comes to the child through the process of toilet training. The child begins to establish an identity as an individual and this process is an essential point of basic ego formation. Because of now present language skills, experiences can be labeled and retained in the conscious. If toilet training occurs before the development of language and the child's ability to be expressive and understand what is being demanded, the experience of toilet training may become associated with tension and anxiety and then stored in the unconscious as an unpleasant event. Premature toilet training not only occurs without the benefit of language and symbolic representational processes, but is also mistimed in terms of the occurrence of biological dominance of the anal area. Freudians saw the restrictive practices of a Victorian society (in which toilet training sometimes began at six months of age) as a particularly negative influence on healthy psychosexual development. It is likely that the influence of Freudian theory (along with the advent of the washing machine) has contributed significantly to later and more permissive toilet training practices in Western, industrialized societies.

Within Freudian theory the anal period is the stage during which the child first confronts the need for conformity to social expectations. The child must increasingly consider the wishes and standards of others. During the oral stage gratification could occur at personal convenience or desire (thumbsucking, mouthing, biting) and, even is social standards were imposed by disapproval, the consequences were not momentous. But as the anal stage ends, the child is well aware that needed gratification cannot occur at will and that there are consequences for ignoring social standards. In the clear awareness of others and the growing distinction of self, the stage is set for the next developmental stage.

The Phallic Stage. The third major developmental stage described by Freud is called the *phallic stage*. It is thought to last from approximately the fourth to the sixth year. During this period, psychic energy is invested in the genital organs and the pleasure that is received through organ manipulation. It is also during this period that some of the most profound psychological changes in the child's personality development take place.

Children who by this developmental stage have established a fairly sound identity of themselves as individuals (with a realization that they are biologically and psychologically separate from others), are faced with increasingly sharpened conflicts with parents. The child develops feelings that grow in magnitude to form a *complex* of interrelated emotions and behaviors termed the Oedipus complex for males and the Electra complex for females. The ultimate importance of this stage is in the resolution or working through of these conflicts and the subsequent development of appropriate sex role identification. Freud believes that the entire dynamic process of child-parent interaction and the resolution of Oedipal and Electra conflicts provides the framework for the basic construction and solidification of the superego (Freud, 1950).

The Oedipus complex takes its name and meaning from the Greek tragedy Oedipus Rex in which Oedipus kills his father and marries a woman who is, unknown to him, his biological mother. On learning of this transgression, he punishes himself by gouging his eyes out. Freud believes that the desire to possess the mother sexually is characteristic of all males during the phallic stage of development. Parallel to the biological changes that take place during this stage, the male seeks the primary and original love object, the mother, and begins to see the father as a competitive force for the love and affection that only the mother can give. The male child's feelings of inferiority are compounded by the results of a comparison between his and his father's genitalia.

Although the wish to possess the mother physically and psychologically is unrealistic in terms of societal taboos, the male child pursues these irrational desires and eventually is forced to confront his father over who will be the primary recipient of the mother's attention. During this subtle yet profound confrontation, the male child eventually recognizes his father's outrage at his motives and becomes fearful that the father will punish him (through castration) for his incestuous behavior. This fear takes the form of what Freud called the *castration complex*, and specifically results in *castration anxiety*, for the boy. In other words, he fears his father will castrate his sex organs, which are now the focal point of his maturational and psychological growth.

This fear (which remains at the unconscious level) is so strong that the male child eventually abandons these obviously intolerable thoughts about his mother and realizes that the necessary gratification can be obtained only through identification with the father and through the vicarious satisfaction obtained through father-son interaction via mother-father interaction. It is primarily through this process that (1) the beginnings of the superego come into being, because the resolution of the Oedipus complex represents a recognition of societal and tribal mores and values, and (2) the child identifies with his father, leading to successful procreation on the child's part and, indirectly, fulfillment of a very general instinct. The Oedipal conflict is thus resolved.

Freud described a comparable Electra conflict for females but did not elaborate. Many Freudians believe that the process is much more complex for girls than the Odeipal situation for boys. For girls, initially, the young female child does not realize there are any distinct differences between the sexes. Through experience (physical and social/emotional contact with both parents), she realizes she does not possess the same organs the the male does. A sense of inferiority over this results in what Freud called *penis envy*. Penis envy amplifies and intensifies her love and attachment to her father, and there is a corresponding rejection of her mother. The girl is assumed to unconsciously hold her mother responsible for her lack of a male sexual organ.

However, the girl is thought to realize eventually that the incorporation of a penis is physically impossible and that direct gratification of her desire for one must be channeled into identification with the mother. Freud was much less explicit in detailing the process of the resolution of the Electra conflict than in specifying the course of the resolution of the Odeipal conflict.

The distinction Freud made between the experiences for males and females during the phallic stage of development is often cited as a chauvinistic view. Whereas the male is concerned with the expression of his sexual desires through the manipulation of his genitals, the female is described as being preoccupied with the inferiority of hers. Although both sexes come through the conflict with the same eventual developmental outcome (development of the superego and a sex role), the characterizations of the male and the female through the process have very different connotations.

The phallic stage (with the central drama focused on the resolution of the Oedipal and Electra conflicts) is considered to result in a number of major events of possibly lifelong significance. First, there is the solidification of the superego, which finally emerges as a significant part of the psychic structure. Second, there is the establishment of appropriate sex-role identity. These are important hallmarks of development. The phallic stage is not smooth for any child, and for most children there is some difficulty. Resolution of the conflict is more likely to be moderately than completely successful. For yet other children the stage is prolonged even past the sixth year of life, when some form of resolution is thought to occur whether or not it is satisfactory.

At the end of the phallic stage, the child's psychic energy has been well engaged. Conflict has been strong, and pressure for resolution has been relentless. The child is psychically tired, and therefore the biological wisdom is for a period of dormancy to begin—hence the period of latency. However, the problems associated with the Oedipal or Electra period and the more or less successful or unsuccessful resolution of the conflicts are just beneath the surface. Indeed, all the problems of the early psychosexual stages, and most particularly of the phallic stage, have been put in storage to be revived during later adolescence.

The Latency Stage. The *latency stage* is characterized by an inhibition of the sensitivity of the erogenous zones. During this period (beginning around seven years of age), much of the energy formerly invested in sexual desires is displaced or channeled to other behaviors. This stage is a lull or regression of sorts, during which the individual's development seems to slow down. The huge amounts of psychic energy that were formerly invested in resolving the conflicts of the first three developmental stages are now focused on developing affection for the parents and on the establishment of strong social ties with children of the same sex.

Freud and his closest followers paid relatively little attention to this period of development. It was assumed that nothing of significant importance was happening in the psychic realm of personality organization or development. Although the child is active and learning and deeply engaged in many kinds of activities, from the psychosexual point of view it is a point of rest from the rigors of the prior conflicts and a period of gearing up for the battles of the next period. Later contributors to psychoanalytic theory, such as Erik Erikson, paid more attention to this period of development. Erikson's views will be detailed in the next chapter.

The length of the latency period is quite variable. Its onset occurs at about seven years of age with the supposed resolution of the conflicts of the phallic stage. The ending of the latency period, and the beginning of the genital stage, is triggered by the onset of puberty, the beginnings of adult-like sexuality, and the reopening of earlier conflicts.

The Genital Stage. For many the *genital stage* is synonymous with adolescence. Although recent writings of Freudians have sought to differentiate the genital stage into several substages, we will treat it as one major developmental stage.

The genital stage begins around the twelfth year and is in one sense the final stage of development. It is characterized by intense psychic activity and the distribution and redistribution of psychic energy. Earlier resolutions of conflicts in preceding psychosexual stages and their resulting distributions of psychic energy again come up for reconsideration. The genital area of the body becomes associated with adult sexuality, and physical sexual development is accompanied by psychic sexual identity and role playing.

The genital stage is a period of serious decisions. Sex-role identity is reconsidered and some real or fantasied forms of homosexuality are thought to occur universally. Freudian theory has traditionally viewed the final election of homosexuality as a form of deviance resulting from the inappropriate resolution of the Oedipal conflict for males and the Electra conflict for females. However, recent treatments of homosexuality within Freudian theory have taken a more complex view (Fisher & Greenberg, 1977).

The ego and supergeo face significant tests during the adolescent period, and inadequate development of one or both has been the supposed cause of adolescent suicide, delinquency, and serious mental disturbances. The storms and stresses of adolescence are the psychic wars of the genital period. When the genital period comes to a close, the adult's mature personality structure has been set in place. According to Freudian theory, changes in personality structure are difficult to achieve beyond this point because the redistribution and transformation of psychic energy typical of the fluid character of earlier developmental periods now require a great deal of effort, usually requiring professional help and intensive therapy.

Instincts and the Developmental Process

Perhaps the best example of how Freud's psychosexual theory can be applied to the process of development is through an examination of instincts and the cycle of gratification mentioned earlier.

In Figure 5-2, the components of this cycle (need or instinct, goal object, goal-oriented behavior, and reduction of tension) are represented, as well as an example of each. Here, hunger represents a basic biological need. Through associations what we called a memory trace formed between the sensation of hunger and the presence of food; the person "knows" what appropriate action (eating) can reduce the tension associated with the need.

This is a simple illustration that shows how the individual takes an active role in satisfying basic needs. It can also illustrate the cyclical or repetitive quality of instincts. Hunger occurs again and again, and the cycle continually begins anew. In fact, most needs are only satisfied temporarily, and the system returns to its original state of tension, again seeking different ways to satisfy more developmentally advanced needs (such as the need for affiliation or emotional support), thereby ensuring uninterrupted progress.

Freud's psychoanalytic theory is often presented only in terms of its implications for personality development, with little attention given to such dimensions as thought or cognition, or other aspects of development. However, there is a subtle relationship between emotions and thought that is integral to the understanding of Freud's theory and the role that instincts play. The problem-solving component of development is a major part of our everyday behavior and it can also be understood within the psychoanalytic model.

All thought, whether it is primary or secondary process thinking, results from the need to reduce tension. In the search for a goal object that will reduce tension

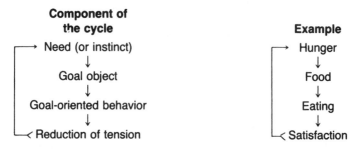

Figure 5-2. The cycle of gratification.

(such as food or sleep) the individual eventually accepts whatever goal object offers maximum reduction in tension and minimal expenditure of energy. The primary dynamic of development is, however, that the *essential* goal object is never really obtainable, and this absence is a source of continual motivation to seek satisfaction. Even when there is no object that can provide complete gratification, there are two possible outcomes.

The first involves an *affective* or emotional discharge of energy. For example, the infant who is hungry and operates with an abundance of id-controlled energy cries when he or she is hungry. The infant is not equipped physically to find food acting alone. This is due to (1) the motor limitations of infants (they cannot feed themselves), and (2) the infant's history of receiving the necessary gratification through some external agent, such as the mother. The very young infant has not yet developed the structural capability to deal with the environment by obtaining goal objects through purposeful thinking. Consequently, an affective discharge of energy in the form of crying serves the important purposes of (1) reducing tension, and (2) alerting someone (the mother) to interact and assist. Although crying is effective (it does release tension), it is only temporarily so, because the need is not gratified and the infant is forced to continue the search. Eventually, however, this affective energy will be channeled into goal-oriented, realistic, ego-controlled thinking.

The second strategy is an outgrowth of the first outcome just described. Affective discharges eventually involve contact with the outside world. The thinking process results from the interrelationship between memory traces and need/object associations. The young child who has a need often finds it fulfilled without much expenditure of energy. Through the satisfaction of basic needs, memory traces and images are formed, and when in the future the child experiences the same or a similar need, the image of the fulfilling object can be recalled and used as a guide in thoughtful pursuit of the goal object. In this manner, through the establishment of a base of memory traces, a complex wealth of associations evolves that provides the individual with alternative goal objects when needed. An individual learns to satisfy a need through a variety of choices.

In some situations, however, the surrounding world may be structured in such a way as to provide for the satisfaction of needs without any investment or a minimal commitment of energy. This is often the case with children or adults who are provided with everything they desire and are not expected to make any investment. Needs are satisfied without any action on the part of the individual. This is potentially a tragic outcome, because no investment of energy means no growth. Theoretically, the higher-order thinking processes (or secondary process thinking) necessary to obtain the goal object can never be developed without the presence of tension.

Sigmund Freud was interested in the clinical treatment of people with emotional problems. In the process of developing a theory to account for a treatment technique, the energy model, the structural components, and the developmental stages were devised. Freud viewed the process of helping someone regain psychological health as involving a restructuring of the distribution of this psychic energy. Behavioral problems were viewed as symptoms stemming from the maladaptive distribution of psychic energy. Freud's patients were motivated by the psychic energy of the unconscious, and thus the unconscious motivations for their behaviors were unknown to them. Successful therapy helps the individual transform the unconscious motivation to the conscious level, to talk about it, deal with it, and reassign and psychic motivation to the conscious level where awareness (ego and superego) is in better control and theoretically is more adaptive and functional for the individual.

It is beyond the scope of this book to treat psychoanalysis as a therapeutic technique or a clinical theory. However, it was Freud's development of the clinical dimensions of psychoanalysis that led to the formulation of a developmental theory. Freud found that in helping transform unconscious energy into conscious energy, a frequent phenomenon was the recall of earlier experiences from childhood. This repeated happening along with the experiences and the similarity of types of events that patients recalled led to his consideration of the importance of early events, and the proposal of the id, ego, and superego as developmental structures.

SUMMARY POINTS

1. Freud's accomplishments provided the first attempt at developing a systematic and global theory of development.
2. Freud was influenced by the principle of conservation of energy.
3. Freud utilized talking out or free association in the treatment of emotional illness.
4. Freud's psychoanalytic model of development consists of dynamci, structural, and sequential components.
5. Freud applied the concept of conservation of energy to human behavior with the identification of psychic energy.
6. The total amount of energy within the system does not change, yet the distribution of the energy depends on many complex factors.
7. Freud postulated that primary sources of energy derive from instincts, which have their origin in the biological needs of the organism.
8. The fundamental goal of early instinctual behavior is the reduction of tension.
9. Instincts have a cyclical quality, and most needs can be only temporarily satisfied until the organism returns to the orignial state of tension.
10. The id contains everything that is passed on from one generation to the next, and is the storehouse of all instincts.
11. The id is an inborn biological structure that has immediate gratification and reduction in tension as its purpose.

12. The pleasure principle states that a primary goal is the achievement of pleasure through gratification.
13. Thought that does not distinguish what is real from what is not real is primary process thinking.
14. The unconscious urges the id to remain active throughout life, but as development proceeds, a smaller proportion of psychic energy becomes invested in the id.
15. The ego results from the interaction of the organism with the environment and the eventual reduction of tension associated with certain needs.
16. Ego processes facilitate gratification through secondary process or rational thinking.
17. The superego is the structure that represents the principles and mores of society.
18. The purpose of the superego is to inhibit the id from expressing impulses that are socially inappropriate.
19. Defense mechanisms serve the important developmental function of protecting us from recklessly discharging the energy necessary for later growth.
20. The sequential component has as its central emphasis the pattern or progression of the organism through different and increasingly adaptive developmental stages.
21. Freud proposed that development consists of a series of five stages, each characterized by a focus of psychic energy on a different area of the body.
22. Freud assumed that these psychosexual stages occurred universally for all children.
23. The cycle of gratification provides a model for understanding the developmental contribution of psychoanalytic theory.

HOW THEY STUDY DEVELOPMENT

Unlike many other developmental theorists, Freud rarely observed children in any kind of clinical setting and almost never conducted any traditionally "experimental" studies. Yet, for a variety of reasons, a substantial amount of empirical research based on his psychoanalytic approach has been completed over the past 80 years.

Since one of Freud's basic assumptions is that developmental change often takes place on an unconscious level with a redistribution of energy, we might want to look at a study that examines how changes in the distribution of psychic energy might affect behavior.

One of the views about aggression in young children is that it is a result of pent-up frustration. This is a psychoanalytic view, where the release of pent-up energy is tension reducing and operates according to the pleasure principle.

The primary hypothesis that was tested in Mallick's study (1966) was whether the expression of frustration produced aggression helped to reduce verbal aggression. In other words, did it provide a suitable outlet?

To test this, the authors had sixth grade "confederates" (children who knew the purpose of the experiment) frustrate some third graders who were trying to complete a block-building task. There was another group of sixth graders who did not interfere with their third grade counterparts' block building and praised them when they were finished. Two measures were used to assess level of aggression: the number of shocks the third grader could ostensibly give the sixth grader to "get even," and rating by third graders on a "like-dislike" scale of the sixth graders.

The general conclusion of the study is that aggressive play, with or without previous frustration, has no effectiveness as a cathartic experience. In other words, participating in an aggressive activity (such as administering shocks) does not provide a suitable outlet for frustration.

FURTHER READINGS

Bettelheim, B. Freud and the soul. *New Yorker*, March 1, 1982.

Freud, S. The origin and development of psychoanalysis. *Journal of Psychology*, 1910, *21*, 181–218.

Freud, S. *The complete psychological works*. London: Hogarth, 1953–1964.

Hall, C. S. *A primer of Freudian psychology*. New York: New American Library, 1954.

Jones, E. *The life and work of Sigmund Freud*. New York: Basic Books, 1953–1957.

Monroe, R. *School of psychoanalytic*. New York: Holt, 1955.

READINGS OF OTHER INTEREST

Stone, I. *Passions of the mind*. New York: Doubleday, 1971.

Fisher S. and Greenberg, R. *The scientific credibility of Freud's theories and therapy*. New York: Basic Books, 1977.

Byck, R. *The cocaine papers*. New York: Stonehill Press, 1974.

6

Erik Erikson's Psychosocial Perspective

The main business of the adolescent is through gentle transaction to stop being one.

Arthur Koestler

This sense of identity provides the ability to experience one's self as something that has continuity and sameness, and to act accordingly.

Erik Erikson

INTRODUCTION AND BASIC ASSUMPTIONS

As Freud's psychoanalytic theory grew in influence, students flocked from all over Europe to Vienna to learn from Freud himself. Some of these students went on to develop specific aspects of theory, while others challenged some parts of it. Most of the variations on Freudian theory focused on understanding abnormal behavior and extrapolating various ideas and principles related to childhood. Two students of Freud who focused directly on children and on the developmental process were Anna Freud, his daughter, and Erik Erikson, an artist and teacher who came under Freud's influence and turned his attention entirely to children. Over the years, Erikson has extended Freudian theory and helped to shape a particular emphasis that was noted for its focus on the ego as a central component in the individual's functioning. His *psychosocial* theory has had a significant impact on the understanding of the developmental process and has focused on the entire life span. In fact, Erikson is often considered the first true "life span" developmental psychologist.

Unlike many other early psychoanalysts, Erik Homberger Erikson never really "left" the Freudian camp by rejecting Freud's initial orientation. He did, however, provide a unique perspective by incorporating many of Freud's primary assumptions while greatly expanding on the model. Erikson broadened the network of factors considered responsible for influencing development.

According to Erikson, psychological development results from the interaction between maturational processes or biological needs and the societal demands and social forces encountered in everyday life (Erikson, 1950b). In doing so, Erikson placed greater emphasis on the dimension of socialization than Freud did. In addition to this distinction, another important difference was Erikson's concern for psychological development throughout the entire life span, rather than just the years from birth through adolescence. Erikson examined the consequences of early experiences on later life as did Freud, but he went farther and described the nature of qualitative change during the middle and later years of life. These later periods of development have (traditionally) been ignored by developmental psychologists. However, recent trends in such fields as gerontology and popular publications such as *Passages* (Sheehy, 1976) and *Transformations* (Gould, 1979) have stimulated thought and research in this area, making Erikson's work even more popular.

Like Freud, Erikson postulated the existence of a series of stages of development governed by underlying maturational forces and the presence of a conflict at each one of these eight stages. He developed the notion and role of conflict resolution to a greater degree than Freud by associating each of the eight psychosocial stages with a definite crisis that had to be resolved in order for the individual to move on to a more advanced stage. Erikson believed that although maturational processes might be the impetus for the onset of different stages, it is the societal demands present from conception through death that act as very powerful mediating and shaping forces.

Erikson never received formal scientific training before he began his career as a child analyst. Most other analysts had degrees in medicine or related areas, but Erikson's training prior to his introduction to psychology was in the fine arts. As an aspiring European artist during the late 1920s, he found himself employed as both a teacher and private portrait painter. Through informal introduction, Erikson came in contact with people who introduced him to the field of child analysis. After receiving his certificate in child analysis in 1933, he departed for Denmark where he practiced for a short period of time until he finally transferred his studies to the United States.

Although Freud based his theoretical approach on the relationship of life energy or libido to the psychological functioning of the individual, Erikson stressed the importance of the ego. He saw the ego as a unifying structure, and ego strength as the glue that bonds together the different aspects or dimensions of psychological functioning. For Erikson, the ego was as Freud viewed it: the executor of realistic goal-seeking actions and the intermediary between the biological urges of the id and the societal constraints of the superego. However, the developmental nature of Erikson's theory made the ego the structure of prime importance through which certain crucial developmental crises are experienced and eventually resolved. When the ego falters and cannot deal with the crisis it faces, development is thwarted and cannot proceed successfully. Erikson, like Freud, felt that although biological imperatives are of great importance, the social pressures and forces we experience are of greater importance. When these forces are examined in detail one gets a picture of what Erikson referred to as *psychohistory*, the history of those events of a social nature that interact with biological processes to produce behavior. Erikson made extensive use of the technique of relating past experiences to present behavior in an effort to understand motivational factors, behavioral outcomes, and future needs of the individual. Freud proposed the existence of *psychosexual* stages, while Erikson's stages are best described as *psychosocial* in nature because of the serious consideration he gives these other factors.

The Principle of Epigenesis

The epigenetic principle forms the theoretical basis for Erikson's work. The principle of *epigenesis* (epi meaning "upon," and genesis meaning "emergence") is based on an embryological model, in which each event during fetal development has a unique time of ascendancy, the plan for which is contained in the organism's genes. Erikson explained epigenesis in a general way as follows: "Anything that grows has a ground plan, and . . . out of this ground plan the parts arise, each having its time of special ascendancy until all parts have arisen to form a functioning whole" (Erikson, 1950a, p. 52). Biologically, the individual has few basic elements at conception, but with time these elements combine and recombine to form new structures.

    Much in the same way, differing psychological parts come together to form an entirely new and qualitatively unique entity. The functioning whole, by definition, can no longer be reduced into the parts that originally formed it (hence this view is not reductionistic). An analogy might be a building, which on completion is more than simply concrete, bricks, and wood. As a unique entity it may be a place to work, a place to live, or a place to play. As a functioning unit it serves a new level of purpose far more complex than the simple structural elements of which it was originally composed. Similarly, the independent reflexes present at birth become organized in such a way as to produce behaviors that are qualitatively different than the sum of all these reflexes.

    According to Erikson, this time plan is controlled by maturational processes by means of the epigenetic principle. During each of the eight stages of Erikson's psychosocial model, a different conflict has particular significance for development. Given that these conflicts result indirectly from a struggle between maturation (biological needs) and the social demands placed on the individual, the ego becomes the primary mediating force in the developmental process. Although Freud believed that the ego is formed as a developmental by-product of the id after birth (based on surplus available energy), Erikson felt that the ego is present at birth in an immature state. For this reason, Erikson is often referred to as an ego psychologist.

Stages of Psychosocial Development

Development takes place through the resolution of crises at different developmental stages. Erikson described these stages in his very influential book *Childhood and Society* (Erikson, 1950a). Table 6-1 shows what each of these stages is, the psychosocial task or crisis associated with the stage, the social conditions that might assist or deter the successful completion of the stage, and the behavioral outcomes that result from successful or unsuccessful completion of that stage. The psychosocial task or crisis at each stage is stated in general terms. Remember that these conflicts are not all-or-nothing situations but represent continua of psychological functioning. The extremes of each continuum are unrealistic, yet part of each extreme is often present in all individuals at any given stage. For example, no child grows up with complete trust or complete distrust, but rather adapts as social demands dictate.

Stage 1: Oral-Sensory Stage. The first of Erikson's eight psychosocial stages is the *oral-sensory stage*, during which the infant experiences the first of many interactions with the immediate environment. The infant needs these outside influences to help regulate basic behaviors.

In the newborn infant's environment, massive amounts of stimulation are present. Information from the different sensory modes of touch, taste, smell, hearing, and sight is processed at a rate and intensity that exceed the capabilities of the relatively immature organism. The oral component of this stage reflects the biological mode through which the child receives most of the gratification. In this as other stages, Erikson nominally combines Freudian terminology with his own. For example, the oral component of the oral-sensory stage maintains an important theoretical connection between Erikson's psychosocial and Freud's psychosexual perspective. In this stage, the psychosocial crisis is the question of whether or not the child can trust the world, and, as you might expect, the focus of this trust is maternal involvement.

The *trust-mistrust* continuum reflects the value of the child's experiences during the first year of life and how the child feels about interactions with outside forces.

Table 6-1 Erikson's Eight Stages of Psychosocial Development

	Psychosocial Stage	Task	Social Conditions	Psychosocial Outcome	
Stage 1 (birth to 1 year)	Oral-sensory	Can I trust the world?	Support, provision of basic needs, continuity Lack of support, deprivation, inconsistency	Trust Distrust	. ✓
Stage 2 (2 to 3 years)	Muscular-anal	Can I control my own behavior?	Judicious permissiveness, support Overprotection, lack of support, lack of confidence	Autonomy Doubt	✓
Stage 3 (4 to 5 years)	Locomotor-genital	Can I become independent of my parents and explore my limits?	Encouragement, opportunity Lack of opportunity, negative feelings	Initiative Guilt	✓
Stage 4 (6 to 11 years)	Latency	Can I master the skills necessary to survive and adapt?	Adequate training, sufficient education, good models Poor training, lack of direction and support	Industry Inferiority	✓
Stage 5 (12 to 18 years)	Puberty and adolescence	Who am I? What are my beliefs, feelings, and attitudes?	Internal stability and continuity, well-defined sex models, and positive feedback Confusion of purpose, unclear feedback, ill-defined expectations	Identity Role confusion	
Stage 6 (young adulthood)	Young adulthood	Can I give fully of myself to another?	Warmth, understanding, trust Loneliness, ostracism	Intimacy Isolation	
Stage 7 (adulthood)	Adulthood	What can I offer succeeding generations?	Purposefulness, productivity Lack of enrichment, regression	Generativity Stagnation	
Stage 8 (maturity)	Maturity	Have I found contentment and satisfaction through my life's work and play?	Sense of closure, unity, direction Lack of completeness, dissatisfaction	Ego-integrity Despair	

Source: Adapted from Erik Erikson, Childhood and society, New York: Norton, 1950.

Erikson emphasized that it is not just the quantity of trustfulness that is important but the quality as well. For example, if the sensory input that children receive is harsh (loud noises, for example) or children are roughly handled, they may feel a sense of distrust and become defensive and necessarily protective from a threatening environment. On the other hand, when the environment is supportive and consistent, children are likely to be trustworthy and to develop confidence in their ability to predict what will come next.

Erikson recognized that although it is adaptive to be distrustful of certain dangerous things in the environment, too much distrust can lead to excessive cautiousness (Erikson, 1950b). Likewise, although trust is very important for the formation of a psychologically healthy individual and essential human bonds and attachments, excessive trust is naive. In this situation children have difficulty discriminating between what is valued and worth pursuing and what is irrelevant or dangerous or a threat to their developmental progress.

The important elements of Stage 1 are shown in Table 6-1. The oral-sensory stage is characterized by the developmental task of determining whether children can trust the world as they know it. It is a question that the child continually asks. The feedback the child receives through social interactions can be supportive and provide for the basic biological and social needs that lead to trust and a sense of confidence. Lack of support, inconsistent interactions with others, and deprivation of basic needs lead to a sense of mistrust that threatens later developmental progress. The child who does not successfully resolve the trust-mistrust crisis at the appropriate time will have a poor foundation on which to resolve later crises. The degree to which successful resolution of a crisis takes place at one stage of Erikson's model affects the degree to which crises are resolved during subsequent stages.

Stage 2: Muscular-Anal Stage. The second stage that Erikson described deals with the child's ability to regulate or control his or her own physical behavior. Most notably, this includes the eliminatory functions associated with toilet training. Indirectly, however, and just as important, during this stage children learn they have input into the forces that affect their lives.

The Freudian counterpart of this stage is the anal stage of development, during which emphasis is placed on the control of specific muscles located in the anal region of the body. These muscles are important in the expulsion of feces and in toilet training. The developmental task of Freud's anal stage is acquiring control of these specific muscles. Erikson's view of this stage, however, goes beyond the specific anal area and generalizes to musculature throughout the body. Erikson notes that control of all the muscles becomes the focus of the child's surplus energy. Not only are children expected to develop control of the muscles that deal with elimination, they are also expected to develop some control of impulses in general. This change leads to a successful feeling of *autonomy* (control over one's behavior),

[handwritten margin note at top: Street children / What happens / when child is / overprotected and / in a sense because / then autonomous.]

as opposed to feelings of _shame_ (less control). The psychological and social components of Freud's theory were distinct from one another, but with Erikson the two are more closely intertwined. *[handwritten: very Western]*

The muscular-anal stage requires children to face the task of defining and discovering the degree of control they have over their own behavior. If children are given the opportunity to explore new avenues and independence is fostered, they will develop a sound sense of autonomy. On the other hand, if children are not given any opportunity to test their own limits and is doted on and overprotected, they develop a sense of shame and doubt their ability to deal effectively with the world. This stage is characterized by a dilemma between holding on and letting go. The successful resolution of this stage helps to encourage a sense of autonomy, wherein children learn to control their own behavior and to some extent their environment.

[handwritten margin note: I cannot, but]

Stage 3: Locomotor-Genital Stage. Freud recognized that during the genital stage of psychosexual development the potential exists for conflict resulting from the Electra and Oedipal complexes. In a similar fashion, Erikson acknowledges that this stage is set by social expectations for independent movement and motivation as a result of new-found autonomy and control. The formulation of this stage exemplifies the way in which Erikson employed and extended basic Freudian theory.

Freud felt that this stage was characterized by the focus of energy on the genital areas of the body. Erikson agreed with this but took the idea one step further to incorporate the psychosocial component as a major part of this biological need. The original Electra and Oedipal complexes involved the resolution of a conflict that focused on a desire to embrace the parent of the opposite sex. The conflict is eventually resolved by constraints placed on the child by society. The locomotor component of Erikson's third stage of psychosocial development represents the child's movement away from the dependency on parents and toward the ability to meet personal needs. Children become capable of initiating more complex actions on their own, resulting in more gratification than was possible earlier when they were more dependent on parents.

[handwritten margin note: Mom houses; in sleeping in same room. Get dressed / shower with clothes on.]

This initiative is important because the child's autonomy is continually increasing, and because the child rejects any guilt that might be associated with not moving in an independent direction. This guilt results from the discrepancy between aspirations for certain goals using new locomotor skills and the acts initiated to accomplish these goals. Table 6-1 shows the locomotor-genital stage to be characterized by the question, "What are my limits, and how can I best achieve my goals?" This is an important beginning step toward independence. If the child is given support for these efforts and encouraged in them, a sense of initiative will be strong. Otherwise, the lack of opportunity and negative feelings experienced by the child who tries to exceed established limits and is punished result in a sense of

[handwritten note at bottom left: ? I doubt a / street child has / these questions / on his mind.]

[handwritten note at bottom right: exacerbated / by mothers who / look to their sons as / men of the household. / sleeping in same / room, love making, etc.]

guilt. Both ends of this initiative-guilt continuum are probably determined more by social factors than by internal or organismic factors.

Stage 4: Latency. Freud believed that the latency stage of psychosexual development is characterized by the child's investment of energy into knowledge and intellectual and social exercises rather than clear biological needs. In other words, the available psychic or libidinal energy is no longer focused on a specific region of the body (as it was in the anal and oral stages of development) but is now focused on less concrete needs, most of which are related to social and cognitive development. As a matter of fact, some speculation exists that the later developmental stages of Erikson's theory are more characterized by social than other biological processes.

Freud viewed this period as psychosexually inactive, but for Erikson it is as dynamic and active as earlier periods. Erikson believes that this time of development is crucial for the child's sense of industry seen as the ability to master the social skills necessary to compete and function successfully in the society in which the child lives. For example, for children who live in an agricultural society, the developmental tasks requisite for successful completion of this stage are those associated with farming. At this stage of development, cultural expectations take precedence over other needs, and the ability to master certain skills and abilities becomes paramount. Erikson describes a child who does so as *industrious.* Industriousness leads to a feeling of completeness or satisfaction. For children who are not even given the opportunity to master their own world or who have their efforts blocked, these unsuccessful experiences lead to a sense of *inferiority*, or lack of worthiness. Inferiority results from the child's perceived lack of importance or inability to deal with the demands of his or her world. For the preadolescent child who is striving for recognition yet finds it unreachable, feelings of inferiority may persist through later stages of development.

There is another reason why this stage of psychosocial development is thought to be so important to later success. The preadolescent invests a tremendous amount of energy inward toward the development of such skills as industriousness and the self-help aspects of growth. This period, which precedes formal adolescence, is a time for reorganizing and regrouping energies to handle the tremendous biological and emotional demands that will shortly follow. When adolescence places demands on the child, the individual who has acquired useful social skills (such as fixing cars, caring for siblings, or milking cows) has the distinct advantage of having completed an important step toward developing a meaningful identity. During the latency stage, the child's question of importance is "Can I master the necessary skills to survive in my community?" If the conditions surrounding the child support the development of these skills such as good educational institutions and adequate models in the home, the child is likely to develop an industriousness that leads to a sense of satisfaction. The social conditions that encourage feelings of inferiority are those that fail to prepare the child for the entrance into life and to provide the tools needed to succeed.

Stage 5: Puberty and Adolescence. Puberty is a time when some of the most drastic changes occur in all spheres of individual development. Up to this time, the child has not experienced such great changes in both physical and psychological capacities and needs. Now, adolescents are expected to begin defining their interests in terms of career choices, further education, trade skills, and raising a family. Both biologically and culturally, adolescence is considered the end of childhood and the entrance into adulthood. This time is one of great change and excitement, and it is also when the individual develops an *identity*, or a definition of self. The child begins to select and define a role and prepare to handle the chosen position.

If development proceeds successfully, then the adolescent should have some sense of security. Through the first four stages of Erikson's hierarchy, the individual has gained some trust, is somewhat autonomous, capable of initiating behavior toward a defined end, and is industrious to the extent that he or she is competent in performing certain skills. The next crucial step is the development of a sense of identity, or asking "Who am I?" and "What ideas, thoughts, or objects do I feel represent my way of thinking?" If the environment is not supportive and if the adolescent finds it difficult to establish a role, the result can be an ill-defined concept of one's own identity, a condition that Erikson calls *role confusion* (see Table 6-1).

In some ways, given the turbulent nature of today's world, it is understandable that some adolescents have great difficulty in defining or adhering to a certain role or set of beliefs. Much of the activism during the late 1960s and early 1970s was attributed to young people not being able to find themselves and developing a kind of "existential guilt," where many of these children felt guilty about their own good fortune while others suffered. This lack of role definition (or role satisfaction) can result from pressures to define a role at an increasingly earlier age to please parents, rather than successfully resolve earlier crises.

Stage 6: Young Adulthood. Because Erikson's theory of psychosocial development is based on the notion of stages and the epigenetic process, development will be optimally successful if the crisis associated with each stage is successfully resolved. Stage 6 illustrates how important dependency on earlier stages is. For the first time, new goals and tasks that directly involve other people are placed before individuals, and they are expected not only to develop and meet career goals, but also to begin the developmental process of interacting with others of the same and opposite sex. Now, at full biological maturity, one of the primary developmental tasks is the formal inception of the family unit through marriage or cohabitation.

This does not necessarily mean that entering into a union or producing children are the only forms an intimate relationship can take. The intimacy that Erikson discusses is a general type of intimacy between people regardless of sex or personal arrangements. From Erikson's viewpoint, such intimacy represents a commitment on the part of individuals to each other so that a warm and meaningful relationship is established. The maturing adult is expected to make a commitment through intimate interaction with another individual. *Intimacy* is the goal of this psychosocial stage. This stage of development is intertwined with the one that precedes it, because role confusion can lead to unsuccessful and superficial relationships and a translucent idea of identity. This need for intimacy supersedes every other need at this stage. But, more important, this crisis represents a giving of oneself to another individual deemed worthy of trust. So Erikson believes that feelings, belief systems, values, and goals become invested in another person with whom one feels intimately involved. An individual must have some degree of autonomy and basic trust in order to enter into such a relationship. He or she must have a real sense of identity that can lead to a level of intimacy that is appropriate.

The consequences of little or no intimacy in relationships is a sense of ostracism or *isolation*. When feelings cannot be communicated or shared, a feeling of being left out and low self-esteem can result. This is harmful to one's self-concept and prevents advancement to the next stage. Development in this stage is characterized by strong efforts to develop real and meaningfully close physical and psychological relationships. Lack of such meaningfulness results in despair, loneliness, and a kind of isolation that sometimes lasts for the remainder of a lifetime.

Young adulthood is the time for another interesting change. As people become more competent, they become less dependent on external agents for assistance and more autonomous and secure. During young adulthood, the social conditions that characterize probable psychosocial outcomes are more internalized and less a result of concrete conditions in the surrounding environment. Therefore, the social conditions that affect outcomes beyond puberty (in young adulthood, adulthood, and maturity) are prescribed within the context of the individual's needs rather than solely social factors.

Stage 7: Adulthood. One of the important elements of Erikson's theory is that development is a continuous, ongoing process. For the young adult who is well on the way to a successful career and intimate personal relationships, the relevant task is to generate whatever is necessary to define a style or life role. This *generativity* might characterize the young woman who, after working for five years to accumulate some savings, may begin graduate school and take the first step toward becoming a physician, or begin to have children and take part in their development. It also characterizes the middle-aged man who feels that a change in occupation is necessary to establish greater congruence between his role expectations and his actual behavior. Often, after twenty years in one profession, individuals suddenly change direction to enter a new aspect of study or adventure. When such people are asked why they changed, they frequently respond by saying something like, "All my life I wanted to do this, and only now have I realized that I can."

What these people may be saying is that their roles in life up to now may have been satisfactory, but not sufficiently fulfilling. A major component of Stage 7 is emphasis on continuity with preceding stages. The sense of generativity that the adult feels comes from efforts to have some part in supporting and encouraging the development of the next generation. Those individuals who cannot lend this continuity to the next generation may become overly absorbed in personal needs, ignore the needs of others, and gradually become *stagnated*.

Stage 8: Maturity. Erikson used the term *ego integrity* to describe older people who have come to recognize, after a lifetime of successfully resolving conflicts, that they have led a meaningful, productive, and worthwhile life. Stage 8 has mystical elements, and Erikson stresses the importance of being "one with your past," and creating and feeling a new love for the human ego and not necessarily for oneself. The older person can dispense wisdom to young children. This wisdom has traveled the hard and difficult road from basic trust-mistrust conflict experienced as an infant through this final stage of realization. If development has proceeded successfully through the years, Erikson considers that this stage consists in taking or gaining a perspective on what has occurred.

According to Erikson, healthy individuals will be able to look back in retrospect on past years and, regardless of their content, feel satisfied. They will view their own being as congruent with the purpose, rhyme, and reason of life and develop a great deal of ego strength or *ego integrity* from this awareness. The strength gained from a high degree of ego integrity also helps one adjust to the aging process and eventual death. This is much like the state of self-actualization that Maslow (1968) discusses. The person who cannot successfully view his or her life as meaningful makes a desperate attempt to compensate for lost time when there is no time left. Such an individual finally realizes that things are not as they should be and that the emptiness that characterized so many of the later years is bound to continue. In such a case, a tragic state of *despair* can develop.

The Appeal of Erikson's Approach

Many practitioners have adopted Erikson's theory of psychosocial development as a useful framework in dealing with parents and children. Here, much of Freud's theory and influence are present, yet there is very little of the controversy surrounding his work. For example, educators have often found the descriptions of the developmental tasks useful in choice and design of curriculum. There is an

careful.

intuitive attractiveness to the commonsense dimensions of Erikson's proposed stages, and because he pays such central attention to schools, neighborhoods, cultural values, and social patterns, his readers find experiences they can identify with. Thus Erikson has proved to be useful to many who deal with children.

Erik Erikson's theory has had extensive appeal, especially to Americans. Perhaps this is so because some of the central elements of Erikson's characterization of the developmental process were influenced by his own transplantation from a European to an American society. As a sensitive observer of the American scene, he developed a sharp appreciation for the influence of social factors on development. Erikson's theory of good development is also consonant with the ideals of a democratic society. His concept of development is almost entirely equated with such democratic principles as freedom to choose different options and the right to privacy.

Throughout each of the eight psychosocial stages we have discussed, the principle of epigenesis is the primary controlling force that integrates the separate parts of human development to form a unified whole. Although the idea of an epigenetic sequence of stages is most firmly rooted in the work of biologists, Kitchener (1978) points out five essential features of epigenesis from the perspective of a developmental psychology.

1. Epigenesis is represented by a *causal set of events*. This means that development consists of events that operate in a preordered sequence in which each event is related to later ones. This is one reason why we call Erikson's model *hierarchical*, because the events that make up each stage (in this case the resolution of a crisis) are related to later crises. More important, however, is how successfully the crisis is resolved, which has a bearing on later adjustment and developmental progress.

2. The concept of epigenesis implies the existence of a *series of stages* that are qualitatively different from one another. Erikson, however, is the only psychoanalytic theorist to postulate explicitly a series of stages across the entire life span. His work represents the increasingly popular point of view of the life-span psychologist who is concerned with the development of the individual from conception through death.

3. Epigenesis is a process through which behavior becomes *differentiated* to form unique elements or parts of a functioning whole. In other words, adolescents who are trying to establish an identity might work toward that goal through the continual refinement of their needs, given the social milieu in which they exist. This is a very important feature of Erikson's theory because it accounts for the way in which new and unique behaviors arise.

4. The parallel process of *organization* takes place largely as a result of increased differentiation. For the individual to develop successfully, and for the whole to become functional, each of the independent units must

be sufficiently well organized to maintain ego-strength integrity. Organization reflects how well underlying mechanisms of development are organized in different individuals. In order for the whole to function, each part of the system must be organized and coherent.

5. Finally, epigenesis is the primary process by which the separate systems that have become increasingly differentiated from one another and then organized become integrated and finally produce a new element to be assimilated by the whole.

Erikson's major contributions to developmental theory have been to popularize the emphasis on psychosocial stages and to stress the importance of strong and healthy ego development. Erikson's book *Childhood and Society* (1950a) is widely read, and the basic assumptions of his theory are probably more easily accepted than Freud's. It is not unusual to find educators, physicians, and parents combining a Gesellian approach with an Eriksonian approach, the first emphasizing the importance of individual maturational factors, and the second extolling the virtues of a loving and supportive environment. When development is not proceeding well, waiting for the child to catch up (the Gesellian stance) is probably less effective than Eriksonian clinical intervention. The clinical intervention would be directed toward identifying the problems blocking growth, removing or remediating those road-blocks to strengthening the ego, and providing the supportive conditions that encourage further healthy development.

SUMMARY POINTS

1. Erikson described eight stages of development that are governed by underlying maturational forces.
2. At each stage there is a conflict that needs to be resolved.
3. Freud proposed psychosexual stages, yet Erikson's stages are best described as psychosocial in nature.
4. According to Erikson, psychological development results from the interaction between biological needs and social demands.
5. Erikson investigated the nature of qualitative change during the middle and later years of life as well as the early years.
6. Societal demands act as powerful mediating forces between biological needs and the total development of the individual.
7. Erikson stressed the importance of the ego as a unifying structure.
8. Development reflects a time plan wherein each individual phase of development is crucial to all subsequent phases.
9. Epigenesis is the basic principle of Erikson's theory, which assumes that all parts of a system have a unique ascendancy within that system.

HOW THEY STUDY DEVELOPMENT

We have mentioned several times in this chapter how one of Erikson's most outstanding contributions was his development of a theory that details developmental change across the entire life span. One of the important impacts this life-span approach has had is to allow psychologists to better understand the process of development during the fast changing and important years of adolescence. With this in mind, let's look at a study that examined the development of self-concept during that period.

One of the prevailing attitudes about the stage of adolescence is that it is a time of great emotional trauma and "storm and stress." These authors undertook a study to determine if indeed this is the case. Their logic was that if they followed young students over a long enough period of time, they would be able to see if there is continuity or stability in the development of one's self-concept, an important part of adolescent development.

Psychologists Dusek and Flaherty (1981) began with 811 students and followed as many as possible over a three-year period, working with children in grades 5 through 12. Each year, the children completed a questionnaire that asked them to choose one of two characteristics that best described themselves. They were given a list of 21 pairs of descriptors, including "relaxed-nervous," "happy-sad," "friendly-unfriendly," and "rugged-delicate."

The analysis of the data indicated that the development of self-concept during adolescence occurs in a stable and continuous way. That is, children who tended to characterize themselves in a certain way at one point in time maintained that same description when tested again in subsequent years. In other words, the notion that adolescence is a stormy and stressful period might not be an accurate description of what actually is happening.

UNDERSTANDING THE PSYCHOANALYTIC APPROACH

1. *What is the major force that influences the course of development?*

Within the psychoanalytic model, the forces that represent a genetic contribution to development interact with the forces that originate in the environment. This is best illustrated by the emphasis that both Freud and Erikson placed on the experiential content of a stage and the way in which outcomes, in terms of developmental progress, often depend on the value or meaningfulness of that content to the individual. For example, Erikson emphasized the social conditions that exist during the different developmental stages and paid attention to the role these conditions play in the resolution of each of the eight psychosocial crises. On the other hand, the major principle on which his theory is based is epigenesis, which stresses that the development of the functioning whole is contained in the genes of the individual.

Freud tended not to focus on the importance of environmental factors as a primary influence on development. This may be because of his background in biology and medicine and his belief that genetic factors are of critical importance in the determination of behavior. Freud well recognized that environmental forces play an important role in development, but, like Erikson, he believed they did not serve as the impetus for development but only as an influence on its direction.

It is important to note, however, that recently released documents find Freud's as confused as many others about the nature-nurture dilemma. Early in the formulation of his theory, he wrote to one of his colleagues, "I have always wondered whether one should suspect, behind these cases, heredity or rather childhood events" (*New York Times*, 8/18/81).

2. *What is the underlying process responsible for changes in development?*

Just as the psychoanalytic model represents an interchange between the forces of heredity and environment, there is a similar subtle interplay between the mechanisms of learning and maturation. To make this clear, we can use the idea of conflict as an example.

Maturation plays a crucial role in the presence of almost all the developmental conflicts or crises. For Freud, each of the stages of psychosexual development centers on a specific location in the body. For example, the sensitivity of the anal region to stimulation is not in any way a function of learning. Children do not learn that part of their bodies is sensitive any more than they learn to grow hair. The focus of stimulation on different parts of the body is clearly a function of maturation. Similarly, Erikson's use of the epigenetic principle emphasizes the unfolding of a time plan, as a result of maturational or biogenetic influences.

But the other side to this issue is the role that learning plays as a mechanism in development. Both Freud and Erikson would probably state that learning plays an important role in the resolution of conflicts as well as in general successful adaptation. When Freud discusses how memory traces form, he is discussing how associations are formed or how they are learned between the goal object and the need. Through repeated associations, these traces assist the individual in recognizing how to fulfill a need without the simultaneous presentation of the goal object. The content of these traces, again, is a function of learning, not maturation.

In many ways, the mechanism of maturation seems to provide the form of the conflict or stage, while the mechanism of learning influences the content. For example, oral needs that are basically maturationally determined, can be satisfied in many ways depending on the content of the environment and what is learned or taught (e.g., breast or bottle feeding, excessive talking, smoking).

3. *What role does age play as a general marker of changes in development?*

The psychoanalytic model tends to downplay the importance of age, either as an explanatory or causal factor in development. Although both Freud and Erikson did specify approximate age ranges during which the individual enters different stages of development, little emphasis was placed on them.

4. *Are there certain sensitive or critical periods during development, and how are they related to the rate of change?*

This is always an interesting question, but especially so from the psychoanalytic perspective. The psychoanalytic model discusses the way in which each stage of development becomes a critical period in and of itself, for it is theoretically the individual's only chance to resolve whatever conflict that might be present at that time. To postpone the resolution of a conflict could cause the individual to remain at a developmentally more immature stage and halt further developmental progress.

The psychoanalytic model assumes that there is a series of critical events in the individual's life, and that these events become major influences on development. Within Freud's theory, the satisfaction of needs is critical, and the goal object (or some form of it) must be present when the need that goal object can satisfy is paramount. Likewise, Erikson believes that the conflicts that are present in development occur at a critical time, when the individual has the facility and motivation to resolve them. What is critical, then, is the individual's receptivity at certain times during development to address these conflicts, and not his or her susceptibility to any major element in the environment.

5. *Is development smooth or continuous, or do changes occur in abrupt stages?*

The psychoanalytic model asserts the sequential nature of behavior and stresses the presence of qualitatively distinct yet related stages. This discontinuous view of development is best illustrated by the epigenetic principle: Erikson clearly identifies eight separate tasks associated with eight separate stages that are all related but are distinct from one another. The principle of epigenesis states the presence of a hierarchy of levels wherein each level is dependent on the others, yet is still unique.

Similarly, Freud's specification of five sequential stages of development, all qualitatively different from one another, fits our description of discontinuity. Freud's contribution provided a prototype for a discontinuous theory. Within the psychoanalytic model the shape of development is discontinuous because the stages within the model are qualitatively distinct from one another, are often influenced by different factors (such as the content of the conflict that is present at a given time), and occur in a somewhat abrupt fashion.

Psychoanalytic theory is also as explicit about the presence of structures to behavior as is any other approach. Erikson did not discuss in any detail the presence and action of structures (although the epigenetic principle calls for an unfolding pattern of structures), but one of the major themes of Freudian theory is the description of the id, ego, and superego. To Freud, behavior becomes a symptom or a sign of the operation of some underlying mechanism that regulates behavior. The structure called the id, for example, strongly determines how and when basic needs will be expressed and fulfilled. When developmental change occurs, it is on a structural level. In other words, any change in behavior directly reflects a change in structure, and furthermore, a change in behavior without change in structure is theoretically impossible.

6. *How does the theory explain differences in development between individuals of the same chronological age?*

Although both Freud and Erikson placed a great deal of emphasis on the importance of biological processes in development, neither ever really attended to the question of innate biological differences. They no doubt assumed that people do come into the world with different constitutions and predispositions, but not to the extent of that endorsed by predeterminists who talk about the pre-existence of attitudes and intelligence.

We can assume instead that both Freud—and especially Erikson—would look to the major environment or social events as determinants of individual differences. For example, as we discussed earlier, during adolescence the establishment of an identity and answers to such questions as "Who am I?" and "What are my beliefs, feelings, and attitudes?" become crucial. If the adolescent is exposed to models such as parents who have a clear understanding of their own personal and professional roles, the child is much less likely to be confused and unclear about what direction identity formation can take. If, on the other hand, the child grows in a supportive environment that entertains his or her trials and tribulations, while providing exposure to consistent and clear sex role models, role confusion is less likely to become an issue and a point of contention later on in life.

FURTHER READINGS

Coles, R. *Erik H. Erikson: The growth of his work.* Boston: Atlantic, Little, Brown, 1970.
Datan, N., and Ginsberg, L. H. (Eds.) *Life span developmental psychology: Normative life crises.* New York: Academic Press, 1975.
Erikson, E. H. *The life cycle completed.* New York: Norton, 1982.
Erikson, E. H. *Identity, youth, and crises.* New York: Norton, 1968.
Erikson, E. H. *Identity and the life cycle. Pshychological Issues,* 1959, *1*, 1–171.
Erikson, E. H. *Childhood and society.* New York: Norton, 1950.

OTHER READINGS OF INTEREST

Blos, P. *On adolescence.* New York: The Free Press, 1962.
Irving, J. *The hotel New Hampshire.* New York: Dutton, 1981.

CHAPTER 7

The Behavioral Model: Basic Assumptions and Behavior Analysis

Heredity is nothing more than stored environment.

Luther Burbank

With a good heredity nature deals you a fine hand at cards; and with a good environment, you learn to play a hand well.

Walter C. Alvarez

I am I plus my circumstances.

Jose Ortega Gasset

INTRODUCTION

The Beginnings of Behaviorism

The different theoretical perspectives we have discussed so far give special attention to a maturational or biological theme. The psychoanalytic model of Freud and his followers and the maturational model of Gesell emphasize the way in which development results from a complex interaction between biological factors across a wide range of settings. All these theorists place some importance on the role of the environment, yet they do not believe that the environment is the major determinant or shaping force behind developmental change. To them, the environment is caused, and not causal. They assume that there are underlying structural components that follow a unique timetable of emergence, and that the presence or absence of these structures affects the direction and rate of developmental progress. Although these structures are not directly observable, their presence is inferred through observing performance on various tasks.

An alternative way of describing how the developmental process takes place is the *behavioral model* or *behaviorism*. Like Freudian theory, behaviorism has many variants. However, behaviorists share the same basic tenet: that development is a process that adheres to principles and laws of learning. Biological givens provide some of the foundation for development, but experience and the opportunity to learn provide the central and necessary elements that give direction to the process. Although much of behaviorism is based on the early work of the Russian physiologist Ivan Pavlov, behaviorism has been characterized as being uniquely American, because it was primarily American scientists who formulated and applied the basic model. In addition, the central location for advanced research and studies within this field is still in the United States.

Most behaviorists believe that the large body of information describing how learning occurs can be applied to the developmental process. Most basic psychology courses devote a considerable amount of time to the study of learning principles, and many students have had experiences in psychology laboratories where they reproduced the phenomena described by the principles of learning, such as conditioning. Although the original evidence for learning came from the laboratory, psychologists have elaborated on these rudimentary learning principles to account for the behavioral repertoire of children and adults.

One other point should be stressed before we begin our discussion of the behavioral perspective. Whenever a group of different theorists attempts to explain any phenomenon, there is overlap in the variables they study, their methods, and (if there is "truth" in science) their findings. Within any theoretical camp, there is always a great deal of variability among the different theorists, yet they are basically tied to the same philosophical assumptions. For example, some people within the broad framework of psychoanalysis adhered to the strict teachings of Freud, while others rejected some of the basic tenets of his teaching and developed their own ideas.

For a variety of reasons, this dimension of the behavioral approach toward development has been slighted. It is sometimes taught that the only type of behaviorism is one that stresses the total and complete control of the developmental process by environmental forces. This viewpoint may be representative of one group of behaviorists, but there are others who believe that internal cognitive or biological processes play an important role as well. In fact, during the past decade some behaviorists have studied the idea that the human acts on the environment, as well as being acted on by it.

In general, not all behaviorists do not place greater importance on biological than on environmental influences. However, many are incorporating more and more of the cognitive and social elements of behavior into their theories, making a rich and diverse set of ideas even more useful.

Basic Assumptions of the Behavioral Model

Behaviorism took its name from the work of John B. Watson, who rejected intro- or self-inspection as a method of studying behavior and declared that only *observable behaviors* were worthy of serious study. Watson believed that psychology was a science just like physics or chemistry, and as a science it should be based on concepts that can be objectively and reliably observed. In this sense behaviorism represents a particular methodological approach to the study of behavior, which is sometimes called *methodological behaviorism.*

But behaviorism also refers to a set of theories detailing how the developmental process is carried out. These theories attribute the control of developmental outcomes more to environmental than biological factors. These theories also share some basic tenets that serve as starting points for most developmental behaviorists. The reason that people fail to distinguish among behavioral theorists and theories may be that all behavioral approaches are based on the same fundamental assertions. This similar foundation provides some continuity between past and present perspectives. The links between today's behavioral theorists and the behaviorists of the early twentieth century are stronger than similar links between their counterparts within other theoretical perspectives. Regardless of what specific theory is being discussed, some basic statements are common to all behavioral views of development.

1. Development is a function of learning. Robert Gagne (1968) defines *behavioral development* as "the cumulative effects of learning." In this context, learning is defined as short-term changes in behavior. When these short-term changes are combined and are "hierarchically organized" (that is, when they build on each other), the result is development. Development, then, is the result of accumulated experiences linked to one another. Development results from learning: Learning does not result from development.

Other behaviorists believe similarly that development is a function of learning, and their theories present detailed analyses of how this learning takes place. For example, Sidney Bijou defines learning as the "relationship in the strengthening and weakening of stimulus and response functions" (1968, p. 2). In this paradigm, processes such as reinforcement and punishment (which will be discussed later) control or govern how and what behaviors are acquired.

2. Development is the result of different types of learning. Robert Gagne defined development as "the cumulative effects of learning. To fully appreciate the diversity and richness of human behavior within the behavioral model, understanding each type of learning that governs the developmental process becomes important. Some of these different types of learning are associated with the theorists who will be discussed in this and the following chapters.

3. Individual differences in development reflect differences in past history and past experiences. Differences in individual development result from past experiences and the value that these experiences had for accomplishing immediate or long-range goals. Behaviorists view the history of the individual as a series of short-term changes that, when linked together, form the foundation for development. The content of these experiences and the way they are organized contribute to the differences between one person's behavior and another's. All children experience something called "child rearing," yet it surely represents a different set of experiences for different people. The difference may reflect the individual's history of learning. The dynamics of how these experiences are stored, recalled, and transferred to new situations are crucial elements of the behavioral perspective.

4. Development results from the organization of existing behaviors. The last two assumptions stress the way in which different types of learning are combined with past experiences to account for individual differences in development. This assumption implies that development is a process of organizing simple isolated behaviors into complex patterns. For example, the healthy infant is born with some very sophisticated reflexes, such as the rooting response, where the young infant turns its head in the direction of the cheek that is stroked. This is clearly an important reflex, because it orients the infant toward the source of nutrition. This reflex and thirty others are the individual elements that form the basis for more complex behaviors. Later development, in all its richness and complexity, is related to these early biological reflexes. This process lends the idea of continuity or consistency over time to this model of development.

The progression from simple to complex behaviors is like a set of building blocks. Each block represents a unit of behavior. All healthy infants have the same basic equipment or biological mechanisms. Over time, different experiences result in a unique organization of these biological potentials. Later in life, these differences become even greater, because the organization of these basically similar experiences undergoes further change. Of course, the developmental process is more complex than simply putting blocks or experiences together in different ways. However, a major source of variation in development does result from differences in past experiences along with how these experiences become organized.

5. Biological factors set the general limits on the kind of behaviors that develop, but the environment determines the behaviors the organism engages in. Within the behavioral perspective, biological influences provide the fundamental systems on which behavior grows. Although biological processes provide a framework, the environment determines the kinds of behaviors that will be acquired.

Even conception is not purely a biological event, because environmental factors influence it. Influences such as the hospitality of the womb, maternal diet, smoking, and alcohol intake become significant factors that can affect development. Although the behavioral repertoire of the newborn infant displays an impressive biological profile of reflexive behaviors, newborn behavior reflects significant environmental influences. Behaviorists have insisted that environmental input affects biological as well as behavioral features.

From a behavioral perspective, if biological needs are met (such as good health care, nutrition, clothing, exercise), developmental progress will depend on the sequencing and relevance of experiences. The nature of these experiences plays a large part in determining the content of behavior as well. For example, in some cultures, school-age children acquire skills such as reading and writing, while in other cultures skills in oral communication are stressed.

6. The development of the individual is not directly related to biologically determined stages. Behavior is not biologically determined, nor is it necessarily tied to or a function of internally regulated biological processes. Behaviorists, however, do not dismiss obvious universal maturational sequences. Being able to balance, for example, is a prerequisite to walking. However, if a child who has this prerequisite is not given the opportunity to learn to walk, walking may be significantly delayed. On the other hand, provision of certain types of experiences can accelerate development.

Behaviorists do not make any a priori claims about the sequence or the presence of stages in development. They do not reject the possibility that an evolutionary history has predisposed the organism toward particular behavioral patterns and sequences.

These six assumptions are not universal among behaviorists. Because behaviorism is an evolving point of view, there are advocates of behaviorism who would qualify these assumptions in various ways. These are not steadfast rules, but only guidelines that can be used as a tool for organization.

CLASSICAL CONDITIONING AND IVAN PAVLOV

Along with Sigmund Freud, Ivan Pavlov made one of the most significant contributions toward making the study of human behavior a science. As a Russian physiologist, his years of studying the digestion processes in mammals earned him the Nobel Prize for Medicine in 1904. As a by-product of this interest in physiology, he questioned the way in which certain biological events become systematically related to changes in the environment that accompany them. Although Pavlov was not a psychologist and was not specifically interested in learning, the results of his research would be applied to understanding how certain behaviors come under the control of the environment. The concepts that started this revolution in thinking about development were *classical conditioning* and the *classically conditioned re-flex*.

Classical Conditioning and the Conditioned Reflex

Classical conditioning is a type of learning that occurs when two different events happen simultaneously and one of these events takes on the eliciting quality of the other (or the original) event. Pavlov presented a good example of this phenomenon in his influential text *Conditioned Reflexes* (1927).

When a hungry dog is given food, it salivates. If the presentation of the food is accompanied or paired (usually more than once) with another event, such as the ringing of a bell, the dog will eventually salivate when the bell alone is presented. The learned response of salivation to a previously neutral event, one that by itself could not cause the dog to salivate, is called a *conditioned reflex*. The process is called *classical conditioning*. Pavlov termed the food an *unconditioned stimulus* (UCS). An unconditioned stimulus is any event that "naturally" (without previous experience or learning) produces an unlearned response. Another example of an unconditioned stimulus might be the knee jerk response, or any reflexive behavior that is controlled by the autonomic nervous system. The dog's salivation (as a response to the unconditioned stimulus) is referred to as an *unconditioned response* (UCR).

There are two other elements in the classical conditioning paradigm that are important to understand. After the unconditioned response of salivation has occurred, the pairing of the food and bell is begun again and, with the introduction of the food, the bell is presented. At this point, the sound of the bell contains no controlling power. After a number of such pairings, the bell is presented alone and causes the dog to salivate. The bell can then be called a *conditioned stimulus* (CS), and the salivation can be called a *conditioned response* (CR). In this example, the unconditioned response and the conditioned response are identical. This is not always the case, but it is likely that these responses will be highly similar to one another. Pavlov's classical conditioning paradigm is illustrated in Figure 7-1. At Time 1, the food alone (UCS) produces salivation, the unconditioned stimulus (UCR). On repeated presentations of the food with the bell (Times 2, 3, and 4 in Figure 7-1), the bell alone elicits the response of salivation and hence becomes a conditioned stimulus. Timing is a very important factor in this process, and the unconditioned and conditioned stimuli must be presented close to each other for conditioning to occur.

An example of classical conditioning in a young child is how a frightening experience such as a nightmare becomes paired with darkness, creating a fear of the dark. Figure 7-2 shows how this relationship is established between the nightmare and the darkness, such that the darkness itself becomes a conditioned stimulus for frightened behavior.

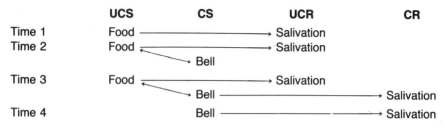

Figure 7-1. The classical conditioning paradigm.

Factors That Influence Classical Conditioning. Our behavior would remain very limited if the simple process described above was all there is to classical conditioning. Since the classical conditioning paradigm could not alone explain the richness and diversity of human behavior, more elaborate concepts are needed.

Pavlov identified two factors that affect the strength of the conditioned reflex: *reinforcement* and *extinction*. He also identified another set of factors that influence the degree of transfer of one conditioned reflex to another: *generalization* and *differentiation*. Reinforcement occurs when the relationship between the conditioned stimulus and the unconditioned response (the darkness and the fearful response) becomes strengthened through repeated association with the unconditioned response when reinforcement is no longer present. In other words, if the child does not experience more nightmares in the dark room, the conditioned response is likely to disappear or become extinguished.

Even though the idea of reinforcement and extinction explain how certain behaviors become more or less likely to occur in the future, these concepts do not explain why our repertoire consists of many different behaviors of all degrees of strength. To account for the complexity of behavior, Pavlov described the complementary processes of generalization and differentiation. Generalization occurs when a conditioned response is given to a conditioned stimulus that is similar to

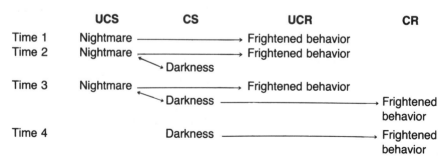

Figure 7-2. Classical conditioning and fear of the dark.

the original. For example, the child who has nightmares may refuse to enter any dark area of the house.

The complementary process to generalization is differentiation, the way in which one stimulus is discriminated from another. This process takes place through the selective reinforcement of certain associations and the lack of reinforcement of others. For example, the child may learn not to be fearful in certain dark settings (such as a movie theater), but may be fearful in others.

The main theme of this chapter is that development results from learning, which in turn reflects one's experiences. Pavlov showed his genius in using the conditioned reflex as a methodology for understanding how a fundamental and important type of learning occurs. In many ways he was the founder of behaviorism, and the essence of his work still continues today in many laboratories around the world. How Pavlov's work on the conditioned reflex applies to the process of development can be summed up by two points.

First, learning is governed by relationships between stimuli in the environment and the organism's reaction to those stimuli (responses). These relationships are strengthened or weakened by reinforcement or extinction. Second, the way one response generalizes to other stimuli (and in turn is differentiated from other stimuli) explains how an organism becomes increasingly complex in its multifaceted relationship to the environment.

THE BEGINNING OF BEHAVIORISM IN AMERICA: JOHN WATSON

The founder of behaviorism in America, John Watson, presented a more detailed analysis of learning than Pavlov and further elaborated some of the principles through which learning occurs. Watson also stressed the necessity of studying behavior objectively as a part of a detailed analysis of the rules that govern the acquisition of simple behaviors.

Up to the beginning of the twentieth century, psychology was characterized by the European tradition of introspection, a technique for focusing on the core of an experience by dealing with the unconscious elements of that experience. The early structuralists, those who used introspection as a technique, believed that this method was highly objective because it consisted of systematic observation and detailed reporting. However, some psychologists objected, claiming that anything that relies so heavily on an individual's interpretation is contaminated by unknown and uncontrollable factors.

John Watson was the first student from the University of Chicago to receive a Ph.D. in psychology. He quickly realized the necessity for studying behavior objectively, rejected the use of "mentalistic" concepts, and dismissed the method of introspection, claiming it to be imprecise. When Watson introduced behaviorism in 1913 as a psychology of objective and observable phenomena, he believed this new brand of psychology should employ the methods of natural science, such as those of chemistry and physics. Watson claimed that through the use of exact and rigorous methods, one could eventually document very precise cause-and-effect relationships between stimuli in the environment and the behavior of the organism. If these same techniques and standards could be applied to the study of human behavior, Watson felt that the mechanisms of behavior and development could be identified.

The Stimulus-Response Connection

Like Pavlov, Watson believed that the basic component of behavior was the *stimulus-response unit*, and that any behavior could be produced (or explained) as long as these stimuli and responses were arranged in the desired fashion. This point of view has far-reaching implications for, and raises some basic questions about, the issues of the control and prediction of human behavior. In one of Watson's frequently quoted passages he discussed this directly: "Give me a dozen healthy infants and my own specified world to bring them up in, and I'll guarantee to take any one of them at random and train him to become any type of specialist I select—doctor, lawyer, artist, merchant chief and, yes, even beggarman and thief, regardless of his talents, penchants, tendencies, abilities, vocations, and race of his ancestors" (1925, p. 104). Watson strongly believed in the total malleability of the individual, and that any outcome is possible given control over critical events.

Watson studied the work of Pavlov and accepted his basic findings about classical conditioning and the conditioned reflex. This provided Watson with a firm foundation to which he added in greater detail his own ideas and beliefs. Watson felt compelled to deal with behavior of all kinds rather than just the reflexive types of behavior that are biological in nature.

Watson defined a *stimulus* as any form of energy that excites a sensory organ. This is an objective definition that specifies both the source of energy (such as a sound), and the measurability of the stimulation. Internal thoughts and feelings are not to be considered stimuli, because they are neither clearly identifiable as sources of energy, nor can they be shown to stimulate any sensory organs. In addition, they are impossible to measure directly. Watson's may be seen as an extreme position, and it is not wholeheartedly adopted in all behavioral circles.

A *response* tends to follow a stimulus and is an observable reaction of some physiological subsystem to a stimulus. These stimulus and response *connections* form the basis for all behavior, influenced of course by the laws of classical conditioning.

Watson's behaviorism stressed that the analysis of complex behaviors should consist of an analysis of the constituent *stimulus-response* units. These responses are not only reactions to stimuli but in turn serve as stimuli for further events. This link between responses and stimuli provides the basis for more extended and complex learning. The classically conditioned reflex (a special type of response) acts as a stimulus for a response that may follow. In turn this provides a linking of one S-R association to the next S-R association and so on, as shown in Figure 7-3, where the response from an earlier S-R association becomes the stimulus for the next. This notion of associations was an important step in the advancement of behaviorism, because it went beyond the simple S-R event and suggested a more complex system of behavior.

Factors Affecting S-R Connections

Like Pavlov, Watson believed that factors beyond the simple S-R association must be taken into account. For Pavlov, these were reinforcement and extinction and the complementary processes of generalization and differentiation. For Watson, these were the *law of frequency* and the *law of recency*, which are elegant in their conception and have far-reaching implications for understanding the developmental process.

The law of frequency states that the more often a person makes a response in the presence of a certain stimulus, the more likely that person will make the same response to that stimulus in the future. For example, after learning that red lights mean "stop," the frequency with which a red light is associated with putting the foot on the brake and stopping the car will increase. The identification of this link in the system (which has many other little links within it such as picking up the foot from the accelerator pedal, placing it on the brake, pressing down) is similar to Pavlov's concept of differentiation. When the light turns green, the foot is taken off the brake, placed on the accelerator, and pressed down. According to the law of frequency, the act of stopping paired with the presence of a red light becomes one of many high-priority associations. It is no accident that stop signs are red, because it is the traffic engineer's purpose to alert people to stop through a dual signal of reading "STOP" and seeing the color red. The engineer assumes that from the driver's experience red represents "take your foot off the accelerator and put it on the brake." The more frequently an association occurs between the two

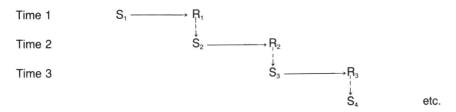

Figure 7-3. A series of S-R associations.

same (or similar) sets of stimuli and responses, the stronger this association becomes. Hence the more likely, given a stimulus or a similar event in the future, the same response will be made.

The law of recency states that the more recently a particular stimulus has been associated with a particular response, the more likely it is that the association will occur again. Where the law of frequency addresses the number of times something occurs, the law of recency addresses the amount of times between the stimulus and the response. For example, the factors associated with certain behaviors are often obscured because these factors occurred so far in the past that no causal role can be attributed to them. The longer the time between the stimulus and the response, the less likely, given the stimulus, that the response will occur again. This is true because as time passes, more mediating events occur to cloud the picture. Similarly, those events that occur most recently following a stimulus are far more likely to become associated with that stimulus than those that occur later. For example, if a child misbehaves, it makes little sense to punish the child "when daddy gets home," because so much time will have passed that any relationship between behavior and the punishment will no longer bear any significance. To extend this example, think how unfortunate it is if the child runs up to the father on his arrival home ready with a hug and a "hello" only to be threatened with discipline for misbehaving earlier that day. The only sense that the child can make out of such an incident is that running up to say hello to dad when he comes home results in being disciplined!

Because the rules of frequency and recency operate simultaneously it is important to consider the events that immediately follow a stimulus and to what degree these events recur. For example, children are often not given feedback consistently (frequency) or soon enough (recency) for it to be an important influence on their behavior. Children should ideally be praised or punished immediately (or as soon after the behavior as possible) to ensure that the associations that are formed are as strong as possible. In addition, parents should be consistent in dispensing both praise and punishment, so that a child always receives support for certain things, yet also learns that other things may be inappropriate or unacceptable. Consistency is the key.

Watson's militant stance regarding the proper methodology for psychology, coupled with his reliance on stimulus-response associations, left a lasting impression on psychology in general and developmental psychology in particular. Watson placed behaviorism squarely on the environmental or nurture side of the nature-nurture controversy. His position was both extreme in its claims and wildly optimistic that a good developmental outcome was ultimately a matter of appropriate control of critical events. It is ironic that in the rush to criticize such extremism, the optimism concerning human potential and the possibilities for fostering optimal outcomes have been largely ignored by many of his critics.

THE EXPERIMENTAL ANALYSIS OF B. F. SKINNER

The Basic Assumptions

With increased pressure for a "better" and more practical psychology in an increasingly technological world, the field of developmental psychology seemed ready for the work of B. F. Skinner. Over the past fifty years, the contributions of this writer-turned-psychologist have made his work as controversial today as Freud was during the early twentieth century. For the interested reader, a fascinating autobiography is available (Skinner, 1976).

The basic assumption of Skinner's theory is that *behavior is a function of its consequences.* In other words, the qualities and characteristics of the stimuli that follow behavior and not the qualities and characteristics of the stimuli that precede it are of primary importance. Skinner believed that through the systematic study and analysis of these consequences, the effects of environmental events on learning could be understood. Since learning is the primary mechanism through which development occurs, then development also can be understood. Skinner, his colleagues, and other behaviorists have invested a great deal of time in defining the rules and conditions that govern the relationship between a response and the events following it. Skinner believes that the consequences of any behavior will cause an increase, a decrease, or no change in the probability or likelihood that behavior will occur again.

In his first book, *The Behavior of Organisms* (1938), Skinner proposed many of the basic concepts that have been applied to the everyday concerns of his audience, which has grown larger and larger with the acceptance and application of these principles. The usage across many disciplines of such phrases as "behavior modification" and "teaching machines" reflects the scope of Skinner's influence. His detailed description of behaviorism as a science turned a full circle from Pavlov's initial work on the classical conditioning of innate reflexes to the broad conception of a utopia represented by *Walden Two* (Skinner, 1948, 1976), a controversial fictional account of communal living.

Respondent and Operant Learning. To fully understand Skinner's contribution to developmental psychology, we need to first discuss the difference between two fundamental types of learning: respondent and operant.

Previous discussions of Pavlov and Watson centered on classical conditioning or *respondent learning.* Respondent learning is subject to the laws of classical conditioning, is automatic in nature, and is not under voluntary control. For example, in Pavlov's work, salivation was elicited by the presentation of meat. Salivation is no more under the control of the dog than a knee-jerk reflex is under the control of an adult, or the sucking response under the control of an infant. These responses are not learned. They are instinctual or species specific behaviors, such as the grasping reflex in humans or flying in birds. These behaviors are not actively transmitted through teaching or any other cultural process, are not learned in the common use of the word, and are elicited or controlled by what precedes them.

Another type of learning, *operant learning*, forms the basis for Skinner's theory of *operant conditioning*. Operant behaviors are those that are controlled by what follows them, not by what precedes them. Further, operant behaviors are not elicited by a stimulus that precedes the behavior, but are *emitted* and are initially under the control of the organism. Because such behaviors are emitted, little emphasis is placed on the stimulus that precedes the behavior. In other words, the stimulus that precedes an operant behavior is not a focus of systematic experimental analysis. Table 7-1 presents a comparison of respondent and operant conditioning across several dimensions.

Why did Skinner choose to study operant rather than respondent behaviors? Respondent behaviors tend to be species specific in nature and limited in their variety and susceptibility to control by environmental events. In effect, they are simply less interesting. This is not true for operant behaviors. Humans exhibit many different types of behavior, and almost all of them are operant in nature. Look at some of these operant behaviors and what may be common consequences of them: brushing our teeth (fewer dentist visits); dressing nicely (attention from other people); cooking a good meal (good taste); or walking to work (good exercise). There are so many different behaviors that are not reflexive, and so many possible outcomes or consequences of those behaviors, that it is no wonder there are such wide and varied individual differences among people. Skinner devoted a great deal of time and effort trying to understand the factors that influence these differences.

Table 7-1 Comparison of Respondent and Operant Conditioning

	Respondent Conditioning	*Operant Conditioning*
What is the origin of the stimulus?	Known and important	Irrelevant
What is the origin of the response?	Response is elicited by stimuli (S^E)	Response is emitted by the organism
Relationship between stimulus and response	Eliciting stimulus precedes response (S^E R)	Reinforcing stimulus follows response (R S^R)
Examples of each	Eye blink, digestion	Driving, mowing the lawn, socializing
Other terms used	Classical conditioning Type S learning Associative shifting Conditioning	Instrumental conditioning Type R learning Trial and error learning Problem solving

The Basic Model

Like other behaviorists, Skinner's concern for understanding behavior (and development) focused on the study of observable behaviors. Figure 7-4 represents a simple model of how the consequences of a behavior become important.

Figure 7-4 illustrates the simple paradigm of a response (R) following a stimulus (S) characteristic of respondent learning. This part of the model is no different from other learning-based models of development that have already been discussed. The difference between Skinner and other theorists becomes apparent when a new element, the concept of the *reinforcing stimulus*, is introduced (Figure 7-4b). This S^R (the R superscript represents a reinforcing event) acts to control behavior that has preceded it and determines with what degree of certainty (or probability) that behavior will occur again. If a stimulus that follows a behavior increases the probability of that behavior occurring again, this stimulus belongs to the general class of stimuli called *reinforcers*. Think of a situation where you have been reinforced for something you have done. For example, if you returned a lost wallet to its rightful owner and received some money as a gesture of thanks, this sequence of events may be reinforcing. In a similar situation in the future you might take the same action.

Sometimes, however, an event that follows a behavior can cause a decrease in the probability that the behavior will occur again. Such events belong to the general class of stimuli called *punishers*. For example, running out of gas and having to walk three miles is an unpleasant experience. People learn that the consequences (walking three miles) of some events (running out of gas) are unpleasant and adjust their behavior accordingly.

Even though people may be aware of the process through which behavior is affected, how do they know what the consequences of a behavior are? Through learning, a storehouse of experiences is acquired and through these experiences stimuli in the environment are identified that are likely to act as either reinforcers or punishers. Through experience the individual learns how events in the environment act as *discriminative stimuli*,—those events that signal that a behavior will be followed by some type of reinforcer or punisher. With the concept of a discrim-

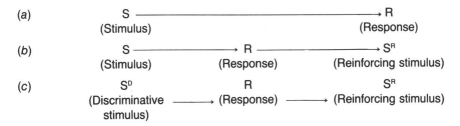

Figure 7-4. The basic operant conditioning model.

inative stimulus, something new is added to the model. Figure 7-4c is basically the same schematic as in Figure 7-4b, but the original S is now an S^D or a discriminative stimulus. This event acts as a sign or a flag for the learner that a behavior will have certain consequences. The discriminative stimulus for the behavior of walking to the nearest gas station when out of gas can be the needle on the empty mark on the fuel gauge. The discriminative stimulus for eating may be the time of day, whether or not a person is hungry. Many different stimuli can take on discriminative qualities, again contributing to individual differences.

Factors that Influence Behavior

The idea that behavior is a function of its consequences can be directly applied to everyday experiences. If the contents (and context) of behavior are examined, those behaviors that have a substantial payoff are repeated, while those not having such an attractive payoff are not. For example, some people enjoy going to class, restoring an old house, or managing a business. On the other hand, those same people avoid things that have a low payoff, such as paying bills, cleaning the house, or working at the office past 5 P.M. It is important to remember, however, that emotions such as enjoyment and discomfort are correlative properties of the reinforcement process. Behaviors, and not feelings or people, are reinforced.

We must consider not just the consequences of behavior, but a host of other factors as well before the operant perspective to understanding human development can be fully appreciated.

The Concept of Reinforcement. The concept of reinforcement maintains that a stimulus event that follows a behavior increases the likelihood or probability that that behavior will occur again.

All reinforcers are classified as stimuli, yet the reverse is not necessarily true. All stimuli are not necessarily reinforcers, because (1) they do not always have the effect of increasing the frequency of the behavior they follow (the primary criterion for a reinforcer); and (2) they are sometimes not easily operationalized or relevant. A Skinnerian psychologist would not spend time searching for such stimuli since they have minimal effects on behavior.

There are basically two classes of reinforcers: *positive* and *negative*. The choice of these terms has nothing to do with a value judgment that positive reinforcers are ''good'' and negative reinforcers are ''bad.'' The use of the terms positive and negative refers to adding a stimulus to a situation (a positive action) or subtracting a stimulus from a situation (a negative action). The terms reflect an action (presenting or withdrawing) rather than a state or judgment (good or bad).

Positive Reinforcers. Positive reinforcers are stimuli that upon their presentation result in an increase in the probability that a behavior will occur again. In other words, they are stimuli that, when added to a situation, strengthen the future probability of an operant response. For example, reinforcing children for cleaning up their room may be a very effective way of maintaining that behavior. Another example might be thanking a friend for a favor. In both examples, the stimulus that followed the behavior, which was added to the situation (the attention and affection), acted as positive reinforcers.

Negative Reinforcers. Negative reinforcers are stimuli that on their withdrawal result in an increase in the probability that a behavior will occur again. Through the withdrawal of an unpleasant or aversive stimulus, the behavior is reinforced. For example, removing a splinter is reinforcing because something is being taken away that is unpleasant. In this case the act of removing the splinter was negatively reinforcing.

At times it may be difficult to decide whether or not a reinforcing stimulus is acting as a negative or positive reinforcer. For example, the removing of the splinter is followed by relief from annoying pain. The key question is always whether or not the removal or presentation increases the behavior it follows. In this case, nothing was really presented, but indeed the splinter (and its associated pain) was removed. Hence it is a negative reinforcer.

Special symbols are used to represent reinforcers. Positive reinforcers are represented using the letter S with a plus sign as a superscript (S^+). Negative reinforcers are represented using the same letter, only with a minus sign as a superscript (S^-). The general class of reinforcers is represented as S^R.

In an environment so full of potential reinforcers, it is often difficult to determine what is or is not a reinforcer. To determine this, Skinner recommends that we observe what follows a behavior. If we are interested in understanding why a certain child keeps raising his or her hand in class, it would be useful to observe what happens after the child's behavior. In this case, perhaps the consequence might be the teacher's attention reinforcing the child's behavior.

Let's apply a more detailed analysis for testing whether a stimulus is acting as a reinforcer with the same example as the one used above. A child continually raises his hand and, when responded to, appears not to have anything to say. Observation of this behavior shows that every time the child's hand goes up, the teacher provides attention. When a question is asked, the teacher provides some type of response. It soon becomes clear that the teacher may be reinforcing the child through a combination of attention and verbal support.

To be sure that the teacher's attention and not some other factor is the reinforcer the following strategy could be applied. For a fixed period of time (perhaps one school week) an observer could record how often the teacher reinforces or gives attention to the child for hand raising. Note that the emphasis here is on the *frequency* of the response. This period of time is the *baseline period*, and the rate of responding (the primary measure of interest here) is the *baseline frequency*. In Figure 7-5 each point represents the frequency of the behavior on one of the five days in the baseline

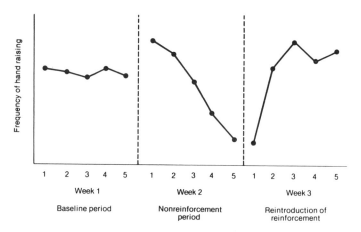

Figure 7-5. The course of an operant behavior when reinforced, ignored, and reinforced again.

week. The line represents a trend. To pursue the hypothesis that hand raising is controlled by teacher attention, the next step would be to remove the attention and examine the effect it has on the behavior. For the next week, the frequency of hand-raising behavior is again observed and recorded, under the new condition of nonreinforcement. The rate of behavior gradually decreases. Although the behavior might initially increase right after the reinforcement is terminated, eventually the level stabilizes.

Now there is one final phase to the test: the reintroduction of the reinforcer to examine the effect it has on the behavior. Why is this important? Even if the behavior did decrease in frequency when the teacher withheld reinforcement, perhaps the child stopped for some other reason (for example, some classmates warned him to stop taking up so much class time). If the rate of responding increases through the reintroduction of teacher attention, then teacher attention must be what is controlling the behavior. If this is not the case, it is time to consider the possibility that another stimulus in the environment is controlling the child's hand-raising behavior. This paradigm is called an A-B-A design, where A represents the introduction of reinforcement, B represents the withholding of reinforcement, and the second A represents the reintroduction of the reinforcer.

Superstitious Behavior. Along with Skinner's extensive laboratory work came another interesting phenomenon called *superstitious behavior*, or behavior that is accidentally reinforced. It is unplanned learning that takes place when a behavior and a stimulus acting as a reinforcer are inadvertently paired together, on the basis of coincidence. For example, one highly successful major league baseball player eats only chicken on a game day. Another puts his uniform on in a certain order and wears "lucky socks." The order of getting dressed, or wearing the same socks, became associated with the team's success. The socks can even take on the value of a reinforcer since they become associated with the powerful reinforcing stimulus of winning. Such practices are also a very powerful influence since people are often reinforced for performing a certain kind of behavior by what does *not* happen to them. For example, some people insist on a certain seat when they travel by airplane. Because the outcome is a safe trip, this further reinforces their behavior of choosing that seat again. Such behavior is of course not related to the safe flight of the airplane. They are, however, behaviors that have been learned through the accidental pairing of the behavior (choosing the seat) with some other condition in the environment (a safe trip).

The Concepts of Extinction and Punishment

Extinction. Clearly, individuals do not continue to do the same things over and over again for no apparent reason. There are other factors influencing operant behaviors that cause them to decrease in frequency or even stop altogether. In the example used earlier (the child who was reinforced by the teachers' attention), ignoring the behavior and withholding any type of reinforcement resulted in a decrease of the behavior. This procedure is called *extinction*, and it takes place when a response is not reinforced. In Figure 7-5, the B part of the A-B-A design (where reinforcement was withheld) is an example of extinction.

Another example is that as young children become more adapted to their environment they quickly learn which behaviors result in a reward. Crying before going to bed or when being placed in the playpen is frequently reinforced be well-meaning yet naive parents. The scenario might go something like this: After dinner and a change of diapers, the baby is played with affectionately and then placed in the crib. No sooner is the door of the child's room closed than the familiar cry begins. The parents let the child cry for a few minutes, and then, no longer able to stand the noise (or their belief that perhaps something is actually wrong), they go into the child's room and while the baby is still crying, pick her up to cuddle. The baby stops crying immediately, the parents feel they did the right thing. They are reinforced by the baby's silence and all is well.

However, when the baby is put back down in the crib the crying begins again. The established cycle is strengthened: the child's crying, attention by the parents reinforcing the crying, and more crying. This is a tiring and exhausting routine that benefits no one. Not only is the baby being reinforced, but nobody is getting any sleep! But how do the parents know that there is not something wrong with the baby? As good parents, they checked to see if the baby was wet or being jabbed with a diaper pin. Interestingly, parents learn very early to distinguish among different cries. The child's quality of crying becomes a discriminative stimulus for going to aid the child (fell-out-of-crib crying), or for ignoring the child (attention-getting crying).

Although it is very difficult for parents to do, attention-getting crying has to be ignored and be allowed to extinguish itself. It might take hours, since the child has learned how well the crying works, and ignoring a crying baby is very difficult.

Punishment. *Punishment* is the decrease of a response on the presentation of an aversive or unpleasant stimulus. For example, if you park in a no-parking zone, a parking ticket may punish your behavior. The ticket (or the fine you pay) acts as a punisher. Punishment can be related to the two classes of reinforcers discussed above. Punishment can be seen as the withdrawal of a positive reinforcer (*negative punishment*) or the presentation of a negative reinforcer (*positive punishment*). Again, the question we ask in deciding whether or not a stimulus is acting as a reinforcer or punisher of either kind is "What effect does the presentation or withdrawal of that stimulus have on the behavior?" If the effect is to increase the probability of the behavior, the process of reinforcement is occurring. If the result of the stimulus following the operant behavior is to decrease the likelihood that a behavior will occur again, it is a punisher. Keep in mind, however, that the qualities of the stimulus are less important than its effect on behavior. It is not the characteristics of the stimulus but the effect it has on behavior that is important.

For example, spanking is used by some parents to dicipline their children. However, until the effect that spanking has on the child's specific behavior is established, it is impossible to determine what role spanking plays. One child in a family might stop running out into the street at a result of a spanking, while another might continue to do so. For the first child, the spanking acts as a punisher (the rate of behavior decreases), while for the second child the spanking acts as a reinforcer (the rate of behavior increases). The second child might have received some degree of reinforcement through the personal attention received as part of the spanking and will probably come back for more of both.

Table 7-2 is a summary of the relationships between a stimulus in the environment and the effects the presentation (addition) or withdrawal (subtraction) of that stimulus might have on future behavior.

The difference between negative punishment and extinction is that in extinction there is no consequence (nothing follows the behavior), while in negative punishment there is a consequence (something is taken away). For example, taking a toy

Table 7-2   Effect of Stimuli on Behavior

	Behavior Increases	*Behavior Decreases*
Stimulus added to the situation	Positive reinforcement	Positive punishment
Stimulus subtracted from the situation	Negative reinforcement	Negative punishment

away from a child who is misbehaving would be an example of negative punishment if the misbehavior decreased.

Schedules of Reinforcement. There is another important factor that deals with the relative frequency at which reinforcers and punishers occur. Behaviors are not reinforced or punished each time they occur. In the natural world, the contingencies on behavior do not occur on so regular a basis. Sometimes people ignore a no parking sign and risk being ticketed to park closer to the stadium. Sometimes they win at poker, and sometimes waiting for the mail carrier pays off with a long-awaited letter. All of these ''sometimes'' imply that the frequency of many of those stimuli that act as reinforcers and punishers are not easily predictable.

Schedules of reinforcement (and punishment) refer to the regularity with which patterns of stimuli follow operants and the effect they have. For example, will there be a difference in good manners if children are given a penny every time they eat nicely, or every third time?

Although over 900 schedules of reinforcement or ways of delivering reinforcers and punishers have been documented (Ferster & Skinner, 1957), there are two general classes of reinforcement schedules, continuous and intermittent. When a behavior is *continuously* reinforced, every response is reinforced. On the other hand, when a behavior is *intermittently* reinforced, the behavior is reinforced according to criteria such as the number of responses or the amount of time between responses.

Table 7-3 illustrates these schedules of reinforcement and shows how they

Table 7-3 Types of Reinforcement Schedules

	When is the reinforcement delivered?		
Continuous		*Intermittent*	
		Interval	*Ratio*
Every time the organism responds.	Fixed	Once per unit of time (e.g., every 10 seconds)	Once per number of responses (e.g., every 10 times)
	Variable or Random	Once on the average per unit of time (e.g., 10 seconds, then 6, then 2 for an average of 6 seconds per response)	Once on the average per unit of responses (e.g., 3 times, then 4 times, then 2 times for an average of 3 responses per reinforcer)

differ in answering the question "When is reinforcement delivered?" In other words, is the reinforcer given every time the behavior occurs (a continuous schedule), or every fifth time (a type of intermittent schedule)?

Continuous Reinforcement. Here a reinforcer is delivered every time the organism responds regardless of the number of responses or the time between them. Although this schedule is less complex than the others, it is certainly as important from a developmental perspective. Through the use of such a schedule, much if not all early operant behaviors are started. Continuous schedules of reinforcement are excellent ways to get a behavior going and to strengthen it in its early stages. They are not, however, especially good for maintaining a high rate of behavior, because they are vulnerable to the effects of extinction and punishment. When an infant begins to babble, that behavior should be reinforced as frequently as possible. Similarly, when a grade-school child is learning a new way of adding figures, until the behavior or habit is established, a continuous schedule of reinforcement is most effective.

Intermittent Reinforcement. There are two dimensions on which intermittent schedules can differ from one another. First, is the individual reinforced on the number of responses (a *ratio schedule*), or on the passage of time between responses (an *interval schedule*)? For example, if a child is reinforced for every five problems completed correctly, the child is on a ratio schedule. On the other hand, if a child is reinforced every half hour for sitting in his or her seat and not bothering other students, the child is on an interval schedule.

The second dimension is whether or not there is an equal amount of time or number of responses between the delivery of reinforcers (called a *fixed schedule*) or there is a variable number of responses or amount of time (called a *variable schedule*) between the delivery of reinforcers. If office workers are reinforced every second day they come to work on time, this is an example of a fixed interval schedule because the amount of time between reinforcers is fixed at two days. On the other hand, if workers are reinforced for every third account that was settled, this would be an example of a fixed ratio schedule.

Variable schedules are somewhat different. A variable ratio schedule delivers a reinforcer based on the *average number of times* a response occurs. An adolescent may be reinforced on the average of every third time his room is cleaned and straightened up. For example, the adolescent would receive $1 for cleaning his room the first time, and then perhaps the fifth time, averaging one reinforcer every three times.

On a variable interval schedule, the important element is the amount of time between reinforcers. A child who is working well alone might be awarded one point toward a prize on the average of every five minutes. This means that she might be reinforced after one minute, and then after nine minutes, but a total of six times over a half-hour period.

Based on laboratory studies with both human subjects and infrahuman organisms (such as rats), Skinnerian psychologists have been very exact in specifying what type of delivery system is best to maintain a certain rate of behavior. It is important to understand the use of schedules of reinforcement because certain behaviors are in part dependent not just on the presence of reinforcement but on the manner in which they are delivered. In fact, one could say that the method of reinforcement (that is, the schedule of delivery) is as important as the fact that the behavior is being reinforced.

Stimulus Control and Stimulus Discrimination. The patterns with which stimuli are followed by environmental events are as important as the fact that consequences occur. In our daily lives, not all the responses that are made are reinforced and, depending on a variety of factors, reinforcers are delivered in different patterns.

Although factors that influence the rate or frequency of a behavior have been discussed, one important question we have not addressed is how novel or unique behaviors are acquired. In other words, how do systems of behavior far more complex than the simple stimulus-response association develop?

The main criterion for developmental change within any behavioral theory is whether or not learning has occurred. Whether in a situation involving classical or operant conditioning, the beginning point of change is often the characteristics of the stimulus itself. We earlier discussed the importance of reinforcers, but the topic of how stimuli become important to the individual still has to be addressed. For example, "Why do I act in a certain way in the presence of some stimuli and not others?" "What is it about the weather that prompts me to take along an umbrella?" These things are, of course, a function of experience. The process through which experiences become valuable and stimuli are associated with certain outcomes is called *stimulus control*. Through this process certain stimuli become highly potent as cues or signs for future behavior and serve as indicators of the relationship between a response and whether or not that response will have any important consequences. These controlling or informing stimuli are called *discriminative stimuli* (represented as S^D).

There are many examples of the way stimuli take on a discriminative power. The sound of the car as it comes into the garage can act as a discriminative stimulus for "Mommy's home" and starting dinner. However, other discriminative stimuli signal the absence of any rewarding condition, and they are abbreviated using the letter S (for stimulus), with a delta or small triangle as a superscript (S^Δ), indicating no change in the probability of that behavior being reinforced.

The original conditioning paradigm presented in Figure 7-1 consisted of a simple stimulus-response bond. With the introduction of the discriminative stimulus as a powerful component of development, the paradigm is expanded. The progression is from the simple stimulus-response association ($S \rightarrow R$), to the stimulus-response association with a stimulus acting as a reinforcer ($S \rightarrow R \rightarrow S^R$), to the point where the reinforcing stimulus (S^R) assumes discriminative qualities ($S \rightarrow R \rightarrow S^R/S^D$). Remember that the initial stimulus represented by the letter S is relatively unimportant. Eating when not hungry (but at lunchtime) is a good example of how, through learning, stimuli (such as the time of day) become discriminative and control subsequent behavior.

More important, this concept of stimulus control illustrates the effective discrimination between those stimuli that are favorable to our survival and those that are not. Individuals learn which situations are life threatening and which are not and incorporate them into their behavioral repertoire.

If the history of a behavior is examined, the stimuli in the environment that have a controlling influence and those that are superfluous can be identified. Given that we can identify those events in the natural world that set the stage for another behavior (but do not have control over that behavior), how do these behaviors become associated with one another to form the complex set of behaviors known as development? Through the processes of *chaining* and *shaping*, discrete behaviors become connected and organized to form an elaborate developmental system.

Chaining and Shaping. Chaining is the process through which a stimulus that acts as a reinforcer for one event becomes a discriminative stimulus for the next. In other words, a chain of behavior is a series of stimulus-response-reinforcement elements wherein the reinforcing stimulus from the previous event takes on the quality of a discriminative stimulus. In this fashion very complex behaviors are constructed. For example, reading is a task that involves the identification and discrimination of certain stimuli and their individual sounds (letters), their sounds as a grouping (words), and the relationship between these words (context). Each of these steps is dependent on the next, and the simple discrimination of a letter eventually leads to a complex behavior called reading through the establishment of a long and intricate chain.

When children learn to swim, they are not expected to be able immediately to coordinate their arm, leg, and breathing movements. Instead, the simplest elements of the chain are learned first and, through practice and experience, these are linked together. Children are taught how moving one arm becomes a discriminative stimulus for turning the head and breathing, while placing the head in the water is another discriminative stimulus for exhaling.

Thus one's many activities throughout the day consist of complex chains of behaviors. From the time that one awakes, stimuli that act as influences on future behavior bombard the individual. The weather report becomes a discriminative stimulus for what to wear that day. Similarly, being tired from getting home late the previous night acts as a discriminative stimulus for getting home early tonight and catching up on sleep.

Where chaining is the process through which individual behaviors become linked together, shaping is the development of novel behaviors through the systematic reinforcement of some responses and not others. Whenever feedback is given to a child or an adult in response to a question, future behavior is being shaped.

Shaping was discovered through the experimental analysis of animal behavior. Skinner found that by successively reinforcing closer and closer approximations to the desired response, he could create almost any behavior that was within the physical boundaries of performance. For example, he taught pigeons a modified game of Ping Pong and even how to provide navigational feedback for guided missiles.

Shaping directly involves the individual as an agent in ongoing changes in behavior. When a young child switches from a bottle to a cup, drinking habits must also change (using the lips properly and holding the cup). No longer can the cup be turned upside down (as could the bottle) because a new behavior has been shaped by means of the gradual and systematic acquisition of behaviors and the process of reinforcement.

Generalization. The process of shaping and chaining explains how behaviors become complex and related sequentially to each other. The next question is how a behavior (or class of behaviors) becomes functional in other settings besides the one in which it was originally learned. A young child might call every female "mommy," possibly because the child thinks that all of these people are actually his or her mommy, but also because the child has generalized beyond the primary stimulus what has been learned.

In generalization, the stimulus or the response changes as a function of the similarity between itself and another stimulus or response. In *stimulus generalization*, a response to a new stimulus is similar to the original response. Take, for example, braking the car at any flashing red light on the road. Here the stimuli are similar (red traffic signal and flashing red light) but not identical. Another example of this phenomenon is shown in Table 7-4a. The female caretaker has been associated with the specific response "mommy." Throughout the process of stimulus generalization, this response becomes associated with other stimuli that are in the same general class yet are different. The stimulus of female caretaker generalizes to any familiar or similar-looking female, and the identical response ("mommy") is the result. Stimulus generalization belongs in the same class as stimulus control, because it concerns the control that a stimulus has on a learning outcome.

There is another parallel process, called *response generalization*, in which the stimulus remains the same but the response to the original stimulus changes. For example, the young child might respond to her mother's using a different term that was learned in another setting but is functionally equivalent, such as "mom," or "mama." Table 7-4b shows an example of this.

Many operant psychologists feel that stimulus generalization accounts for the development of concept learning or concept formation in the young child. Through continual exposure to similar yet somewhat different stimuli, the child forms a

Table 7-4a   Stimulus Generalization

	Time 1	Time 2
Stimulus**	Female caretaker	Any female offering interest
Response*	"Mommy"	"Mommy"

Table 7-4b   Response Generalization

	Time 1	Time 2
Stimulus*	Female caretaker	Female caretaker
Response**	"Mommy"	"Mama," "Mom," or name of caretaker

*Remains the same.
**Changes.

concept, defined as a class of objects that have similar characteristics or functions. For example, the young child who at first thinks that all four-legged, furry things are dogs (overgeneralizing) begins to learn that there are other classes of animals as well, such as cats and even lions. Either over- or undergeneralizing is not productive and illustrates the need for continual feedback from socializing agents such as parents and teachers.

The Application of Experimental Analysis

To understand development through the application of the behavioral model, it is important to realize that the concern of the developmental psychologist is not with development as a stage-related phenomenon, but as a process that operates according to the principles of learning. The concern is with understanding how the various laws of learning affect the individual and contribute to different behavioral outcomes. In behaviorism, individual differences are unique because of the environment, not because of any inherent biological process. Skinner helped to develop and refine behavioral laws to a sophisticated degree, and although he did not deal directly with the process of development in humans, he provided the foundation for later, more process-oriented theorists.

The Skinnerian perspective views development as a reorganization of simple, classically conditioned and operantly learned behaviors. Infants are not totally devoid of predispositions, but, in accordance with the assumption of a blank slate (tabula rasa), these inherited tendencies reflect only biological reflexes. Through such processes as stimulus control, chaining, shaping, and generalization, behaviors become related to one another to produce a sequence of interconnected stimuli and responses. As a unit, these connections become the stimuli for later development. The behavioral approach assumes the individual is passively susceptible to factors in the external environment, and that the consequences of a behavior may be determined not by what is wanted, but by what the environment has to offer. For example, few parents want to abuse their children. Strange as it may seem, however, the contingencies in the environment are often such that this behavior accrues some kind of benefit to the parent.

Behaviorism began as an effort to understand human behavior through understanding the principles of learning. The developmental process itself may be intricate and difficult to untangle, but the theory and assumptions are straightforward and highly operationalized. Skinner believes that the individual reflects the constraints and opportunities that the environment offers and contributes nothing on its own other than biological functions and preparedness.

The application of behaviorism has been highly valuable as a technique for modifying and analyzing individual elements of behavior as illustrated in the "How They Study Development" feature for this chapter. It also has great social relevance. The task now is to further expand on this basic perspective, adding insight to the process of learning and considering it as more than a short-term process of change but rather long-term extended process of development.

BEHAVIOR ANALYSIS: SIDNEY BIJOU AND DON BAER

In 1961, Sidney Bijou and Don Baer published *Child Development I: A Systematic and Empirical Theory*, which has been influential in offering a new perspective on the study of developmental psychology. In the early 1960s, the concepts of operant psychology were just becoming widely popular, and operant applications to the area of child development seemed appropriate and necessary. Harold Stevenson (1983) points out how Skinner "did nothing to adapt his theoretical position on operant conditioning to encompass variables that are to be important in discussing children's behavior" (p. 227). At that time, Bijou and Baer's book was probably the most comprehensive statement regarding development from a behavioral perspective. Its focus is on explicit and operational systems within the developmental process and is the first step in the presentation of a theory of development using behavioral ideas and terminology that relate operant principles to everyday developmental occurrences, such as language development or social interaction.

Although some critics of this approach believe that it is belittling to view the developing individual as mechanistic and the process of development as reductionistic, Bijou and Baer present this perspective as a straightforward and systematic presentation of how events in the environment shape and modify behavioral outcomes. Their most recent statement, *Behavior Analysis of Child Development* (1978) offers an even more comprehensive treatment of the role that learning plays in the developmental process.

Bijou and Baer believe that psychological development is represented by the "progressive changes in the way an organism's behavior interacts with the environment" (1961, p. 1). Behavior is not a function of either environmental or biological factors, but the result of an interaction between the two. The task of the developmental psychologist is to explore the nature of the changing interaction between the behavior of the organism and associated environmental conditions. The center of this interest becomes how the environment changes and what effects this change has on the organism. Likewise, the way in which the organism changes the environment and the ever-changing interaction between the two become important concerns as well. For example, if understanding the early adaptive behaviors of the infant is important, both the biological repertoire of the child (such as cooing and smiling), as well as the conditions in the environment that might affect such behaviors (such as the caretaker's attentiveness) are considered.

Bijou and Baer expanded on earlier behavioral perspectives and presented a broader interactionist approach. Most previous behavioral theorists had envisioned the human being as somewhat passive and acting only as a receptor of influences originating in the external environment. Within the behavior analysis perspective of Bijou and Baer, the human organism uses these forces to determine subsequent responses and behaviors; development thus is defined by interactions. Bijou and Baer's contribution to understanding the developmental process was to specify the different elements of these interactions and how these elements affect changes in behavior.

Making Behavior Meaningful: Stimulus Functions

In the formulation of their theory, Bijou and Baer identified a concept that goes beyond the notion that stimulus-response associations are the building blocks of development. Their concept of *stimulus function* takes into account the functional relationship between a stimulus and a response such that, for a certain stimulus, a response tends to serve a specific function. In a specific setting, a relationship is established between events. For example, the ringing of the school bell is related to a specific response, such as going to the next class. The response of getting out of the seat and moving to the next class defines the function of the stimulus. Behavior thus becomes a result of which stimuli in the environment take on functional significance.

All stimuli cannot, of course, be functional, and there are many events that go unnoticed and therefore have no functional significance. The term "functional analysis of behavior" refers to an analysis of the relationship between a stimulus and a response (behavior), and the nature of the functional relationship between them. For example, parents quickly learn to correlate a child's fussy crying with hunger. That S-R event will eventually take on some functional significance for parents. Similarly, if people are untrained in a skill, such as automotive repair, they are not likely to relate noises in a car engine to burned-out valves or a faulty carburetor.

On the other hand, there are some stimuli that are indeed nonfunctional. For adolescents, who tend to focus on social and peer pressure, an adult's opinion might be not only unwarranted but also meaningless in the general context of what is occurring. To quote Bijou and Baer, "Stimulus functions concentrate simply and objectively upon the ways in which stimuli control behavior: produce it, strengthen or weaken it, signal occasions for its occurrence or non-occurrence, generalize it to new situations and problems, etc." (1961, p. 19). It is important to point out that many different stimuli might indeed have the same or similar stimulus function. For example, talking with a receptive friend, supportive parents, or others might all serve as reinforcing events that strengthen the behaviors that produce them. This perhaps is one of the most important advantages of the concept of the stimulus function: It allows the information of a general class of environmental events and defines their functional relationship to present and later behaviors.

BASIC ELEMENTS OF BEHAVIOR ANALYSIS: STIMULUS AND SETTING EVENTS

Within the historical tradition of the behavioral approach to development, Bijou and Baer believe that the laws of natural science can best explain the development and progression of behavior from one level to the next. This is a natural science point of view, and it is not uncharacteristic of many behavioral theorists. By adopting such a viewpoint, they attempt to reduce the general class of environmental influences to more specific classes of *stimulus events*, or changes in the environment that have a measurable impact on behavior. The term "measurable" is very important, because the only real clue that some change in the environment has occurred is whether or not a change in the individual's behavior can be reliably observed.

Stimulus Events

The first class of stimulus events that Bijou and Baer identified are *physical events*. Physical events are those stimuli that are produced by humans or occur naturally. For example, a television set, rain, automobiles, rock music, and cornflakes fit into this class. The second class of stimulus events, called *chemical events*, includes environmental stimuli that act at a distance from the organism, such as the smell of fish or the stinging of iodine on a cut. *Organismic* stimuli are next, and this general class includes biological or maturational events that provide stimulation for the organism. The onset of puberty, dentation, and the action of the respiratory system are examples of this class. The last class of stimulus events is *social events*, involving the appearance, action, and interaction between living organisms, such as daily conversation with a colleague or interaction with a child.

Whether these different types of stimulus events occur alone or in concert with one another, each of these classes of behaviors can be looked to as either producing or being directly involved in the developmental process. In fact, most environmental events that eventually establish some type of functional relationship with a response include many stimuli from each class of stimulus events interacting with each other. Behavior in the morning may consist of a functional relationship between feelings of hunger (organismic), the smell of coffee (chemical), greetings to family members (social), and deciding what to wear (physical). These different classes are by definition separate, but practically they overlap to form a complex system of stimuli to which organisms respond. You might be able to use this idea of stimulus events to identify influences within your own environment that affect your behavior. Again, this concept helps us organize and systematically assess environmental factors, which are the crucial factors in the developmental process. Keep in mind, however, that many stimuli in the environment never became stimulus events because they hold no discriminative value.

All the different stimuli in the environment can be classified into one of the above four categories. Remember that just because the proper class of stimulus events can be identified, it does not mean that any event has any functional significance. Besides the content of a class of stimulus events, two other factors are important. First, stimulus events deal with the here and now. It is important to specify the relationship between the stimulus event and the current behavior. Second, specific stimulus events have a history of occurring in certain situations, and past history should be taken into account as well. Take, for example, the aroma and holiday festivity that surrounds Thanksgiving. Here a significant relationship between stimulus events and certain behaviors has become established over many years. In sum, the stimulus events that are associated with past behaviors become very important. Both past and present influences are of paramount importance in the development of the individual.

Each of these four different types of stimuli can serve one of three different functions as it relates to a change in learning or development. They can serve to *elicit* a response, act as a *discriminative* event, or *reinforce* some outcome. The value and role that stimulus events play is well grounded and depends on the past reinforcement history of the individual.

Setting Events. As you might expect, different stimulus events precipitate different kinds of behaviors. For example, people move out of the path of an oncoming car; people are greeted by friends. But what is the mechanism through which these different stimuli and their associated responses become part of the developmental process? Bijou and Baer offer the following explanation. A stimulus event accompanied by a certain response becomes a *setting event* for another stimulus-response interaction. That is, one event or occurrence helps to set the conditions for the occurrence of subsequent events that become related to each other. This adds a sense of continuity to the progression from one stimulus to a response to yet another stimulus and so on.

Development, however, is much more than the basic process of chaining that was discussed earlier. It is not just the association or linking of stimuli and responses to one another in a coincidence of time and space. For example, the child who comes home from school and inadvertently slams the door (receiving a mildly disconcerting look from his mother) finds the stage set for subsequent behaviors, such as a short talk from mom about closing the door quietly. This short talk in turn can become a setting event for subsequent behavior. Setting events, then, are occurrences that set up or prepare the individual for a subsequent interaction with the environment that is determined by the current state of affairs (e.g., some form of scolding for slamming the door). Figure 7-6 illustrates the relationship between stimulus events and setting events. Although a stimulus event is simply a factor influential in soliciting a response (whether the stimulus event acts as a respondent or an operant), a setting event unifies a series of stimulus events and helps provide continuity. Setting events give meaning to certain stimulus events, and therefore act as effective influences on development.

Ages and Stages and Behavior Analysis

There is at least one question that comes up again and again when the developmental process is discussed. Does development occur in a series of well defined, age-bounded stages (highly related to biological or internal growth mechanisms), or does it occur as a continuous set of changing behaviors, unrelated to that psychological variable called age?

This argument is a familiar one, because it parallels the nature-nurture or heredity-environment issues. Such theorists as Gesell and Freud, representing the maturational and psychoanalytical models respectively, believed that development is a series of age-related changes in which age is defined as the passage of time, a convenient and easily understood marker variable. Very few psychologists will argue with the idea that with time, certain changes in behavior become increasingly apparent. However, such an idea does not necessarily mean that changes in age are the primary determinant. Although age might be a convenient (and often the

Stimulus Events		Setting Event
Class	*Event*	
Chemical	Smell of soup	
Physical	Table setting	
Organismic	Hunger	Eating dinner (which in turn can become a
Social	Time to eat, rest of family at table	stimulus event for subsequent behavior)

Figure 7-6. The relationship between stimuus and setting events.

only) variable along which a child's behavior is categorized, it is imprecise and nondescript. To many people, developmental psychology is synonymous with the idea of age-related change, and some even believe that the reason and explanation for change in behavior is in itself a change in age. Such a viewpoint provides the framework for many traditional child-oriented activities. Baer, along with others, finds such an explanation imprecise and impractical. Instead they believe that a sequence or programmatic presentation of experiences is the important factor in understanding the developmental process.

In his article, "An Age Irrelevant Concept of Development" (1970), Baer describes an experiment carried out by Wendell Jeffrey in which the way children learn the difference between left and right. For the group of four-year-olds selected for the study, this learning proved to be difficult. Jeffrey eventually trained the children to effectively discriminate their left from their right sides using a set of programmed sequential exercises employing motor and verbal cues. As Baer points out, children may be expected to distinguish between right and left when they become older (and the natural environment has had a chance to teach them the difference), but because virtually no time passed between the four-year-olds' lack of discrimination skills and their sudden acquisition of these skills, a very important case is made for the idea that development is not meaningfully related to the passage of time. Therefore, identification of those experiences or factors that can account for changes in behavior is important for understanding the developmental process. As Baer contends, "It is the process of development, not merely the outcome of development which should be our subject matter" (1970, p. 239).

Children experience many different things in the course of development. Most of these influences, however, occur in a random rather than a systematic fashion. When events are arranged in an orderly fashion, we can then begin to see the effectiveness of structuring experiences and their potential impact on growth and development.

Many popular works on child rearing and child development often mention such stages of development as the "terrible twos," or "troublesome threes," and they seem to imply that the children's behavior is a function of their chronological age. A child may very well have some biological imperative or need that must not be approached by the parent in a different way from when that child was younger. However, it is often the demands of the situation that encourage one child to behave in a way different from another. Where one child is encouraged to take advantage of these newfound skills through exploring the environment, another child might be restricted in exploratory activities and not given the opportunity to enlarge their behavioral repertoire. Instead, this later child may be given the wrong messages, and his or her behavior may become contingent on those discriminative stimuli that some parents associate with troublesome behavior.

The individual comes to the environment equipped with certain types of basic mechanisms or reflexes. The influences in the environment facilitate development in one of many directions. Development is not a by-product of the child's age but a result of the child's interaction with those forces in the environment that are often controlled by people such as parents and teachers.

SUMMARY POINTS

1. Behaviorism does not refer to a single theory but encompasses a wide range of approaches that vary in the degree of influence attributed to the environment.
2. Development results from the organization and reorganization of existing behaviors.
3. Biological factors set the limits of development, but the environment determines the kinds of behaviors in the individual's repertoire.
4. The development of the individual is not fixed by biologically regulated stages.
5. Ivan Pavlov, the Russian physiologist, was the first scientist to study the direct relationship between behavior and events in the environment.
6. Through repeated pairings, previously neutral stimuli become conditioned stimuli and responses.
7. The concepts of reinforcement and extinction are related to the strength of a conditioned response.
8. The concepts of generalization and differentiation are related to the number of responses in the individual's repertoire.
9. The more frequently a connection occurs between a stimulus and a response, the stronger the association becomes (law of frequency).
10. The more recently a certain response is given to a certain stimulus, the more likely it will happen again (law of recency).
11. Respondent behaviors are controlled by what precedes them, and operant behaviors are controlled by what follows them.
12. A positive reinforcer is a stimulus that is added to a situation, and a negative reinforcer is a stimulus that is subtracted or removed from a situation.
13. A punisher is a stimulus that follows a behavior and decreases the likelihood of that behavior occurring again.
14. Superstitious behaviors are those that are accidentally reinforced.
15. Extinction of a behavior occurs when the behavior is not followed by any consequence and decreases in frequency.
16. There are two basic classes of schedules of reinforcement: continuous (every response is reinforced), and intermittent (responses are reinforced according to time or rate).
17. Different stimuli in the environment assume discriminative qualities and control subsequent behavior.
18. Learning is generalized from the original setting to another through stimulus and response generalization.

19. A functional relationship is established between a particular stimulus and a particular response so that a response tends to serve a specific function.

20. Stimulus events can be physical, chemical, organismic, or social, and they have a measurable impact on behavior.

21. A setting event consolidates a series of stimulus events and serves to prepare the individual for another stimulus-response interaction.

HOW THEY STUDY DEVELOPMENT

A primary theme of this chapter has been how the behavioral psychologist emphasizes the importance of environmental influences as contingencies on observable behaviors.

One of the most useful applications of behavioral theories of development has been in the area of behavior modification. Here highly specific behaviors are identified and then modified through the systematic application of various principles of operant learning. The following study (Allen, et al., 1966) is an excellent example of such an application.

The purpose of this study was to determine whether the use of adult attention (used as a social reinforcer) would have an effect on increasing a child's play relationships with peers.

As with most behavioral interventions, both adult attention and play relationships were defined in measurable terms. Adult attention was defined as "a teacher's going to, talking to, smiling at, touching, offering and/or giving assistance to the child." The other focus of the study, play relationships, was defined as looking, smiling, touching, helping, or working with another child.

As in many behavioral studies, only one subject, a four-year-old pre-schooler was used. An objective record was made of how much this child spent by herself, with adults or alone. After establishing a "baseline" frequency of how much time was spent, reinforcement procedures were begun. The teacher would praise the child and encourage her participation in groups, and would turn away or ignore her when she sought adult attention.

To insure that it was the attention of the adults that originally maintained her lack of involvement with other children, the situation was then reversed. Under this condition, the child was not encouraged or praised when she played with other children. This reversal resulted in an increase in isolate behavior as would be expected if the child's behavior was under the control of the social attention. Again, the conditions were reversed once more, and the child's behavior returned to the goal set by the teachers, high rates of contact with other children and a decrease in attention seeking from adults.

This is a simple, yet very powerful example of the impact that the systematic application of environmental contingencies can have on a child's behavior. It also illustrates how much of behavior and the process of development can be explained through the application of those principles illustrated here.

FURTHER READINGS

Bijou, S. W., and Baer, D. M. *Behavior analysis of child development*. Englewood Cliffs, N.J.: Prentice-Hall, 1978.

Bijou, S. W., and Baer, D. M. *Child development I: A systematic and empirical theory*. Englewood Cliffs, N.J.: Prentice-Hall, 1961.

Kendler, H. H., and Kendler, T. S. Discrimination and development. In W. K. Estes (Ed.), *Handbook of learning and cognitive processes*. New York: Halstead, 1975.

Pavlov, I. *Conditioned reflexes*. London: Oxford University Press, 1927.

Skinner, B. F. *About behaviorism*. New York: Knopf, 1974.

Skinner, B. F. *The behavior of organisms: An experimental analysis*. New York: Appleton-Century-Crofts, 1938.

READINGS OF OTHER INTEREST

Skinner, B. F. *Beyond freedom and dignity*. New York: Knopf, 1971.

Skinner, B. F. *Walden II*, New York: Macmillan, 1948.

CHAPTER 8

Social Learning Views
of Development

Experience enables you to recognize a mistake when you make it again.

Franklin P. Jones

Experience is not what happens to a man; it is what a man does with what happen to him.

Aldous Huxley

A parent's job is to be the person who can see over the hill.

James L. Hymes

THE DEVELOPMENTAL LEARNING APPROACH OF ROBERT SEARS

In the first seven chapters of this book, we have seen how theorists sometimes share the same basic assumptions concerning the process of development. One example includes the theories of Freud and Erikson, and how both proposed a set of stages through which each individual passes.

We have also seen how there are theories that share very little in common with one another, and for many years psychologists and educators have discussed how these different theoretical views might be combined. More often than not, however, these efforts have not resulted in any real significant advance, since philosophical differences were too great to allow for a meaningful dialogue.

In the work of Robert Sears, however, we have a genuine (and most people would say a successful) effort at bridging the gap between the psychoanalytic and the behavioral approaches to understanding development. His training and experience in the psychoanalytic domain, with a special interest in the process of identification, was combined with his studies of behavioral theory to produce what might be the first and only eclectic view of development to stand the test of time.

The Theoretical Outlook

Robert Sears has spent the major part of his academic career as a professor of psychology at Stanford University, where his most significant contributions have been in the area of the effects of child rearing on personality development. His training as a psychologist took him from Yale University to the University of Iowa's Child Welfare Research Station, where a great deal of the information available about child development at that time was being generated. It was, however, his relationship with one of his instructors at Yale, Clark Hull, and other behavioral psychologists that greatly influenced the development of his own theoretical growth.

Like most behavioral theorists, Hull believed that the basic building block of learning was the simple stimulus-response (or S-R) action. He elaborated on this by postulating that a set of *intervening variables*, placed between the stimulus and the response, have an important influence on behavior. To better understand Sears' approach to social learning, let's briefly review the major characteristics of intervening variables identified by Hull.

The most important of all the intervening variables in Hull's model was called *reaction potential*. Reaction potential is the potential for making a certain response, given the presence of a certain stimulus. For example, with an environmental event such as a parent being present when the baby awakes from a nap, we can consider the likelihood that the baby will or will not begin to interact verbally with the parent.

The strength of this potential is determined by five different factors. The first is called *drive*, and represents any kind of primary need such as hunger or thirst. When such drives are associated with previously neutral stimuli (such as the sight of a milk bottle for a hungry baby), the neutral stimuli take on the characteristics of the original drive and become what is known as *secondary motivators*.

The second factor that contributes to the strength of the reaction potential is the *intensity of the stimulus*. It is much more likely that even when we are not hungry, we will be receptive to one of our favorite foods, rather than something about which we feel ambivalent. The lower the intensity of the stimulus, the less likely we are to respond.

Incentive motivation is another factor that determines the likelihood of a response occurring, since it refers to the amount of reward that is given for the behavior. We are much less likely to work for a low wage, since our knowledge of the payoff for our work will affect our judgment and future actions. Incentive motivation can be a very powerful factor since it focuses on the anticipation of rewards and their value.

The fourth component is *habit strength* or the number of times a certain behavior has been rewarded in the past. This component has special applications to Sears' theory where it takes on the new name of *experience*. For example, the one-year-old baby who is beginning to talk continues to make all sorts of noise at everyone's pleasure because of the rewards of attention and warmth that it brings.

Finally, the last factor deals with the resistance to repeating responses, known as *inhibitory potential*. This is the degree to which an individual may be motivated not to respond. For example, although there may be a reward for misbehaving (attention), there are also reasons *not* to misbehave (such as punishment!).

All five of these factors, when summed together in a mathematical model, allowed Hull to make predictions as to the actual likelihood or probability that can be associated with a particular behavior.

It's clear that Hull pursued an objective approach to the study of behavior and the factors that lead up to its change. We will see traces of Hull's influence on the development of Sears' theory as we continue our discussion.

Although Hull had a profound impact on Sears, he was also influenced during the 1940s by the psychoanalytic approach to understanding development. Although it was hard for him to believe that the psychoanalytic model was satisfactory as a theory of development, there were certain components that led him to attempt some bridge building between his own behavioral approach and what psychoanalysis had to say. Perhaps this is one reason why the majority of his work has been in the area of child rearing and child-parent interaction, historically primary interests of psychoanalytically oriented child developmentalists. During this same period, he was also strongly influenced by the application of behavioral principles to social problems by such psychologists as John Dollard and Neal Miller.

Like other behaviorists, Sears focused on the effect that the consequences of a behavior have on future behavior. He believed that whatever consequences a behavior might have, these in turn become the cause for later behaviors. This *cycle of behavior*, beginning with innate or instinctual needs and tempered or shaped by the child's experiences, is one of the most significant components of his approach. Over time, these experiences take on value as secondary reinforcers. Indeed, the individual differences that we see in behavior are theoretically the result of how different individual experiences affect the value of a particular reinforcer. For one child it may be "worthwhile" to verbalize at a high rate (since she receives encouragement for such), yet another child might be passive and relatively nonverbal.

Some Basic Assumptions. We've already mentioned how Clark Hull was one of the first American behaviorists to propose the idea of an intervening variable. Robert Sears in his research and teaching believed that social influences (especially the home environment and parental attitudes) were the most important of these variables.

As we will shortly see, he had a very strong interest in the nature of dyadic (two person) interactions as well as the developmental nature of these interactions.

Before we can discuss this, let's first focus on some of the basic assumptions of Sears' social learning theory approach.

Initially, *all behaviors begin as an effort to reduce tension that is associated with some biological need.*

The first assumption clearly reflects some of the training and interest that Sears had in psychoanalytic theory. If you remember from your reading about Freud's view of development, a major emphasis is placed on the role that biological needs play in the development of the child's affective and cognitive systems. In addition, there is a cyclical nature to development and to instincts in particular, such that the primary goal of development is to learn how to reduce tension and then incorporate that learning into a repertoire of behaviors.

While it is true that all of us tend to have highly similar biological needs, a major source of differences between people is the way that these needs are satisfied.

Behavior (and development) is a function of interactions between people— most important, in the form of a dyad.

Sears' primary research interest was in the area of child rearing. Perhaps his best known work, *Patterns of Child Rearing* (Sears, Maccoby, & Levin, 1957), reflects this long and intense interest in understanding why parents rear their children using one method rather than another.

As part of this research (see "How They Study Development") Sears focused specifically on the interaction between the mother and the child. It was his belief that the primary sources of socialization and training came about as the result of an interaction between these two people. (During the late 1950s, fathers were not known to have anywhere near the influence on their child's development we know about today.)

Children often mimic their parents yet, at other times also show original or novel behaviors. On the other hand, parents, and especially the mother, encourage (or reinforce) or discourage (or punish) certain behaviors, so that the child eventually learns what is acceptable and what is not. Later in life, the family and then society take over these teaching functions, but initially it is the child-parent interaction that helps build and strengthen the basic blocks of the child's developmental course. Since a dyadic interaction is the most common one the young child experiences, Sears reasoned that this is the place to look at most closely to understand the dynamics of how social forces affect learning.

The third assumption is that *drives present at birth provide the foundation for later development.*

It's difficult to see how any theorist would argue with this statement. Surely, our basic behaviors (such as reflexes) must come from somewhere, and the repertoire present at birth in the form of reflexes is as solid and universal a starting point as any.

Sears, however, took this assumption one step further in believing that primary drives (such as hunger) play a major role in being "contiguous" or paired with, other initially neutral events in the environment. Hence, these previously neutral events take on the quality of a *secondary motivational system*. For example, the child learns that controlling his or her bowels can be a pleasant physical and social experience because of the approval given from parents and others in the immediate environment.

These drives (sometimes called instincts in other theoretical approaches) seem to be one of many building blocks that the developing child uses again and again. They are constantly being linked with social events to form an increasingly complex pattern of behavior.

Behavior is the cause and effect of later behavior.

Behavior, whether it be simple or complex, cannot occur in isolation without affecting other parts of the individual's behavioral system. When a behavior is established, it is invariably linked with other behaviors. Sears emphasized how complex patterns of social behavior (such as child rearing) are formed through the constant refinement of parental behavior based on some chosen strategy and the effects on the child's behavior.

This process is like the chaining of behaviors we discussed in Chapter 7. Chaining is where discrete behaviors become linked together to form a behavioral system. So it is in Sears' social learning view of development as well, where various behaviors can take on the power to elicit additional behavior which in turn elicits others, and so on. The complexity of the pattern depends on a variety of factors, the most important of which is experience.

The last of these assumptions is that *the quality of a behavior (in terms of what reinforcement value it holds for the child) is a result of experience and learning.*

The reinforcement value of a behavior is very similar to Hull's concept of incentive motivation. Earlier we defined this as the amount of reward that accompanies a certain behavior. For Sears, it is the history of the individual that determines how valuable it would be to perform a certain behavior to that individual. A good example of this is the teacher who knows what some of the things are that the child likes to do. If jumping rope is one, time to do this can become an effective reward for time spent at seat work. Similarly, in a household where children are not rewarded for certain behaviors, parents cannot expect them to perform these tasks spontaneously. If children are encouraged and rewarded for cleaning their room, the reinforcement value will help encourage the child to continue.

The Developmental Nature of Sears' Social Learning Theory

A major difference between behavioral theories and other approaches such as the psychoanalytic or cognitive-developmental theory (which we will discuss in the next chapter) is that behavioral models usually do not postulate the existence of stages of development.

The primary reason for this is that if one believes that development occurs in some kind of stage sequence, it follows that development takes place as a discontinuous process of plateaus and abrupt changes when the individual reaches a certain point. On the other hand, a traditional behavioral approach endorses continuity of behavior, where earlier behaviors are related to and (as we have seen above) to some degree become a causal factor in later behaviors.

Sears incorporated the idea of stages in his theory by proposing a three "phase" model of (1) *rudimentary behavior*, (2) *secondary behavioral systems*, and finally, (3) *secondary motivational systems*. Table 8-1 illustrates what these stages are, their time frames, and the focus of the stage.

Phase I: Rudimentary Behavior. Phase I takes place between birth and 16 months of age and is characterized by the infant's innate needs being satisfied and the kinds of behavioral learning that takes place as a function of those needs.

Through the reduction of tension associated with basic biological needs, infants begin to amass the kinds of behaviors that are necessary to become somewhat more independent from a caretaker. The infant also begins to develop a wide range of social and interpersonal skills. Since the child is so "inexperienced," a great deal of the reduction of these needs takes place through simple trial and error learning. If the infant finds that vocalizing a certain way does not get the desired kind of a response from a parent the baby is likely to try another strategy that might be more successful.

After being successful at one strategy, the infant is likely to repeat that strategy and perhaps generalize it to other settings when a similar (but not identical) need arises. For example, the child might learn that the most effective way of getting attention is through loud and direct verbalization to one or both parents. If that is effective, it might also be the strategy that is used at the day care center or with other relatives. This generalization is an important step, because the child is reaching out and developing skills in other settings through interactions with new people.

What probably is most overlooked at this stage, and this is especially true for parents, is that a reciprocity is established between the parent and child such that

Table 8-1 Sears' Phases of Development

Phase	Age	Focus
I. Rudimentary Behavior	birth–16 months	Innate needs
II. Secondary Behavioral Systems	16 months–5 years	Family centered learning
III. Secondary Motivational Systems	5 years +	Extra familial learning

the child acts in a way that encourages certain parental behaviors as well. It is not just the parents' innate desire to provide warmth for their new baby that encourages them to rock and cuddle the infant, but the endearing responses and "cuteness" of the infant's behavior that encourages such behavior. For example, children in the later months of this stage (around one and one half years) are quite mobile, can get around well on their own, and are also quite verbal. In effect, children at this age behave in such a way as to encourage certain behaviors on their parents' part, all of which are advantageous to their growth and development.

It is easy to see by these examples how important the dyadic or one-to-one relationship is during this early phase of development. It might also help to explain how children who do not have some of their basic needs met are slower to develop, especially in the area of social skills.

Phase II: Secondary Behavioral Systems. This second of three phases within Sears' theory lasts until about five years of age and focuses primarily on the interaction between the child's developing physical and intellectual skills and the social conventions of the family. Rather than just associating "mom" or "dad" with the appropriate solution to whatever concern the child has, the child now needs to reach out and align the satisfaction of primary needs with that which the environment offers. For most children around this age, school is not a full-time activity. The development of a place within the family system, however, may very well be one. It is now more than just the satisfaction of needs, but the reduction of tension associated with what we described earlier as secondary sources of reinforcement. Eating with the family not only satisfies the basic need of hunger, but also begins to teach the child the correct way to behave at the table, how to ask for certain things, rules of conversation, and so forth. This is a time when the children are reaching out to their parents and family for guidance on how to satisfy needs that are growing more complex every day.

One example of this process is toilet training. During this phase almost all children learn to control their bowels. At one point, especially during the rudimentary phase, it wasn't important or particularly socially valuable for a child to be trained. Parents understand this and treat the child accordingly. Now, however, things have changed. At a certain age, parents expect their child to be out of diapers, and the pleasureable physical sensations and autonomy that were present earlier become somewhat tempered by the demands of the other member of the dyad, as well as by society. This is a perfect example of how a primary need for elimination becomes linked with a more secondary source present in the environment: the approval of parents *and* others.

Phase III: Secondary Motivational Systems. Besides all the other things that happen around age five or six, the most important for both the child and the family is the beginning of formal education. It is clear to almost every parent that the moment children begin school, their child's behavior is shaped by an entirely new set of potential reinforcers. The dyadic relationship a mother or a father had with the child is simply no longer possible at that same level. Instead the child enters the world of socialization, with many different types of peers with which to play, different behaviors to try, and different sources of potential reinforcement for all these kinds of behaviors.

The child has progressed from a reliance on one person during the very early stages of development to a reliance on the family during Phase II. During this last phase, the child is now faced with the prospect of self reliance.

The Relationship Between The Three Phases of Social Learning

As someone very interested in the socialization processes that surround childhood, Sears believed that these three different phases cannot stand alone. Rather, anything affecting any one affects the other two as well.

For example, in Figure 8-1 we can see how these three phases can be seen as three concentric circles with the rudimentary stage being the smallest (and first to be formed), and the secondary motivational phase being the largest and last to be formed. The child at birth only has the parents available as a source for fulfilling basic needs. As the child ages, the family becomes a more critical socializing agent. Finally, the largest circle, that representing society's contribution, reflects the importance of this phase of development. It is the largest because it is likely that there are more "sources" of socializing influences located in society than anywhere else.

When one event occurs within one circle, like a pebble hitting a pond of water, there are ripples or reverberations throughout all the different phases. For example, the death of a parent will have an impact on the child's socialization within the family structure itself, but also what experiences he or she brings to the more general environment as well.

As the child gets older, other changes in the relationship between these phases change as well. As you can see, the boundaries between the stages become less definitive, and the area encompassed by any one stage changes as well. For example, for the 15-year-old who is very much involved in developing a set of mores in line with the expectations of society, the phase emphasizing social concerns is relatively large in size. Similarly, for the younger child, the first phase is more central to development and assumes a "larger role."

Although the work of Robert Sears is a significant contribution to our understanding of the developmental process, it is interesting how it has never really become as popular as some of the other theories and approaches we are discussing throughout this book. There may be several reasons for this, such as the difficulty any psychologist has in combining aspects of different developmental theories. Or perhaps Sears' approach was not unique from what was already available. We should not overlook, however, how his major contributions toward applying psychoanalytic principles within a behavioral model probably provided the framework for many of the behavioral theorists who followed him and placed a special importance on factors other than those that are directly responsible for change.

HOW THEY STUDY DEVELOPMENT

Long before it was fashionable to be concerned about families and how children are raised, Robert Sears and his colleagues undertook a large scale study that is still thought as a hallmark contribution in developmental psychology.

As we discussed in this chapter, one of Sears' major interests is in the different strategies that parents use to raise children. He was also very interested in trying to build a bridge between the psychoanalytic and behavioral approaches to development, and the methods used in this study reflect this dual orientation.

Sears and his colleagues set out to answer the following three straightforward but, up to that time, unanswered questions:

1. How do parents rear their child?
2. What kinds of effects do different types of training have on children?
3. Why do mothers chose one way of raising children over another?

This study interviewed 379 mothers of five-year-old children, who reported in great detail their feelings about being a mother, their child rearing "philosophy," and their perceptions of their own child's behavior. Each mother was interviewed using a set of 72 questions that generated many different responses in such areas as permissiveness, discipline, praise, and use of punishment.

What did they find? It would be convenient perhaps, to be able to report that one or another type of child-rearing practice resulted in a certain outcome. But, as in many studies of human behavior, there are a variety of different factors that might contribute to any one pattern of behavior.

One important finding of Sears and his colleagues (1957) is that the mother's warmth toward her child is an important factor. For example, maternal warmth related to many of the child's behaviors, while maternal coldness was associated with bed wetting and feeding problems. Perhaps most interesting was the answer to the question about the effectiveness of punishment versus rewards in training children. As the results of the study revealed, punishment is much less effective than rewards. For example, physical punishment was strongly related to aggressiveness and feeding problems.

As you may know, more and more research is now focused on the family and, specifically, child-rearing practices. The work by Sears and his colleagues provided an early and very useful model for continuing this work, as well as contributing some of the first reliable information about the effects of parenting.

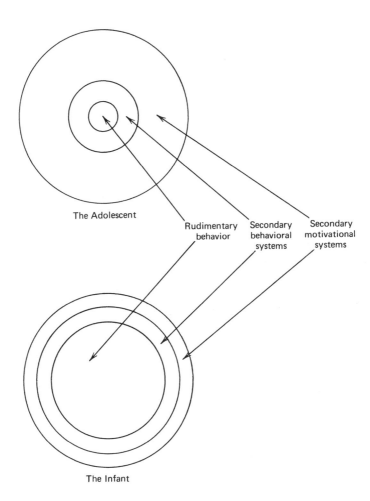

Figure 8-1. Sears' three different phases of social learning.

THE COGNITIVE-SOCIAL LEARNING THEORY OF ALBERT BANDURA

With the completion of the theoretical and empirical research by Sears and others, the behavioral tradition entered an important new era. The idea that individuals were nothing more than passive hosts having little direct control over their fate became less and less acceptable as an adequate explanation for development. Since the application of the intervening variable in applied settings, behavioral approaches were no longer tied to the unidirectional model that only the individual is affected by the environment, and there is no reciprocity.

Even with Sears' important contribution, questions still existed about how human beings learn so many complex behaviors in so relatively short a time without *obvious* practice. For example, the acquisition of language cannot be explained as the arduous process of children hearing every possible combination of nouns, verbs, and adjectives and being reinforced for copying these combinations. Rather, it is a result of predetermined potentialities enhanced by a supportive and properly programmed environment. Likewise, people participate in other classes of behavior that do not appear to be the result of direct instruction. For example, parents often practice the same philosophy toward rearing their children that their parents practiced. These practices are not directly taught. This type of learning takes place through an entirely different process and is called *vicarious learning* (Bandura, 1971).

Albert Bandura and Richard Walters developed a theoretical perspective that views the individual as an *active mediator* who operates on the environment in accord with certain expectancies and contingencies, but with foresight or knowledge as to what the consequences of his or her behavior might be even before the behavior occurs. This is a radical change from the traditional or fundamental S-R conception of learning. Indeed, Bandura and Walters (and later Bandura alone) developed a system that proposes a merging of separate S-R bonds or elements into unified patterns of behavior. Further, much of the direction (but not the cause) of behavior is attributed to the individual's own internal behaviors, referred to primarily as *mediating processes*.

The Theoretical Outlook

As we have seen, most theories of development within one general model tend to build on one another. For example, Erikson's theory of psychosocial development was different from Freud's psychoanalytic theory, yet it embraced many of the same basic concepts. This does not mean that a later theory is simply a logical extension of an earlier one, but that some theories incorporate certain concepts and ideas that have already been established. For science to advance and not just to keep reproducing itself again and again, this building process is a necessity. This has also been true with social learning theory. Social learning theory incorporates the basic rules and terminology of S-R learning, along with the fundamental tenets of S-R psychology, including the notion of stimulus-response bonds, respondent and operant behaviors, and schedules of reinforcement, all of which are important elements of social learning theory.

Another important assumption of social learning theory is that significant learning takes place through the process of imitation or modeling. This assumption is common to traditional S-R theories; the way in which people imitate or model behavior and receive reinforcement for that action has been discussed. However, the process of imitation here becomes more complex, because the individual has an active role in determining what classes of behavior are to be imitated, with what frequency, and with what intensity. Perhaps the most important difference between the traditional S-R view of imitation and the social learning theory view is that within the social learning theory, certain classes of behavior can be learned *without the benefit of direct experience*. Put another way, *vicarious* or indirect reinforcement is as effective as direct reinforcement for facilitating and promoting imitation.

The significance of this assumption cannot be overestimated. For many years, behavioral psychologists dealt mostly in a framework wherein the effects of imitation were bound to the temporal qualities of an event. Imitation was thought to be a process tied to the learner (or the person doing the imitating), who was reinforced as the behavior was taking place. Social learning theory presents an entirely new outlook, wherein reinforcement can occur in an indirect fashion. Although experience might be the best teacher, the experiences of others are important as well. People do not drive through intersections when the light is red because they are aware of the consequences of doing so even though they may not have experienced them directly.

As another example, we often hear the parental demand "Do as I tell you!" From a social learning theory perspective, people are more likely to do as they see others do. Children are often told not to do certain things (such as smoking, showing bad manners, or having uncontrollable temper tantrums), yet when they revert to these behaviors adults wonder where they learned them. Parents are probably the most powerful models in a child's life and are therefore potentially the best teachers. This is true not only because of the high degree of frequency and intensity with which the child and parent interact, but also because of the high regard children have for parents and their desire to be like them. Of course, the easiest way to be like another person is to copy his or her behavior, which is a process that operates extensively throughout the life span.

Social learning theory ascribes special importance to the operation of *internal mediational processes* in development. This is a major distinction between the social learning theory perspective and other behavioral viewpoints. Specifically, this assumption emphasizes the importance of the operation of internal mediating processes in learning. That is, between the sensory input that forms the basis of all learning and the final act of behavior, internal operations affect the ultimate outcome. If this assumption is accepted, one can no longer view development from the unidirectional approach that is presented in other S-R theories. Radical behaviorism's fundamental assumption is that individuals are relatively passive in their actions and have little to do with determining their own course of development.

The social learning theory perspective goes beyond this, and assumes that the impetus for behavior is environmental in nature, but the developmental process is bidirectional, characterized by a reciprocity between the individual and the environment. Bandura called this viewpoint *reciprocal determinism* (1977). At the most simple level, this view assumes that sensory input does not automatically produce behavior unaffected by the individual's conscious contribution. In essence, this process of reciprocal determinism can be described as follows: The learner does not acquire a set of S-R bonds or associations simply through being reinforced for copying a model. Instead, the individual processes information from the model and develops a set of symbolic representations of the behavior that, through trial and error learning, is later matched. Attempts to match this template using feedback occurs until the learner's behavior is on target. It is not simply a process of the learner perceiving a model and then imitating the behavior, but a much more complex series of steps wherein an approximation of the model's behavior occurs through the internalization of what the model represents, followed by the learner's attempts to match that representation.

The Role of Reinforcement in Imitation

One of the most important concepts in behavioral development is the process through which reinforcement acts to influence behavior. Certain important factors determine the strength of a reinforcer and its effect on subsequent behavior. One of these is the immediacy with which the stimulus event (or reinforcer) follows the individual's behavior, and another is the schedule of reinforcement or frequency with which these reinforcing events occur. These are important components of the learning process.

When the traditional S-R perspective is examined, one realizes that reinforcement is a very efficient tool in the modification of behavior, but not necessarily one that can be used to create or facilitate the development of novel behaviors.

Within the traditional behavioral perspective, reinforcement plays a very important role in modifying behavior. Social learning theory, however, goes one step further, ascribing two important and distinct functions to reinforcement: *information and motivation.*

Informative Qualities of Reinforcers. The first of these functions is that reinforcers have informative qualities. The act of reinforcement and the reinforcement process itself can tell the individual what behavior is most adaptive. People do not grope in a haphazard fashion until something in the environment comes at the right moment and reinforces a response. They act with intent. In a sense, they learn through experience what to expect in advance, and by learning in advance they become better at predicting what behaviors maximize their chances for success. Before a job interview, for example, people are aware of the potential outcome (getting the position) and have learned to maximize their chances (by dressing appropriately, for example).

Some of the most impressive empirical work based on social learning theory treats this very point regarding expectations. If this idea is valid, one would expect learning to be "better" or faster when some advanced knowledge is present. And, in fact, much more effective learning does occur when the individual is aware of what behavior is being reinforced. Thus knowledge of the consequences of a behavior can be a great help in optimizing the effectiveness of a learning program or explaining a complex process such as imitation.

If people are informed as to what behavior will be rewarded under what conditions, the likelihood of successful learning can be greatly improved. For example, in a school setting, children are not handed a pencil and paper and allowed to make random marks until letters of the alphabet are produced. Instead, they are shown models and instructed what to do. Similarly, the adult is informed of what the expectations of a job are and what is necessary to complete the work to obtain payment or whatever reward or reinforcer is being offered.

This informative function of a reinforcer also allows some insight into the consequences of a behavior prior to commitment. For example, in a strange situation people often do not know what behaviors are acceptable because they have very little information about the new setting. It is often difficult to be aware of the appropriate behavior to reach for as a goal. The informative aspect of a reinforcer depends to a large extent on the amount of previous experience that has been established within that setting.

Motivating Qualities of Reinforcers. The second important difference between the S-R view and the social learning theory view of imitation is that reinforcers have *motivating* as well as informative qualities. People learn to anticipate what the reinforcers will be in certain situations, and the beginning step in many developmental sequences is this initial anticipatory behavior. This is one element within the very large context of cognitive or mediating operations that occurs within the individual in its reciprocal relationship with the environment.

People do not possess psychic powers to see into the future, but they do learn from other people's good and bad experiences. For example, children are (or should be) inoculated before there is a chance of polio or diphtheria infection. These tragedies do not have to be experienced before parents take action. Likewise, cars are not parked in towaway zones, because, if they are, they will be towed away and the owner fined. Future consequences of behavior can act as motivators to provide direction to behavior. This notion in itself makes the social learning theory view of development very powerful in helping us to understand day-to-day behavior. The informative and motivating qualities of the reinforcement process are two dimensions that distinguish the traditional S-R view from the social learning view of imitation. There are also, however, other important differences best described through a comparison of the two viewpoints.

Two Learning Theory Views of Imitation

One important distinction is the different roles that reinforcement occupies in the traditional S-R perspective and in the social learning theory view. Reinforcement-based theories of imitation postulate the need for direct reinforcement, in that behaviors must be directly reinforced in order to be learned. In other words, imitating a behavior without being reinforced for the behavior results in incomplete or no learning. Within the social learning theory approach, however, imitation occurs through the observation of a model, without the learner necessarily receiving direct reinforcement, or actually modeling the behavior.

In Chapter 7, we discussed the idea that direct reinforcement is an effective way to facilitate change in behavior but not necessarily a way to understand the formation of new behaviors. Social learning theory does not consider reinforcement alone to be a sufficient explanation for imitation. It is only a component that facilitates learning, along with covert processes such as attention, organization, and rehearsal.

If one accepts the basic premise of the traditional S-R perspective that, in order for learning to occur, the individual must directly experience the consequences of an action, then the scope of behaviors that can be explained is limited. This is true because it is obvious that we could not possibly learn all we know only through those events we directly experience. Vicarious learning is the process through which we are indirectly reinforced or punished. For example, seeing a child being punished can deter other children from running into the street. Direct instruction is probably critical in learning many skills, such as swimming. We could, however, also learn how to swim by recalling what the instructor has said and the images of the instructor's actions in the water, and by putting these thoughts and images into action.

Individuals do not need to be told or shown all the time whether they are correct or incorrect in order for further learning to take place. It is because of this, that social learning theory is considered to be so powerful in its explanatory role. It helps to account for the large amount of learning that can take place without direct exposure to a model.

We can contrast the S-R and the social learning perspectives in a schematic diagram (see Figure 8-2). The traditional S-R viewpoint (Figure 8-2a) shows imitative behavior reinforced as the behavior is taking place and in the presence of the model ($S_{modeling\ stimuli}$). It leaves little room for any contribution by the individual other than previous experience, represented by a storehouse of earlier S-R associations. Within this model, reinforcement acts to strengthen earlier imitative be-

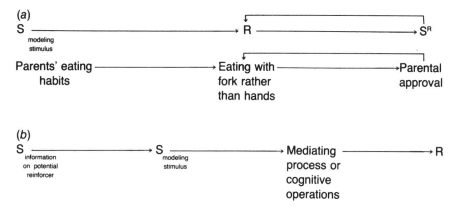

Figure 8-2. Imitation from the traditional and social learning theory views.

haviors in the presence of a model or a modeling stimulus. For example, a child might imitate his or her parents' table manners, and if reinforced (or punished) for this behavior within a reasonable amount of time, the conditions for simple imitative learning are present. Reinforcement (or punishment) of the behavior and the behavior itself occur in close physical and temporal proximity.

The social learning theory viewpoint (Figure 8-2b) represents a more complex approach. As before, there is a model that will be imitated ($S_{modeling\ stimulus}$) and a resultant behavior (R). Initially, however, the individual acts on the basis of some awareness of what is and what is not worth imitating and anticipates an outcome ($S_{information}$) that is potentially advantageous. People are frequently in situations in which they choose not to imitate a model, because the anticipated reinforcers are not worth the effort or hold no value for the individual. This anticipatory behavior provides much of the motivation for modeling a specific behavior or class of behaviors. Young children learn the significance of imitating the speech patterns of their parents very quickly, because they often receive a great deal of reinforcement for this behavior.

Another unique component of the social learning theory view is the individual's attention to the modeling stimulus ($S_{modeling\ stimulus}$). One crucial difference between social learning and traditional S-R views is that of *mediating or internal cognitive operations*: where the individual acts on the information available based on the observation of a model. It is a process of encoding information about the model to make it available to the individual, storing it to be used at a later time, rehearsing the order of the elements so that they can be correctly reconstructed when necessary, and finally transforming these congnitive acts into actual behaviors that are rep-resented as a response (R). Most social learning theorists describe these internal operations as mediators and tend to shy away from such terms as "thinking." The idea of a mediating influence is much more clearly conceptualized than is some general operation called "thinking." The social learning theorist is as concerned with operationalizing behavior as the traditional behaviorist and finds such terms to be nondescriptive.

Although the significance of direct reinforcement from external sources is not a cornerstone element in the social learning theory approach, it is still important. Beyond this however, the major force that operates within the social learning theory view is vicarious reinforcement (Bandura, 1971). In other words, through a variety of mechanisms behaviors are reinforced without direct experience. You should be able to see how this position does not assume that the organism is passive and waiting for the environment to have an impact on behavior.

Social Learning Theory as a Process

Four processes are necessary for imitation or observational learning to occur: attention, retention, motor reproduction, and motivation. Without any one, the social learning theory model is incomplete and successful imitation is less likely to occur.

The individual must be capable of *attending to* or paying attention to the event or to its different elements. For example, children who have attentional deficits (such as poor impulse control) may not be able to sit still long enough to pay attention to the stimulus. They may pick up an element of an experience, but they may be unable to process all the elements necessary to represent the entire event. Not properly attending to a model is frequently the primary reason why teachers contend that if children would only pay attention, they could learn. Bandura believes that such factors as past history of reinforcement, sensory capacities, and complexity of the modeled event are also important influences on the attention process.

Another important operation in imitation is *retention*, or being able to remember the critical features of an event. These features can then be recalled and utilized as necessary. For example, the sequence of steps for changing a tire becomes activated when we learn we have a flat tire. The use of the jack, removing the hub cap, and so on, are all recalled. If one cannot remember what the different steps are in a sequence of event, then a behavior cannot successfully be modeled. Retention involves processes such as symbolic coding and rehearsal. These elements of memory make it possible to internalize an event and recall its sequence at a later time.

A third process involves the *motoric reproduction* of modeled behaviors. Here it is necessary for the learner to be capable of physically performing the behavior. For example, learning to hit a baseball consists of watching a ball, swinging a bat at it, at the correct angle and time. Swinging the bat and hitting the ball are global behaviors that include many simple steps, such as keeping your eye on the ball, keeping the feet stationary, placing the hands in the proper position on the bat, and maintaining the correct swinging level. When batting instructors teach people to hit, they do more than ask the student to watch. They discuss the different *constituent behaviors* described above and check to see that the learner can at least perform these different individual behaviors before any attempt is made to combine (or correct) them. The learner must be able to perform all the discrete behaviors before successful imitation can take place.

Finally, the last necessary component is some form of *motivation*. According to Bandura, motivation can take the form of external (direct), or vicarious (indirect) reinforcement. The first of these two different motivational influences is the same type of reinforcement present in the traditional S-R model of imitative or observational learning. The last, however, places the social learning theory perspective apart from earlier theories. Vicarious reinforcement makes the individual more autonomous and less dependent on direct environmental influences. Immediate reinforcement is not necessary every time a move is made in a direction toward the completion of a goal. Behavior is regulated and individuals find a comfortable medium between self-generated reinforcement and that received through external sources. Gratification is necessary for a behavior to reach fruition, even if that gratification is self-generated. This ability to reinforce ourselves can be used in a clinical setting, where therapists teach people to reinforce their own behavior and increase their self-esteem. *older and younger students — who uses machines safely*

Vicarious reinforcement results when there is an increase in a behavior that a potential learner has seen reinforced in others. This type of reinforcement is a very powerful force in explaining how so many new behaviors can be acquired with so little direct experience. Experience might be a great teacher, but the human organism is so complex that everything that is learned could not be the result of direct experience and direct reinforcement. For example, the adolescent's latest craze may be the result of peer group behavior. The reinforcer here may be acceptance by the peer group, which for the teenager is a powerful one. Likewise, the middle-aged adult may dress and act like a young adult in an effort to recapture past feelings and experiences. Imitating the behavior of a younger generation can be a powerful motivator in its false promise of bringing with it the feeling of being young again.

Just as reinforcement is delivered vicariously, punishing experiences can occur the same way. People do not have to overdose on sleeping pills or drive a car with an almost empty fuel tank to understand the consequences of their actions. They have learned through other people's experiences what the outcomes are. By watching others, one can quickly learn what behaviors are punished (or what behaviors are reinforced) without the painful experience of actually receiving the punishment. We raise our hand in class rather than shout, because we know one is rewarded and the other punished.

Four operations—attention, retention, motor reproduction, and motivation—

are all necessary for imitative or observational learning to take place. But how do
these operations interact with one another? Although attentional operations are
probably the first step in observational learning, it is doubtful that there is an actual
sequence to these four operations. The four might be represented as parts of a
diagram with the performance of the individual itself as the center of the diagram.
For modeling to occur, there must be an initial stimulus to copy. Figure 8-3 represents the relationship between the four necessary operations of attention, retention,
motoric reproduction, and motivation, and the outcomes of the modeling (called
observational learning). You should note that all of these "circles" or influences
do not contribute equally since one or more processes are often more important
than others.

Imitated behavior rarely exactly matches the model's behavior, but instead
approximates it to fit the learner's needs. For example, if a certain technique for
carving wood is learned, it is likely that one individual's own personal style will
contribute to the uniqueness of the borrowed technique. In the same way, imitation
can have other effects on behavior. It is not only new things that are learned through

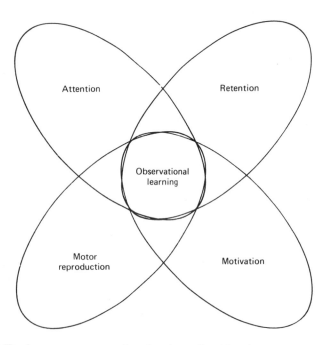

Figure 8-3. The four necessary operations for observational learning.

the process of imitation or observational learning, but the modeling process also precipitates behaviors that are already in our repertoire that were not necessary at an earlier time. The observation of models can have three distinctly different effects on present and future behavior: modeling effects, disinhibitory/inhibitory effects, and eliciting effects. *What is learned*

When the learner behaves in a novel way (does something new), the *modeling effect* has taken place. For example, a toddler who picks up an old rag and begins to dust the furniture like his parents illustrates a new behavior without any clear association with other behaviors the child has shown in the past. It is very difficult to say whether any behavior is totally novel in the sense that no part of it existed as an element of another behavior. Perhaps the child's housecleaning help is just a combination of other established behaviors such as rubbing a hand over the surface of the wall and holding a rag. Combined, these become a new behavior called dusting. New behaviors are usually defined as a recombination of already existing elements that have not been combined in that fashion before.

Next, there is the *eliciting effect*. Very often the model will serve to elicit or precipitate a behavior that already exists in the repertoire of the learner but that up to now has not been called on or actively stimulated. Many behaviors are not facilitated unless they become necessary. This is an example of using old or previously learned strategies in a new and different setting. For example, people can drive a rented car that resembles their own. Behavior becomes an approximation of some target behavior, and for this reason it may be difficult to identify (without any prior knowledge of the individual's history) which behaviors are new (modeling effect), and which behaviors are already established yet not active (eliciting effect).

Finally, the last effect that Bandura discussed is the *inhibitory/disinhibitory effect*, which is a special case of the eliciting effect. Observing a model can act to disinhibit (encourage), or inhibit (discourage) a behavior. For example, take the child who in the past has been very aggressive. Because aggressive behavior is in the child's repertoire, the circumstances at a certain time might determine if this behavior is modeled. Perhaps aggression is highly reinforced. In other words, behavior is *disinhibited* through interaction with other models. On the other hand, behavior can be *inhibited*: sanctions can be placed on being aggressive, and the child can decide against aggressive behavior. *DEF OF LEARNING*

These three effects combine with the four processes (attention, motoric reproduction, retention, and motivation) to provide a framework through which the acquisition of behavior by means of a series of complex reciprocal interactions between the organism and the environment can be understood. The importance of the organism's active participation in the social learning theory perspective cannot be overemphasized. This is not just because this distinguishes it from the traditional S-R viewpoint but, most important, because it underlies a view of development that opened up a new way of viewing the developmental process.

Rel between learning and development

HOW THEY STUDY DEVELOPMENT

A very powerful concept in social learning theory, if not the most powerful, is that of *vicarious learning*. As you remember in our discussion in this chapter, vicarious learning is a special kind of learning that takes place without direct reinforcement. This is so powerful because it provides an explanation for how our behavioral repetoire can be so rich and diverse without necessarily experiencing all those things we know or do.

One of the most famous and best illustrations of vicarious learning and the effect of modeling follows. This study by Albert Bandura and his colleagues provided a foundation for many of the social learning theory experiments in the last 20 years.

The way that aggressive behavior is acquired or learned is of great interest to developmental psychologists since it is present in some form at all levels of development, and is one of the issues that often becomes a part of the nature-nurture debate. The primary interest of the authors of this study was to determine if exposure to aggressive and nonaggressive models would make a difference in the rate of children's aggression when they were in a situation without the model.

To accomplish this, 36 boys and girls enrolled in a preschool were divided into eight groups. Each of the children was placed in a room with an adult model. Half the children observed same sex models and half observed opposite sex models. The child and the model were led into an experimental room, and the model seated at his or her own table did one of two things.

If the child was in the aggressive condition, the model would play with some of the Tinker Toys that were available and then begin to act aggressively toward a five foot inflated punch doll (that returns to an upright position when hit). The model would hit the doll, punch it in the nose, and sit on it. These aggressive acts were also accompanied by verbal aggression directed at the doll. If the child was in the nonaggressive condition, the model would simply continue to play with the toys provided, and not pay any attention to the doll.

To test for aggressive modeling or imitation, each of the children was then placed in a room containing a variety of toys, including a three foot inflated doll of the same type as described above. Each child spent 20 minutes in the room, where a judge recorded the child's behavior every five seconds in one of several predetermined categories. The measures that were used to evaluate the child's aggressiveness were physical aggression, verbal aggression, nonaggressive verbal responses, mallet (or hammer) aggression, sitting on doll, punching doll, nonimitative physical and verbal aggression, and aggressive gun play.

The results showed that children who were exposed to aggressive models showed a significantly higher amount of aggression than those children who were exposed to nonaggressive models. In addition, boys showed more aggression than girls when they were observing a male aggressive model.

In recent years, a great deal of concern has been voiced about the effect of television on the development of aggressive and prosocial behavior in children. Studies such as the one discussed here increase our understanding of those effects as very powerful influences.

Understanding the Behavioral Approach

1. *What is the major force that influences the course of development?*

Probably the most important thing to remember about the role that hereditary and environmental influences play in the behavioral approach is that biological factors set the absolute limits for development and the environment determines the content or types of behavior within those limits. This is one of the central assumptions of behaviorism noted at the beginning of Chapter 7. If we look at some of the specific theorists we discussed in the last two chapters, it is clear that the central ideas of each uses environmental factors as a benchmark. For example, Skinner's definition of operant behavior includes an examination of the way in which a behavior "operates on the environment" as a result of what follows that behavior. For Skinner, these consequences originate in the environment, where they can be objectively and accurately defined.

Bijou and Baer extended the application of operant psychology and included other factors that, even if not solely controlled by environmental change (for example, a biological setting event such as a fever), result in a functional relationship with some event in the environment. Likewise, Bandura's concept of reciprocal determinism stresses the interactive nature of the relationship between heredity and environment but still makes clear that the environment is a more critical influence on the individual's development than what the individual brought to the situation.

For the early behaviorists such as Pavlov, the role of the environment was much like the role maturation played in Gesell's theory: overwhelmingly predominant. Over the years, however, with the advances made in some substantive areas of development (such as personality theory), theorists have been more likely to acknowledge a biological contribution, even if not as a primary component of the theory.

2. *What is the underlying process responsible for changes in development?*

Each of the behavioral theorists we have discussed proposed that a different type of learning is the foundation of development. But regardless of the type of learning they specified, it is clear that maturation is not a primary mechanism in development. For example, Pavlov's focus on classical conditioning and Watson's emphasis on the connection between the stimulus and response gave little credit to the contribution of maturational forces to development. Not until the work of Skinner were biological or maturational processes ascribed any role and, even then, not until the work of the social learning theorists was the process of maturation considered essential for certain types of learning to take place. The motoric reproduction element of social learning theory clearly requires a certain level of neurological development to be completed.

The role of maturation in development is to prepare the developing individual *[handwritten margin notes: "lack of needs basic", "Baer -", "development (learned or natural (behaviorist) or nature (other))"]*

to receive what the environment might have to offer. For this reason, we should strive to provide the basic needs for all children (such as food, clothing, and health care) to maximize their potential for optimal development within different environments.

3. *What role does age play as a general marker of changes in development?*

In many ways, age assumes the same importance as maturation. Baer's notion of age as an "irrelevant" component of development characterizes the behavioral position. Age is not a causal or an explanatory concept, and at best it is used as a general marker to indicate what we can expect of children. It is so general, however (for example, infants do not talk but twelve-year-olds do), that it almost becomes useless. In many ways this reflects an appealing characteristic of the behavioral model, because it does not constrain the child's behavior with age expectations, but instead lets the child be judged on his or her own terms rather than in comparison with others.

4. *Are there certain sensitive or critical periods during development, and how are they related to the rate of change?*

What is "critical" to development within the behavioral approach is not so much the period of time frame within which an event may occur, but the fact that the event occurs. We should talk then of "critical events," and not critical periods. As in any other model, the individual is of course sensitive to biological threats (such as the German measles during pregnancy), but behaviorists consider development to be made up of learned phenomena. The individual may be more ready to learn at one time than at another, but unless the critical event occurs to facilitate that learning, development is likely to be somewhat haphazard and possibly delayed.

Our discussion of maturation and learning as mechanisms in development stressed that learning is the predominant force, but that the individual does need to be at least physically competent to learn. Critical events originating in the environment occur throughout development and have a major impact on the direction that development takes.

5. *Is development smooth and continuous, or do changes occur in abrupt stages?*

From the beginning of our discussion of the behavioral approach to development, we have stressed that the changes that take place over time are the result of learning and that there is little if any recognition of stages or qualitatively different levels of development.

It would be extreme to say that development is only the quantitative addition of more and more connections or learned events, because there is certainly a quality of change from one point in the life span to the next. Most of the work in developmental psychology produced over the past fifty years has not focused on detailing the qualities of the environment. The degree of continuity (if it does exist within the behavioral model) most likely would be identified as quantitative transitions in the environment surrounding the individual and not as qualitative changes within the individual as presumed in other more stage-oriented theories.

We should not forget, however, that Sears did provide a phase framework. Perhaps the difference here is that while phases deal with time periods, stages are more bound by biological changes and constraints.

We can often get a clue about the underlying assumptions of a theory by understanding the method that is used to examine the theory. Behaviorists focus on the frequency of a behavior and pay little attention to the presence of any underlying structures. In fact, if there are unseen structures that do change as a function of learning, these structures are not within the realm of direct inspection (such as hypothesized phychological structures), or they take place purely on a physical level.

For a perspective such as that of the social learning theorist, mediating responses or internal events may be an important part of the developmental process and reflect qualitative change. These internal happenings, however, are not based on structures in the sense of controlling learning, but are a result of learning. It becomes a chicken-and-egg problem: Which comes first—structural change or learning? For most behaviorists, structural change and learning are synonymous. For the more cognitively oriented behaviorists (such as the social learning theorists) structural change results from, not in, learning.

6. How does the theory explain differences in development between individuals of the same age?

One way that we could answer this question is to return to Baer's argument that age is an irrelevant concept for understanding the developmental process. Instead, it is the sequence of events that is important, and the similarities and differences that we observe in people has a great deal to do with the quality and the quantity of both current and past experiences.

We have mentioned several times throughout Chapters 7 and 8 how we are all born with the same "basic" equipment, most commonly called reflex behaviors. The influence of environmental factors and the quality of mediating forces result in the direction that one's individual developmental course might take. For example, the difference between the child who receives attention for misbehavior and the child who does not have different reinforcement histories, yet both have the same general goal in sight of receiving some adult or peer attention.

The challenge to behavioral scientists is to develop a method for systematically studying the vast array of factors in the environment that can influence our developmental patterns.

SUMMARY POINTS

1. Robert Sears combined experiences and theory from psychoanalytic and behavioral settings to form a social learning theory of development.
2. All behaviors begin as an effort to reduce tension that is associated with some biological need.
3. Behavior is a function of interactions between people that most frequently occur in dyads.
4. Drives that are present at birth provide the foundation for later development.
5. Behavior is the cause and effect of later behavior.
6. The "quality" of a behavior depends on its potential for reinforcement.
7. Dollard and Miller present a set of six postulates that are based on the role of conflict as a basic drive in human development.
8. Bandura and Walters addressed the important question of how people learn so many things without direct or obvious reinforcement.
9. Vicarious learning—the type of learning that Bandura and Walters emphasized—takes place through imitation or modeling.
10. Significant learning takes place through the process of imitation or modeling.
11. Certain types of behavior can be learned without the benefit of direct experience.
12. Social learning theory as defined by Bandura places a great deal of importance on reciprocal determination, the reciprocal relationship between the individual and the environment.
13. Reinforcers are both informative and motivating.
14. The social learning view of imitation is different from the traditional view, which stresses the need for direct or immediate reinforcement for modeling to take place.
15. Vicarious learning accounts for the way various behaviors are learned without direct experience.
16. Attention, retention, motor reproduction, and motivation are four processes that must be present for imitation to occur.

FURTHER READINGS

Bandura, A. *Social learning theory*. Englewood Cliffs, N.J.: Prentice-Hall, 1977.

Bandura, A. *Principles of behavior modification*. New York: Holt, Rinehart and Winston, 1969.

Jacobsen, S. W. Matching behavior in the young infant. *Child Development*, 1979, **50**, 425–30.

Meltzoff, A., and Moore, M. K. Imitation of facial and manual gestures by human neonates. *Science*, 1977, **198**, 75–78.

Sears, R. R., Maccoby, E. E., and Levin, H. *Patterns of child rearing*. Stanford: Stanford University Press, 1957.

Sears, R. R., Rau, L., and Alpert, R. *Identification and child rearing*. Stanford: Stanford University Press, 1965.

OTHER READINGS OF INTEREST

Burd, A. P., and Milewski, A. E. Matching of facial gestures by young infants: Imitation or releasers? Presented at the Society for Research in Child Development, Boston, 1981.

Miller, N., and Dollard, J. *Social learning and imitation*. New Haven, Conn.: Yale University Press, 1941.

9

The Cognitive-
Developmental
Approach

Play is child's work.

Jean Piaget

Action is the basis for thought.

Jean Piaget

Any subject can be taught effectively in some intellectually honest form to any child at any stage of development.

Jerome Bruner

Previous chapters have described the maturational, psychoanalytic, and behavioral views of development. A fourth general class or family of developmental theories places an increased importance on the active role that the individual plays in the developmental process. For the cognitive-developmental psychologist, development occurs in an ordered sequence of qualitatively distinct stages and is characterized by an increase in complexity. The role of the developing person is active, not reactive. The cognitive-developmental view of development is relatively new to this country and is best represented through the work of Jean Piaget, the Swiss psychologist who has written extensively about the child's quest for knowledge. As part philosopher and part biologist, he combines these two areas into a comprehensive and stimulating view of how development happens.

JEAN PIAGET: INTRODUCTION AND BASIC ASSUMPTIONS

No other psychologist has had as profound an impact on the understanding of the developing child's acquisition and use of knowledge as Piaget. Trained as a biologist, he applied the scientific method to philosophical questions that were answerable when subjective methods were used. His efforts helped to bridge the gap that often exists between philosophy and science.

He filled this gap by focusing on one special branch of philosophy called *epistemology*, the science of knowledge and how it is acquired. The contribution that his studies made to understanding the developmental process is best demonstrated by the type of questions that his approach encouraged Piaget to ask. For example: What is learning? Is the way things appear really the same as what they are? What is the process through which knowledge is acquired? What roles do direct experience and innate reasoning play in development? How do children differentiate between an idea and what the idea represents? Piaget actually created his own branch of epistemology, called *genetic epistemology* (Piaget, 1950a). The term ''genetic'' denotes the developmental progression from one level to the next. Piaget's study of the science of knowledge was a developmental study of the way in which knowledge changes over the course of individual development.

The study of knowledge and its acquisition did not so much form the central core of Piaget's theory as dictate the questions he should ask. Genetic epistemology does not suggest or proscribe a method, nor does it define the variables that are important to examine. It establishes a domain of inquiry to which rigorous and objective methods can be applied.

A Definition of Development

Piaget stresses that the developing individual is *active*, rather than reactive. This proposition raises questions, such as: What is development? How does it differ from learning? Do learning and development occur simultaneously or parallel to one another? How does the individual and not the environment determine what is learned? Development, for Piaget, is a broad spontaneous process that results in the continual addition, modification, and reorganization of psychological structures.

By defining development as a spontaneous process, Piaget (1970) emphasizes the individual's inherent capability of being dynamic, not remaining static. In many of his works, Piaget relates biology (and its role in intelligence) to the changes that take place in the individual. This interaction between the individual's internal motivational system and the demands of the environment forms the essence of development. Piaget termed this striving for order or balance *equilibration*, a self-regulatory process that keeps the individual on the right track. This right track is not a genetic predisposition toward a specific behavior (such as laziness, prejudice,

[handwritten marginal notes: "paper - development into a result of conflict and how it resolve" and "When conflicts are not resolved?"]

or impulsivity, for example), but a characteristic of the entire development of the individual.

Equilibration as a Model for Development

Piaget's idea that living organisms continually seek a state of equilibrium was not a new one. Just as Freud borrowed his notion of dynamic energy from work being done in thermodynamics, Piaget saw the foundation for this component of his model in the field of physics. Like Freud, others believed that development resulted in part from a conflict between opposing forces. If there is a common thread uniting many theoretical perspectives, it is that development is a result of conflict and how it is resolved. A simple example of this is the way people avoid or approach a problem until some resolution is established. Physiologists refer to this general phenomenon as *homeostasis*. Just as the hungry infant seeks satisfaction through the reduction of tension, the grown adult may seek out companionship when alone. Through the process of equilibration individuals seek a *state of equilibrium* between their psychological structures and how well those structures meet changing needs. Equilibration is the primary motivating force behind development. Sometimes the forces that produce disequilibrium originate in the environment ("do your homework"), and sometimes they are internal (hunger). In either case, the result is the same: the resolution of conflict and some corresponding qualitative change.

　　The child is the agent active in seeking out those situations or elements in the environment that will produce equilibrium. Different things motivate different children. Beginning with his own children, Piaget kept elaborate diaries of developmental progress. He recorded their behavior in a very systematic fashion and used this information as the basis for identifying the different stages of development through which children pass. This is called the *taxonomic* or *descriptive* task of developmental psychology. If the observer understands a child's placement in the developmental sequence, the demands of the environment can be adjusted to assure that the optimal degree of disequilibrium is present. Too much incongruity between what a child is capable of and what the demands of the task are leads to excessive tension and an unfortunate association between unpleasantness and learning.

What Development Is

Development is a spontaneous process in which the organism plays an active role. Piaget describes four factors that define development: maturation, experience, social transmission, and the unifying factor of equilibration (Piaget, 1970).

　　Maturation is the process through which biological change takes place. It is controlled by innate mechanisms. The primary role that maturation plays in Piaget's theory is to account for the neurological changes that occur through physical growth and for the sequencing of qualitative changes. However, the effects of maturational forces represent a wide range of potential outcomes that depend on other factors.

The second factor is *experience*. For cognitive growth to occur, the child must interact with the environment. For development to proceed (for the child to adapt successfully to changing environments and demands) the individual must be active. This experience does not have to be directly physical but can be any kind of mental activity such as perception or problem solving.

Social transmission occurs when information, attitudes, and customs are transmitted from one group (such as parents) to another (such as children). This is a general factor that accounts for many of the events in the developing child's world that affect the developmental process.

The fourth and last factor is the process of *equilibration*, the most crucial of the four factors because it plays an integrative as well as a motivational role.

Development is a combination of biological growth, directed activity or experience, the process of teaching or transmitting information, and an inherent tendency to seek a state of harmony or balance. Figure 9-1 illustrates that although development is a function of all four factors, equilibration is the unifying force. The bidirectional arrows represent the mutual interactions between the factors. Keep in mind that no matter what importance is assigned to any one of these four factors, development is incomplete without the other three. For example, unless the child is biologically mature enough, no amount of experience, whether physical or mental, is sufficient for him or her to learn a given task.

Clearly, within this perspective, learning is a necessary but minor component. From Piaget's perspective, the most crucial distinction between learning and development is that development is spontaneous (almost automatic), natural or inevitable, and learning is precipitated or invoked. Although learning is a narrowly defined process that involves the acquisition of certain skills and information (often in response to highly specific stimulus conditions), development is a broad general process through which learning takes place. In other words, learning is a function of development.

The Process Component

The child's progression through a set of qualitatively distinct yet interrelated stages of cognitive development is central to Piaget's theory. To fully understand this sequence of events, however, some of the basic processes of development should first be discussed. These processes are not characteristic of any one stage or period of development, but operate continuously.

This section begins with a discussion of a schema (plural "schemes") and the processes of organization and adaptation.

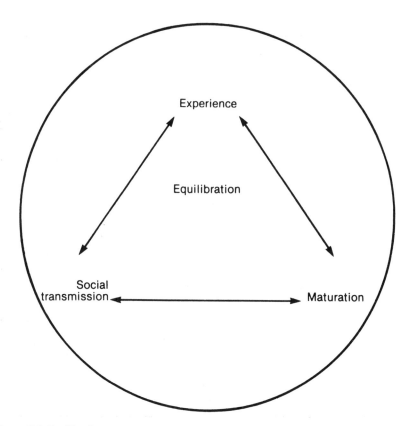

Figure 9-1. Equilibration as a unifying process.

Processes of development:

Schema or Schemes. It is Piaget's contention that the individual acts on the environment in such a way as to construct his or her own concept of the world. The changes that occur through this process are structural ones reflected in what Piaget calls *schemes.*

A schema is the primary unit of mental organization and the structure through which people adapt to the environment. Schemes are flexible in both quality and quantity and are the "mental blueprints" of experience (Kagan, 1971). The earliest schemes (such as sucking and grasping) are reflexive in nature. However, even these reflexive behaviors change depending on the demands of the environment. For example, sucking changes in form when a spoon is used for feeding. Here the schema for sucking has changed its structure but not in the function it performs. The infant is born with many schemes, and through the processes of organization and adaptation develops new ones and changes existing ones.

Organization. *Organization* is the tendency to combine physical and/or psychological processes into a coherent whole. Even for the newborn child, a sophisticated system of communication exists between different biological systems. If this were not so, the child could not survive. For example, the circulatory system circulates blood to capillaries in the air sacs in the lungs, where the respiratory system exchanges carbon dioxide for oxygen. Similarly, touching a hot stove acts as a signal to the nervous system to pull the hand away, which combines the skeletal and muscular systems. These systems are coordinated with each other. All living things have an inherent tendency to organize and synthesize their independent systems. Failure to do so results in biological death.

There are counterparts in the cognitive domain as well. The infant comes into the world with a set of limited but functional schemes such as sucking, tracking with the eyes, grasping, and some twenty-five other primary reflexes. As maturation occurs and biological and psychological structures begin to change, organization tends to relate different schemes to one another, expanding the individual's potential for successful intellectual growth.

One of the early signs that the young child is beginning to act on the environment (rather than the environment acting on the child), occurs when he or she begins to coordinate different schemes (such as grasping and looking). With the coordination of schemes successful behavior begins.

Organization is not something that is learned, but is a functioning, vital component of the living system. Organization is an important life force that acts as one type of mortar to bond the materials of development together.

Adaptation. *Adaptation* takes place simultaneously with organization. Like organization, adaptation is a process that has its theoretical roots in biology. Adaptation is the individual's adjustment to the environment.

The plant and animal kingdom abound with examples of adaptation (also called adaption). The female cardinal is colored a dull brown (while the male is bright red) so she is minimally conspicuous and in less danger of being killed (a threat to the survival of the species). The beautiful colors of spring and summer flowers attract insects that are part of the reproductive process that takes place through pollination.

Adaptation is a very complex process that involves the modification of the individual or the environment to fit the needs of the individual. The process of adaptation can be broken down into two complementary processes: accommodation and assimilation. Assimilation and accommodation are complementary and both operate simultaneously, yet one can take precedence over the other depending on the demands of the environment or the developmental level of the individual.

Assimilation. *Assimilation* is the process through which the individual incorporates new experiences into already existing schemes or structures. It is the transformational component of Piaget's theory through which all knowledge is acquired. An example of assimilation is the way in which young children place everything in their mouth whether or not it is food. This exemplifies the use of one schema regardless of the demands of the environment. In this case, the child changes the environment to fit his or her internal needs.

When assimilation occurs, the schema into which the new event or experience is being assimilated grows (gets larger) but does not qualitatively change. When a young child classifies lions, tigers, and foxes into the same general class of "kitties," he or she is adjusting an experience (seeing lots of animals that look like "kitties") to fit a preexisting notion or schema of four-legged furry animals.

Assimilation is such a pervasive process that Piaget has identified three different kinds, all facilitating development in different ways (Piaget, 1952). *Reproductive* or *functional assimilation* is the tendency to repeat certain actions. It is as if the child is repeating things for the sake of practice until the behavior is sufficiently integrated into the schemes that are already available. In fact, the behaviors that are repeated most frequently are those that are immature or underdeveloped. This type of assimilation accounts for young children's repetitive behaviors, which to untrained eyes may seem to be only repeated random movements. The saying "practice makes perfect" characterizes even the beginning of intellectual development.

The second kind of assimilation is called *generalizing assimilation.* The child will grasp a finger, a rattle, or a clump of hair to exercise a particular schema, and these schemes are exercised on new objects, thereby broadening the schema's utility. In other words, the specific schema tends to generalize to other objects.

Finally, the third type of assimilation is *recognitory assimilation.* Here the child discriminates between those stimuli that are adaptive or useful and those that are not. For example, any child will suck repeatedly on a variety of objects (indicating reproductive and generalizing assimilation), but will focus more intently when that sucking has a different purpose (such as during feeding).

These three different types of assimilation correspond to three important outcomes. They are (1) the repetition of patterns of behavior; (2) the generalization of those patterns of behavior to new objects; and (3) the differentiation between different objects depending on the individual's needs. All three of these outcomes are critical to the successful transition from stage to stage.

Accommodation. The counterpart of assimilation, *accommodation,* is the process of modifying existing schemes to satisfy the requirements of a new experience. Accommodation is the process through which new schemes are formed. When the child accommodates, a qualitative change in the type of schemes occurs. When the child says "kitty," he or she may be corrected by some adult saying, "No, it is a lion." The child can do one of three things: reject this explanation and employ his or her own rules of logic (even if they seem illogical to the adult); form a new schema called "lions"; or expand the already existing schema of "kitty" to include other types of kitties and thereby make it qualitatively different from the previous schema. Accommodation is the process through which changes in the child's intellectual development correspond to reality.

The Relationship Between Assimilation and Accommodation. Assimilation and accommodation are inextricably bound together. Yet it is an outstanding characteristic of the very young child that these two functions are not yet complementary but almost indistinguishable and undifferentiated from one another. The child at a very early stage of development does not possess even the rudimentary ability to separate the object of a certain activity from the activity itself. In other words, the two functions of grasping a new object and adjusting the grasp to fit that object are initially fused with one another. This state of affairs corresponds with what Piaget calls the beginning of *egocentrism*, or a preoccupation with one's own views.

Another important point about the relationship between assimilation and accommodation is that one does not occur earlier (in a developmental sense) than the other. It might be convenient to think that the individual first tries to fit a new experience into an already existing structure (assimilation) and if this is not successful tries to change the existing schema to meet the demands of the environment (accommodation). But in fact these are not sequential processes but simultaneous ones. Elements of a new experience are assimilated and accommodated simultaneously. There is usually something familiar about a new experience, which allows the assimilation of some part of that experience, and something different as well, which places new demands on already existing structures. People generally do not attend to those things that have little inherent interest, nor do they understand those that are too far removed from already existing patterns of behavior.

Finally, assimilation and accommodation comprise the process of *adaptation*. Adaptation and organization are called *functional invariants* (or invariant functions) to denote that these processes are operative at all levels of development and never vary in their general purpose (Piaget, 1952).

Egocentrism

Egocentrism can be defined as the inability to differentiate the subject and the object from each other. Depending on the specific stage of development, this lack of differentiation assumes different forms. As each of the major stages of Piaget's theory is described, the different forms that egocentrism takes will be described. For now, however, a mention of some general observations about egocentrism will serve as a useful orientation.

The failure to differentiate between the subject and the object involves different elements of the child's life space at different developmental levels. Whether it is the inability to differentiate the self from surrounding objects (a type of early infantile egocentrism), or reality from fantasy (a type of adolescent egocentrism), egocentrism encourages assimilation rather than accommodation, because the child focuses on his or her own thoughts or feelings and uses his or her own knowledge as a base of operation (Flavell, 1963). The egocentric child cannot take the perspective of another person (this is especially characteristic of the young child), and "assimilates experiences from the world at large into schemas derived from his own immediate world, seeing everything in relation to himself" (Beard, 1969, p. 25).

Egocentrism, however, should not be confused with selfishness. The selfish child is aware of other people's feelings, but the egocentric child is not. Furthermore, the type of behavior shown by egocentric adults (preoccupation with the self) should not be confused with the construct that egocentrism represents. Egocentric adults focus on their own needs. Elkind (1974) believes that the study of egocentrism may provide a crucial link in the understanding between the cognitive (or thinking) and affective (or feeling and attitudinal) elements of development.

Egocentrism is a powerful construct that characterizes each of the periods Piaget describes. It affects the way the developing child approaches the world, what he or she constructs from the information taken in, and influences development in such areas as interpersonal relations, attitude formation, and social adjustment.

The Sequential Component

One of Piaget's most outstanding contributions to the understanding of cognitive development is his description of a set of qualitatively distinct yet interrelated stages. The notion of stages, however, is not unique to Piaget. The use of stages as an organizing unit (infant, teenager, and so on) sometimes reflects the most important developmental changes that occur during a certain period of time. The theories of Gesell, Freud, and Erikson are excellent examples of this, and in many ways their notion of stages is not different from Piaget's, except for one critical point. Where Gesell and Freud employed the concept of stages in a descriptive sense (a detailed account of what occurs when), Piaget's notion of stages, like Erikson's, is closely related to the concept of structural change. Hence Piaget's stages are models, not just descriptions.

Gesell's notion of stages was based on a description of behavior. On the other hand, Piaget's theory stresses the process that goes on during a stage, not its content. As a biologist, Piaget strongly believed that cognitive mechanisms are an extension of already existing biological systems. Hence the parallel between physical stages of growth and psychological or structural change becomes a plausible and attractive way of conceptualizing development.

Before Piaget's four stages of intellectual development are described, it is important to understand the assumptions of the stage notion of development. Figure 9-2 is an illustration of the progress that one individual might make as he or she advances from one developmental stage to the next. Although Piaget is being

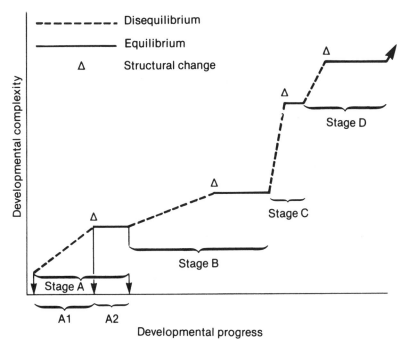

Figure 9-2. The transition from disequilibrium to equilibrium.

discussed in particular, the following eight statements are characteristic of the cognitive-developmental approach in general. In Figure 9-2, the horizontal axis represents the degree of developmental progress, which in most cases roughly corresponds to age. The general form of the curve within the graph suggests that developmental complexity is positively related to developmental progress. As development progresses, the process tends to be accompanied by (to subsume) increasingly complex structural change.

1. The organism begins in a state of disequilibrium. The dotted lines in Figure 9-2 represent periods of disequilibrium in which a sharp discrepancy exists between the internal organization of the organism and environmental demands. There is a conflict between what the organism can do and what it is expected or needs to do. Disequilibrium is the most important motivational factor in Piaget's theory of intellectual development, and it is absolutely necessary if development is to proceed.

2. States of equilibrium do not last as long as states of disequilibrium. The developing organism is in states of equilibrium for less time than in states of disequilibrium. Hence the solid lines in the figure (it projects onto the developmental progress axis) are shorter than the dotted lines, which represent disequilibrium. (Compare the length of lines A1 and A2, for example.) If the process of equilibration is the primary motivator, one might theorize that the organism spends more time in a state of imbalance than in a state of stability. Certain periods of growth (such as adolescence) are characterized by abrupt changes in such things as physical appearance and attitude. These changes, however, are usually preceded by some stability.

3. The organism does not remain in a state of equilibrium or disequilibrium for equal amounts of time at each stage, nor is the rate of progress from stage to stage constant. Individual variability is an important factor in understanding the developmental process. Not only are the dotted and solid lines within any one stage different in length (statement 2), but the slopes of the dotted lines (indicating the rate of disequilibrium) are different as well.

4. Disequilibrium terminates in structural change. The dotted lines have a positively accelerating slope that ends in structural change indicated by a delta (Δ). This structural change places the organism in a position of stability, but the stability lasts for only a short period of time. How long this period of equilibrium lasts (or the length of the period of disequilibrium) depends on a host of related influences that will be discussed later.

5. From the beginning of structural change through the end of the next period of disequilibrium, a trend from maximum stability to maximum growth is represented. The general development progression is from disequilibrium to structural change to equilibrium, and the cycle then begins anew. Within this cycle, the maximum amount of change or development that can take place does take place. This cycle repeats itself in an effort to satisfy the changing structural needs of the organism.

6. The order of stages is fixed. Stage A always precedes Stage B, Stage B always precedes Stage C, and so on. Piaget used the word "invariant" (meaning uniform or lacking variability) to emphasize the point that these stages occur in all individuals in a fixed sequence. Piaget stresses the order and not the rate of progress.

7. Individual stages of development cannot be skipped or omitted from the sequence. Stages occur in a fixed sequence, and an individual cannot progress from an earlier stage of development to a later one by skipping an intermediate stage. According to the illustration, each stage leads into the following one, with no irregular or discrete jumps from stage to stage possible. This does not mean, however, that once individuals pass through a certain stage they no longer possess the structural characteristics that defined an earlier stage.

8. Successive stages are qualitatively different from one another, and later stages are based on the elements and experiences of earlier stages. The reasons that stages of development cannot be skipped is that later stages of development depend on earlier ones for a foundation. For example, in the construction of a new house, pouring the foundation and laying the flooring are separate steps, but it would be impossible to put down a floor where there was nothing to support it. In much the same way, the individual proceeds through a set of stages that are interrelated, and successive stages are a combination of all the characteristics of the earlier stages, plus new additional components.

Figure 9-2 describes progress through a series of stages. Each stage is characterized by a repetition of disequilibrium, equilibrium, and then some degree of structural change. The length of these solid and dotted lines differs in different individuals. It is no surprise that some children develop more sophisticated problem-solving skills earlier than others or that some develop a certain level of social skill later than similarly aged children. Also, the demarcation between periods of disequilibrium and equilibrium are not as abrupt or uneven as Figure 9-2 implies. The figure emphasizes that changes do take place. In reality, the different processes overlap, and some degree of both disequilibrium and equilibrium is present within any stage of development.

The Different Stages of Development

Piaget described four stages of intellectual development:

1. The *sensorimotor stage* (lasting from birth through age two).
2. The *preoperational stage* (lasting from age two to age seven).
3. The *concrete operational stage* (lasting from age seven to age twelve).
4. The *formal operational stage* (lasting from age twelve through adulthood).

Age ranges are specified for convenience. Piaget stresses that these ages represent a normative range and that they are more clearly definable and understandable when their content rather than when they began is examined.

Piaget's notion of stages reflects and emphasizes the structural transitions that take place during different developmental periods, rather than a simple description of different behaviors at different times. Throughout each of these stages there is a continuous interplay between the functional invariants of organization and adaptation. Stages of development are convenient organizers, because they help place behavior at different ages in perspective, but Piaget points out that these stages are not bound by anything other than very general time guidelines. That is, the age range is approximate and should be treated as such. Table 9-1 lists all four of Piaget's stages, the approximate age span, and the major characteristics of each.

Table 9-1   Piaget's Stages of Intellectual Development

Stage	Approximate Age	Characteristics
I. Sensorimotor	*0–2 years*	Intelligence based on perceptual experiences
1. Reflexive	0–1 month	Reflexes become more efficient; lack of differentiation
2. Primary circular reactions	1–4 months	Repetition of certain pleasureable behaviors and the formation of habits, coordination of reflexes
3. Secondary circular reactions	4–10 months	Intentional repetition of events discovered through chance, notion of cause and effect
4. Coordination of secondary schemes	10–12 months	Application of old schemes to new situations, object permanence, first clear signs of intelligence, instrumental activity
5. Tertiary circular reactions	12–18 months	Discovery of new means and repetition with variation for novelty's sake, experimentation on cause and effect situations, hypothesis testing
6. Symbolic representation	18–24 months	Internalizes actions and begins to think before acting, represents objects and images through imagery, invention of new ideas
II. Preoperational	*2–7 years*	Onset of sophisticated language system egocentric reasoning, thinking is perception bound
III. Concrete operational	*7–11 years*	Thought is reversible, and ability to solve concrete problems develops; conservation becomes operative; logical operations develop; thinking is experience based

WORKSHOP KIDS – EXAMPLES (handwritten annotation)

Table 9-1 Piaget's Stages of Intellectual Development

Stage	Approximate Age	Characteristics
IV. Formal operational	11 years to adulthood	Formulation and testing of hypotheses, abstract thought, deductive reasoning, hypothetico-deductive reasoning, thought no longer perception bound.

The Sensorimotor Stage. The sensimotor stage of development begins at birth (and possibly even conception) with the simple reflexes of the neonate and terminates at around two years of age with the onset of symbolic thought representing early childlike language. Within this stage of development, Piaget documents six separate and independent yet interrelated substages. Through an examination of these individual stages, we can see how the child develops from a relatively passive organism that acts without any systematic goal into a thinking being who shows the beginning elements of intelligence.

Substage 1: The Use of Early Reflexes. The infant's innate equipment and preparation for the world is limited. The child cannot distinguish between his or her action on an object and the object itself and is dependent on reflexive behaviors such as grasping, sucking, and reactions to loud sounds as the primary sources of acquiring knowledge about the world.

Although the infant's behavior during the first month of life is not entirely random, it lacks goal directedness. For example, an infant in this substage will use the same reflex over and over again (demonstrating reproductive assimilation), without any apparent accommodatory change in structure. He or she will suck a blanket or a rag toy in the same way. Similarly, the child may grasp everything within reach and use the same schema (grabbing) again and again.

There are two important characteristics of this substage. First, there is no differentiation between the self and the external world. Second, as the infant has increasing experience using different reflexive schemes, he or she tends to become more adaptive to the increasing demands of the environment. Even at this first stage of sensorimotor development, the basic building blocks of cognitive development—the reflexive schemes—are becoming more complex and adaptive.

Substage 2: Primary Circular Reactions. The stage of primary circular reactions lasts approximately from the first to the fourth month of age and is characterized by what Piaget calls (as borrowed from biologists) *circular reactions*. These are called "primary" circular reactions, because the infant's focus is on its own body rather than on external objects.

The term "circular reaction" means the repetition of a sensorimotor act, such as repeated sucking, grasping, or beating of a block with another block. The purpose of any circular reaction is the modification of existing schemes, which is a hallmark of intellectual development.

During this substage of development the child is adept at demonstrating different reflexes, and these reflexes become coordinated with one another. For example, while tracking an interesting object with the eyes, the child begins to reach out to grasp that object. This substage includes a great deal of trial-and-error learning, and chance becomes an important factor. It should be emphasized that the child is not a conscious learner, and intentionality, a hallmark of what Piaget calls intelligence, is not characteristic of the child's behavior at this stage.

Even though the child is relatively non-goal-directed (as compared to later stages), the coordination of different circular reactions has another impact on intellectual development. Through trial-and-error learning, the child develops some notion of causality. He or she may not be able to identify a specific cause-and-effect relationship, but understanding the idea of cause and effect is initiated.

Substage 3: Secondary Circular Reactions. The major characteristics of this substage is the child's preoccupation with the events and objects located outside of his or her body (hence the term "secondary"). The child tries to produce experiences and make them last. It is as if the child has found something new and wants to practice it over and over. This may indeed be the case, because this is a time when functional or reproductive assimilation is a major operating force. During this period the child's development reflects Piaget's assertion that the child's world is constructed, not given.

The primary distinction between primary and secondary circular reactions is the focus of the child's behavior. During the primary circular reaction substage, the child is concerned with objects and events in and around his or her body, but during the secondary circular reaction substage, the concern is with objects and events that are external to his or her body. The child is becoming less self-centered (or less egocentric) and more dependent on things other than him or herself as a source of information about the world. Behavior during this substage can be characterized by a type of early intentionality, in which there is some awareness of what factors cause an event to occur. "The accomplishments of this stage . . . constitute the first definite steps towards intentionality or goal orientation" (Flavell, 1963, p. 102). Keep in mind, however, that this is not the stage at which actual intentional behaviors occur.

Intentionality is an important component of Piaget's theory because intelligence is equated with intentional or goal-directed behavior. During the third substage of intellectual development, the child begins to understand that certain events in the outside world are under the control of the child's own behavior, but true intentionality is not achieved until the next substage. Through the process of trial and

· Elements·
· LANDMARKS
· STAGES
· DEFINITIONS
· CULTURALLY INFLUENCED
· TESTING PROCEDURES.

error, the child is exposed to a variety of combinations of cause-and-effect situations. Given the structural changes that are always occurring, these cause-and-effect experiences eventually take on meaning for the child.

Substage 4: Coordination of Secondary Schemes. Two major landmarks take place during the tenth and twelfth months of the child's cognitive development. The first is when the child begins to use already learned (sometimes called habitual) behavior patterns and more than one schema to prolong events that are novel or unusual. For example, if the child is faced with a new type of problem, he or she will repeatedly try to solve it in spite of barriers that are put in the way. The substage 3 infant, who does not have as clear a picture of what cause and effect represents (Piaget uses the term "means-end"), would be less likely to persevere. The substage 4 child, however, has a clear concept of what causes things to happen, and Piaget believes this to be the first true sign of intelligence.

The second major landmark is the infant's realization that objects in the environment are clearly separate from him or herself and have distinct qualities of their own. This happens, in part, as a result of increasingly sophisticated motor skills that enable the infant to examine objects more intimately for a longer period of time. Along with this increased perceptual awareness comes the development of *object permanence*. Up to this point, anything removed from the child's immediate perceptual field (hidden under a pillow, for example) would no longer exist. The child equates "out of sight" with "out of mind."

The concept of the object is now developed so that the child is aware that if something is removed from the visual field, it does not actually disappear. This is a landmark in the child's cognitive development, because he or she is no longer tied to the perceptual characteristics of a situation in order to act.

Substage 5: Tertiary Circular Reactions. During this substage of development, there is a reversal of the means-end relationship that characterized substage 4. Where the younger child uses old means in new settings, the substage 5 child (twelve to eighteen months) uses new means to solve new problems. Here the child is examining the cause-and-effect relationship between events through experimentation, sometimes called "groping accommodation" (Flavell, 1963). Events are repeated, but beyond this simple repetition comes a degree of variation and the discovery of new properties and experiences.

These reactions are called *tertiary* to distinguish them from the two earlier types of circular reactions. During primary circular reactions, the child was concerned with actions in and around his or her own body. During secondary circular reactions, the child focused on objects in the external world. In tertiary circular reactions the child is engaged in experimental thinking. He or she hypothesizes about the relationship between new causes and their eventual effects.

Again, increased motor skills are a contributing factor in this more sophisticated relationship between the individual and the object. This is the age when most children begin to walk. When a child begins to have a high degree of mobility, the possibilities for new experiences are greatly increased. The child is in much better control of the environment and demonstrates this by effectively manipulating it to ends that to him or her are novel.

Substage 6: Symbolic Representation. During this last substage (eighteen to twenty-four months), there is a major breakthrough in the child's ability to understand relationships between objects and the activities associated with the objects without direct experience or experimentation. The child begins to represent events internally, and *symbolic thought* becomes the primary mode of thinking. This is a time of incredible growth in the child's qualitative capacities, for he or she begins to invent new ideas rather than simply reformulate old ones. Piaget refers to this period as the stage of *reprsentational intelligence* (Piaget, 1952) because the individual begins to represent external events internally. The beginnings of language (a type of symbolic thought) become apparent. Object permanence is now fully operative and the child is on the doorstep of sophisticated linguistic skills.

Egocentrism during the Sensorimotor Stage. If young infants could verbalize their thoughts, they might say something like, "My world is my actions." Sensorimotor children are unable to differentiate themselves from the external objects that they encounter. As Elkind describes it, the primary developmental task at this stage is the conquest of the object (Elkind, 1974). By this by means the distinction between what constitutes the real world and what constitutes the operations and thoughts internal to the child. In some ways this is almost a distinction between reality and fantasy.

The newborn infant is basically a mass of uncoordinated reflexes who has basic needs that must be met. Indeed, our society is structured (or should be) so that the well-cared-for infant can be fed when hungry and changed when wet and uncomfortable. The infant's helplessness, however, points out that it is totally egocentric. The theme of *undifferentiatedness* first becomes manifest in the sensorimotor stage of development with the child's inability to separate physical self from objects.

Summary Description of the Sensorimotor Stage. The term that Piaget used to describe the first of the four periods of his theory—"sensorimotor"—communicates the essence of what happens to the child from birth through the second year. Intelligence and action during this period are the result of perceptual and sensorimotor based experiences. The most crucial component of a child's development is the opportunity to act on the environment in any unrestricted way.

During the first month of the infant's life, behavior is characterized by reflexive activity, with no differentiation between "self" and experience and things that are "not self." In the second substage of intellectual development, an increased separation between these behaviors becomes apparent (hence the idea of a circular reaction). During the third substage of the sensorimotor period, the child focuses on objects and experiences external to his or her own body and repeats certain things over and over again as if to practice them. During substage 4 the child applies already existing means to new problems and forms an object concept that enables him or her to realize that objects removed from the perceptual field (out of sight, for example) do not acutally cease to exist. In substage 5, increased motor skills— such as walking—aid the child in his or her exploration of the world. The child has more control over the environment and begins to experiment with no apparent goal other than the process of experimentation itself. The child might take a mouthful of milk and let it seep out of the mouth at different rates. Such behavior is sure to have some results on the parents' behavior and is one way for the child to gain control over a previously alien environment. The last substage during this period of development occurs when the child becomes capable of representing objects internally, without any need for direct experience. This is the beginning of representational intelligence, symbolic thought, and language.

The Preoperational Stage. The young infant develops from an almost entirely reflexive organism to one that can intentionally manipulate symbols that represent objects in the real world. Imagine the tremendous amount of growth that is now possible, given these new tools for exploring and experiencing the environment. The child is no longer bound by perceptual experiences but can go beyond what the environment offers. The child is progressing from a sensorimotor type of intelligence to a symbolic type of intelligence. Whereas the first was limited to direct interactions with the environment, and second is characterized by a manipulation of symbols that represent the environment: thus the beginnings of language. The onset and development of language is the most significant event during this stage.

The Importance of Operations in Piaget's Theory. An operation is an action wherein an object or experience that was transformed can be returned to its original form. An operation is reversible. It is also an action that is performed mentally (Piaget, 1950b). The preoperational child is incapable of performing such operations and this characteristic is a primary distinction between the preoperational child and the child in a more advanced stage of cognitive development.

The processes of addition and subtraction represent a good example of an operation. The fact that 2 plus 4 equals 6 is logically the same operation as 6 minus 4 equals 2 may seem obvious, but it is not obvious to the preoperational child. The preoperational child cannot mentally rearrange a sequence of events into the reverse order from that in which they originally occurred. One of the primary outcomes of Piaget's long and intensive research into this lack of operationality is the child's failure to conserve the relationship between different dimensions of an event. If one dimension of an experience changes (such as the shape of one of two pieces of clay), the preoperational child cannot understand how the mass, weight, or another dimension can remain the same. Technically, this is the invariance of one dimension while there is a change in another.

Figure 9-3 illustrates three common conservation tasks. In a conservation of number task, the child is presented with a row of objects (such as a row of pennies), as illustrated in Figure 9-3a. He or she is asked to construct a second row of pennies to match the first row exactly. What the child is being asked to do is to establish a type of perceptual equivalence between the two sets of objects. After this task is completed, the experimenter changes the spacing between the pennies in one row so that one row is shorter than the other. When asked which row then has more pennies, the child confuses the dimension of length with that of number and says that the row that is longer has more pennies in it. This is clearly a contradiction of what the child did earlier, when he or she matched each of the pennies in his or her own row with each of those of another row. Yet now the child believes that one row has more pennies than the other. This is a good example of how the child's use of language at this age reflects an immature level of thought.

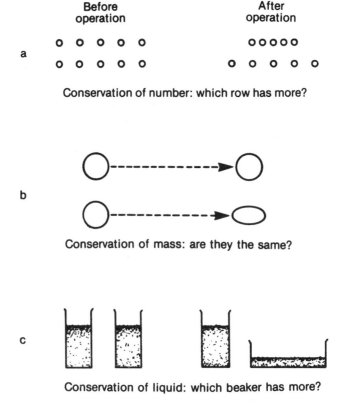

Conservation of number: which row has more?

Conservation of mass: are they the same?

Conservation of liquid: which beaker has more?

Figure 9-3. Different kinds of conservation.

Conservation of mass tasks (Figure 9-3b) are similar in design. For example, a child will be given two balls of clay that are exactly the same shape and size. The experimenter forms one of the balls into another shape (from a circle to a sausage, for example). Again, the child believes that the mass of the two are now different and that one is "more" than the other. In fact, the child cannot reverse the process that has taken place or mentally make the comparison between the two shapes before and after the manipulation took place.

Finally, as the last example, conservation of liquid provides a dramatic demonstration of how the preoperational child is lacking in the ability to reverse an event mentally. In this task (Figure 9-3c), the child is shown two beakers of water, both containing the same amount of liquid and having the same shape. The child is then shown two empty beakers, a tall narrow one and a short wide one. In full view of the child, water from one of the original containers is poured into the tall narrow beaker, while water from the other original container is poured into the wide shallow beaker. As a result of this, it appears to the child as if there are different amounts of liquid in the containers. The child's preoperational logic dictates that the difference that now is apparent is a result of water being lost (or gained) and not a result of a change in the shape of the containers.

The preoperational child cannot conserve or understand that just because one dimension of an experience is changed, other qualities of that experience do not have to change as well. The preoperational child has a difficult time simultaneously relating two dimensions of a situation to one another. For example, the preoperational child cannot understand how she can be both a "good girl" and someone's "little sister." In other words, the child does not yet possess the cognitive structures necessary to recognize that a change in one dimension of an experience does not necessarily mean a change in the others. Because of this, the child is still somewhat perceptually bound and cannot manipulate symbolic elements in a reversible sense. In essence, the child believes that what you see is what you get.

Egocentrism in the Preoperational Stage. The most important aspect of this phase of intellectual development is the child's increasing use of symbols to represent objects and the development of a complex and sophisticated system of language. It is no surprise that the primary task the child is faced with in the developmental course of egocentricity is the *conquest of the symbol*. Now that the child has been separated from the world of sensorimotor egocentrism and can distinguish between self and external objects, the next task is differentiating between symbols and their referents. In other words, the child's world is a function of the way in which the child chooses to represent the world. The child cannot assume another perspective than his or her own, and it is doubtful whether or not the child even knows another perspective exists.

Piaget and his colleagues developed an ingenious task called the three mountain task (Piaget & Inhelder, 1956) to examine this lack of perspective by preoperational children. Figure 9-4 shows a physical setup similar to the task they used; the top view, and the four side views (A, B, C, and D) of a table with three dimensional set of "mountains" on it. Depending on one's position around the table, one sees a different view of the three mountains. For example, view A reflects a configuration seen from seat A. A child is seated at one of four positions, and a doll is placed at one of the other positions. The child is then asked to choose the picture that the doll sees from a set of pictures representing all possible views. If, for example, the doll was sitting in seat D, the correct response would be view D. Preoperational children almost invariably choose the view that represents their own position rather than that of the doll. This illustrates that the preoperational child cannot assume a perspective other than his or her own. In contrast, the older child almost never fails at this task, and, if incorrect, the error will not be egocentric but non-egocentric, such as choosing view C or view B.

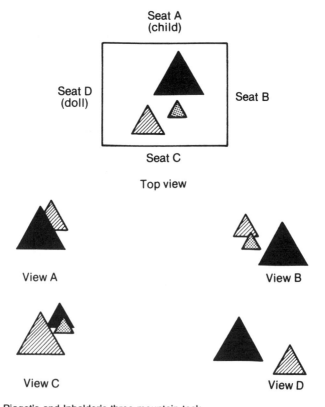

Figure 9-4. Piaget's and Inhelder's three-mountain task.

Another dimension of preoperational egocentrism is the way that language is used. Although Piaget believes that language is a necessary prerequisite for the development of adaptive behavior, language alone is not sufficient. Language has some obvious advantages over sensorimotor functioning, such as the more rapid speed with which events can be processed. However, without the structural changes that take place at this time, language cannot be a primary component of logical thought. Language serves the important function of manipulating and rearranging different symbols (and experiences) without the inefficiency of direct physical activity, but language is restricted by the illogical rules the preoperational child applies to it. The preoperational child uses language in an extreme literal sense. For example, he or she may be confused by a statement such as "He has grown a foot," thinking that indeed someone has actually grown another foot.

The preoperational child also illustrates what Piaget calls *egocentric speech*, in which there is no differentiation between the child and other people. Even though the child is talking with other children, there is a *collective monologue* wherein no meaningful transmission of information takes place. Language progresses during this period from being basically egocentric, where the child's verbalizing has no real communicative purpose (that is, he or she talks at instead of to other people), to *sociocentric* or *socialized* speech, where the communication consists of transmitted information.

Egocentric language parallels the way preoperational children follow rules while playing. Even though they often do not follow the rules, they insist that they are correct. Given that the only set of rules they are aware of is their own, it is logical for them to believe these rules are correct. When two preoperational children play a simple game with each other, each of them changes the rules as they go along to fit his or her personal needs. They are playing for themselves and have no knowledge that a set of outside rules might apply to their behavior.

Summary Description of the Preoperational Stage. The preoperational stage is a distinct turning point in the course of cognitive development. For the first time, thought becomes a symbolic process for understanding the world. The most obvious example of this is the development of language.

The world of the preoperational child is bounded by direct contact with concrete objects. The child benefits most from experiences with nonabstract elements and events, because his or her ability to manipulate events or objects that are not directly tied to perceptual experiences is limited. The child cannot reverse an operation and has difficulty understanding the importance of cause-and-effect relationships in solving certain types of problems.

The preoperational child is in a transitional period. While his or her perspective on the world expands rapidly, there is still some confusion in the evaluation of cause and effect. The child makes inappropriate generalizations and attributes his or her feelings to inanimate objects, assuming for example that clouds cry to make rain.

The Concrete Operational Stage. Up to the age of seven years, the child's cognitive capabilities are characterized by three attributes: the inability to assume another perspective (egocentrism), the centering on only one dimension of an experience rooted in perceptual information (centration), and the inability to perform an operation requiring reversibility. During the stage of concrete operations, these three attributes change in structure, and this change represents a dramatic transition from illogically based thought to logically based thought.

The term "preoperational" defined the child who is in a stage prior to the development of operations, with conservation problems as an example of this lack of cognitive maturity. The concrete operational child, on the other hand, can conserve, perform certain operations, and conquer a variety of cognitive tasks the preoperational child cannot.

The primary reason that this stage is called *concrete* is that most of the child's operations at this point are still tied to concepts that are bound by the limits of perception (including those concepts with which the child has had some direct experience). For example, the child can perform simple operations such as subtracting one class of objects from another when the materials are available to see or manipulate. However, the child cannot perform certain operations that are purely verbal without the benefit of previous experience. The problems are too abstract. So even though the child possesses a new set of more advanced cognitive structures, he or she cannot really escape the limits of perception.

Classification. The concrete operational child can create hierarchies of different classes, and understand the relationship between the members of these classes. For example, the child can understand the two major classes of animals and plants that belong to the larger (or supraordinate) class called "living things" and understands that "living things" can in turn be reduced to two subcategories called "animals" and "plants" (notice the reversibility). Understanding this *hierarchy of classes* is an important accomplishment, since it marks the transition between preoperational and operational thought. The child is beginning to understand the relationship of the elements in a class (plants and animals) to the class itself (living things).

Another example is the task that Piaget frequently used in his research. Imagine a group of objects that differ in characteristics such as color or shape (twenty red wooden blocks and ten blue wooden blocks). The entire group of blocks is physically separated into two groups by color. When asked if there are more red things or wooden things, the preoperational child cannot perform the logical operation of the addition of two subclasses and is tied to the perceptual experience associated with the color of the blocks rather than the general category of blocks (wooden). The concrete operational child, however, performs this task readily.

Operations. Piaget has defined four properties of an operation (Piaget, 1950b).

   1. *Operations are reversible.* ✓

The red blocks plus the blue blocks make up the general class of wooden blocks, and if the red blocks are taken away only the blue blocks will remain. That is, x (red blocks) $-x'$ (blue blocks) $= y$ (all blocks).

In this example, y represents a new class of objects, those that are wooden, are blocks, and are either red or blue. This type of equivalence symbolizes the majority of addition and subtraction problems that the early concrete operational child is expected to be able to solve.

   2. *An operation assumes that some type of conservation is taking place.* ✓

The primary characteristic of conservation is maintaining the equivalence between two objects even though one dimension of the object undergoes some change. In this case, regardless of the number of blue versus red blocks, they are all members of the same general class of wooden blocks.

   3. *An operation never exists alone.* ✓

This is almost necessary for definition, because an operation consists of the reversibility of a process. If it is true that all the blue blocks and all the red blocks equal all of the blocks, all the blocks minus the red blocks must equal the blue blocks. Another reason that an operation never exists alone is that it is a component of a structure that consists of many different operations and schemes that are related to each other. This is in part what makes the transition from one stage of cognitive development to another so exciting an aspect of human development.

   4. *Operations are internalized actions that can be carried out in thought as* ✓ *well as in action.*

Although the concrete operational child can solve problems through the use of mental operations, he or she still has to have some action-oriented referent in order to successfully perform the task. The concrete operational child cannot deal with hypothetical or purely verbal problems without any perceptual reference point.

Seriation. Another important characteristic of concrete operational thought is the ability to *seriate* or to order a series of events in succession. For example, a child is given a set of six cylinders of different heights. Without "hands on" examination (but with the cylinders in direct sight) the child can order them according to their height and can surmise correctly that if the five-inch canister is larger than the four-inch canister, and the four-inch canister is larger than the three-inch canister, then, by equivalence, the five-inch canister is larger than the three-inch one. That is, if $A > B$ and $B > C$, and $A > C$. For the first time, the child can mentally manipulate the relationship between objects. In constrast, the preoperational child could not successfully order a set of objects along a dimension such as size. The schema for size at the earlier age is simply not yet operative, let alone the operations for understanding the relative equivalence between pairs of objects of different heights.

Egocentrism during the Concrete Operational Stage. The outstanding characteristic of the concrete operational child's egocentricity is the "lack of differentiation between assumption and fact" (Elkind, 1974, p. 79). Concrete operational children are more likely to alter the facts of a situation than to alter their hypotheses about that situation. In this sense they are rigid and restricted. They cannot separate the perceptual qualities of an experience from the reality of the situation. This is an interesting type of egocentrism, because the major discrepancy for the preoperational child was between self and others, which now parallels the discrepancy between self and fact. Even though concrete operational children are less self-centered, they are concerned about the correctness of their own assumptions in comparison to the demands of the real world.

In his description of concrete operational egocentrism, Elkind (1974) describes *assumptive realities* as a strategy used by the child to offset the discrepancy that exists between assumption and fact. In general, an assumptive reality is a child's changing of facts to fit a hypothesis regardless of the presence of clear contradictory evidence. For example, if a child has a hypothesis as to why changing the length of a watch chain will decrease the arc of its swing, he or she will modify the reality of the situation rather than change his or her hypothesis. One of the most striking examples of an assumptive reality pointed out by Elkind is called *cognitive conceit*. In this case, concrete operational egocentrism leads children to believe that they are smarter than their parents. The child believes that parents are not bright or powerful in the sense of knowing what to do. Such cognitive conceit is a part of the child's awareness that parents are not superhuman but have flaws and make mistakes much as anyone. The concrete operational child, however, assumes that he or she does not make any of those same mistakes.

Summary of the Concrete Operational Stage. The concrete operational period of Piaget's theory represents a transition between the preoperational and formal operational stages. Although the preoperational child does not yet possess the structures necessary to reverse an operation, the concrete operational child's logic allows such operations, but only on a concrete level. The child now is a *sociocentric* being (as opposed to an egocentric one), who is aware that others have a perspective on the world that is different from his own. Interestingly, the concrete operational child may not be aware, however, of what the content of that perspective is (an awareness that comes during the next stage of cognitive development).

Concrete operational children lack the ability to perform an operation that is not tied to a perceptual experience. They do not wonder about abstract issues such as liberty or the first amendment, because these are difficult concepts to tie to concrete experiences. Educational strategies aimed at the concrete operational child should not assume that the child can learn without the benefit of action-oriented experience. Although concrete operational children can solve problems that are abstract to a limited degree, they are still dependent on perceptual information to formulate and test hypotheses. Finally, the stage of concrete operations has the characteristic of reversibility while the preoperational stage does not. The concrete operational child understands that the order of an operation can be reversed and the characteristics of an earlier situation recovered.

The Formal Operational Stage. This final stage of intellectual development in Piaget's theory covers the age range from around 11 to 15 years. Cognitive development does not cease after the fifteenth year, but any major structural or qualitative changes have hypothetically already occurred. After this time there will be very few new schemes added to the system, the majority of changes that are likely to take place will be modifications of already existing schemes.

The most outstanding difference between the concrete and formal operational stages is that formal operational children are not only bound by perceptual experiences in the here and now but also use past and future deliberations when confronted with new situations. The concrete operational child deals with problems of the present; the formal operational child deals with problems in all time frames.

A second characteristic of this stage is that children begin to function like scientists, and to become capable of (1) accepting assumptions (without any physical evidence to validate the assumptions); (2) developing hypotheses (an "if . . . then" statement or a test of a cause and effect); (3) actual testing of these hypotheses; and (4) reevaluating and restating the hypotheses if the outcomes of the testing are not congruent with earlier assumptions. For the first time, systematic scientific thought replaces the variety of other modes of thinking that were minimally effective but limited the potential for expanded intellectual awareness.

The following problem is one used to demonstrate the way in which formal operational thought differs from earlier stages of cognitive development. Five glasses containing colorless, odorless chemicals are placed before the child. A certain amount of chemical from two of the beakers is poured into an empty glass and the liquid turns yellow. The child is asked to reproduce this color, using any or all combinations of the various liquids. The only thing he or he knows is that the liquid that turned yellow contained chemicals from two out of the five containers.

There are distinct age differences in the approach to solving this problem. Infants up to two years old pay no attention to the problem situation and merely play with the apparatus as toys. Children in the preoperational stage randomly combine chemicals and make no attempt to keep track of what they have done. Between the ages of seven and eleven years, children begin to combine chemicals systematically but tend to become confused after several steps. They too do not maintain a good record of what they have done. Children over eleven years old, however, are able to approach the problem with a logical and complete plan. They take chemicals from the containers two at a time, keeping a record of those that do not work so that they do not repeat themselves. One of the characteristics of this stage of intellectual development is the child's ability to formulate and consider all the possible outcomes of a situation.

During this last stage of cognitive development, there is little differentiation between the organism's structural equipment and the demands of the environment. This does not mean that the child is in a state of equilibrium. In fact, adult and adolescent thinking are characterized by disequilibrium as well as equilibrium, but the pushes, pulls, and transitions that occur do not seem as extreme as when the individual was younger.

The formal operational thinker has the ability to consider many different solutions to a problem before acting on any one. This greatly increases the individual's efficiency, because potentially unsuccessful attempts at solving a problem may be avoided. The formal operational person considers past experiences, present demands, and future consequences in an attempt to maximize the success of adapting to the world.

Egocentrism During the Formal Operational Stage. The type of egocentrism characteristic of this stage results from a lack of differentiation between two different elements: the individual's own thoughts and the thoughts and feelings of others. The formal operational thinker fails to differentiate between his or her own thoughts and what others are thinking. Elkind (1974) believes that the task here should be called the *conquest of thought*, because formal operational children see themselves in the way they think that others do.

For example, many adolescents are self-conscious and sensitive to what others think about their clothes and their physical appearance. There is often no reason to believe that others disapprove of a dress style, but it is difficult to separate one's thoughts from those of others. This might be one reason why teenage children are so susceptible to fads. In addition, this type of egocentrism ensures some degree of social validation, because the child believes that he or she is thinking like others.

Summary Description of the Formal Operational Stage. Teenagers develop what Piaget calls formal operational thinking, which is the systematic analysis, exploration, and solution of problems. Adolescents can comprehend combinations, rearrangements, and permutations of objects and events, which most concrete operational thinkers cannot.

Adolescents differ in other ways from younger children. Most of them can deal skillfully with abstract questions or questions that are contrary to fact, such as "What would have happened if the United States had not entered the Vietnam War?" The more literal, concrete operational child insists that questions of this sort are invalid because (in the context of the question) the war would not have been a factor.

During the teenage years, young people realize that thoughts are private and that no one else knows that they are thinking. They value friendship and sincerity highly and spend time trying to understand people's real motives. They are more aware than the younger child that events can be interpreted in many different ways and then there is no definitive form of truth. They are also sensitive to the discrepancy between reality and ideals. Their understanding of politics and attitudes toward arbitrary rules of conduct are different from those of a younger child. If a rule proves unworkable, they are likely to advocate change, while the younger child recommends increasing the punishment for disobedience as if the rule were inviolate or sacred. In summary, adolescents' thinking is characterized by sensitivity to others, the ability to handle contradiction, and the ability to handle the logic of combinations and permutations. This mature system of thought allows the mastery of complex systems of literature, mathematics, and science. It makes possible the planning of future goals and the integration of past and present into a realistic self-identity, all abilities that are necessary for adultlike socioemotional adjustment.

The Developmental Nature of Equilibrium

As the child develops, he or she tends to move from a general state of less equilibrium to more equilibrium, and his or her interactions with the environment become more broad, generalizable, and stable. The child is learning how to adjust for changes in the environment even before they occur, and in becoming a thinking organism he or she can alter behavior to meet anticipated needs. Thus the child can adapt to a new situation with fewer disturbances to already existing schemes, and in doing so, he or she forms an increasingly solid foundation for future exploration and growth.

At all stages of development, and in all states of equilibrium, the processes of adaptation and organization are operating to seek out new experiences. For this reason, the more active a child is, the more likely a state of coherence and stability will be established. One of the most important educational implications of Piaget's theory is that the action of the child is a primary force.

Equilibrium is a state that the individual actively seeks as part of mastering new parts of the world. It is an underlying theme of all development, and although different stages of development are characterized by differing degrees of equilibration, the process of equilibration is continually going on.

The Developmental Nature of Circular Operations

Earlier in this chapter, three different types of circular reactions were discussed: primary, secondary, and tertiary. A circular reaction is a repetition of sensorimotor acts that facilitate new adaptations. Its purpose is to encourage the individual to reexperience events (some of which occur by chance) and increase the scope of experience. This scope of experience is a crucial variable in cognitive development, because the more active the individual is, the more likely attempts that adaptation will be successful across a wide range of experiences.

Table 9-2 shows a comparison of the three different types of circular reactions, the age at which they occur, the focus of the activity, and an example of the form that the circular reaction might take. Primary circular reactions, which take place during the first through the fourth months of life, have a focus of activity in and around the child's own body. Children at this stage cannot differentiate their activity from the experiences or objects involved in those actions. The child's world is undifferentiated. Sucking for sucking's sake provides a good example of this type of reaction. Such early circular reactions are sensation oriented, and their focus is entirely on the infant's own body.

The onset of secondary circular reactions changes the direction of these repetitive acts from a focus entirely on oneself to behaviors that are now focused outward toward control of objects in the external world. There is no real connection between what the child is doing and the outcomes or consequences of that behavior. In other words, there is no conscious connection between behavior (cause), and the result of that behavior (effect). Piaget viewed the presence of this connection, which he called intentionality, as the first real sign of intelligence. This second type of circular reaction involves direct manipulation of the environment but little if any cognizance that such action has a specific effect on the environment. The child of four through eight months is still considered a naive "scientist" who simply is fascinated by the fact that certain things occur again and again, without any real concern for how or why.

During the twelfth through eighteenth months of life, a dramatic change in the child's cognitive apparatus becomes apparent. The child does not simply repeat activities now for repetition's sake, but begins to vary these repetitions, observe different outcomes, and form a very basic notion of cause and effect. An example of a tertiary circular reaction is when a child drops food to see where it lands. The child varies the amount and type of food to see what the different results are and uses these experiences to understand what the world represents.

The concept of the circular reaction is a good example of the way in which structural change provides the foundation for a later alteration in cognitive development, yet is qualitatively different at different stages.

Table 9-2   Three Types of Circular Reactions

Type of Reaction	Approximate Age	Focus of Activity	Example
Primary	1–4 mo.	In and around infant's body	Sucking
Secondary	4–8 mo.	Directed outward toward the control of the objects in the external world yet no real conscious connection between behavior and result.	Hitting a stick on a pan over and over again.
Tertiary	12–18 mo.	Repetition as in secondary but with some degree of variation. Real exploration begins here.	Playing with food.

Table 9-3 The Developmental Course of Egocentrism

Stage	Goal	Accomplishment
Sensorimotor	Conquest of objects	Object permanence
Preoperational	Conquest of symbols	Language
Concrete operational	Conquest of reality	Cause and effect
Formal operational	Conquest of thought	Distinction between reality and fantasy

The Development Nature of Egocentrism

Table 9-3 shows the developmental course of egocentricity from the sensorimotor stage through formal operational thought. It shows the distinct goal of each type of egocentricity and the task that is associated with the goal. Although different types of egocentricity are characteristic of different stages (and therefore are somewhat stage related), egocentricity is a pervasive construct throughout development.

The sensorimotor child who cannot differentiate between self and physical objects has as a goal the conquest of the objects. The preoperational child who has clearly separated objects from the activity involved with those objects has as a goal the conquest of the symbol. In conquering the symbol and moving on to useful and productive language, the child begins to differentiate between symbols and what they represent. The child's specific concern changes, but the underlying theme is one of the degree of differentiation that exists between two elements.

For the concrete operational child, the goal becomes the conquest of reality, or the ability to differentiate between assumptions and facts. This child can understand that cause and effect is a process but is not interested in the relationship between the elements, because the concrete operational child does not yet have the ability to function independently of experience. Finally, formal operational children cannot differentiate between their own thoughts and the thoughts of others. A good example of this is adolescents' belief that the way they feel about themselves is the way that others feel about them. The goal of the formal operational child is the conquest of thought, or the differentiation between personal thoughts and the thoughts of others. This progression of increasingly abstract differentiation is considered a developmental phenomenon because it occurs at all stages of development and substantively changes in form yet is still based on the same issue: the degree to which the individual can differentiate between certain elements.

A MODEL OF DEVELOPMENT

From what has been discussed in this section on the cognitive-developmental theorist Jean Piaget, the basic information is at hand to construct a model that represents the process of development. Figure 9-5 shows three basic components to Piaget's model of intellectual development: content, structure, and function.

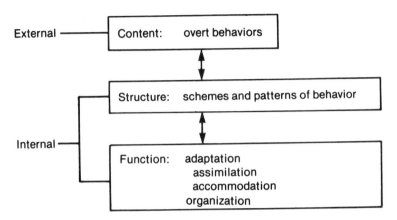

Figure 9-5. Piaget's model of development.

The *content* of a child's intellectual development refers simply to overt behaviors, such as picking up a toy and putting it down, solving a difficult mathematical problem, or using a spoon to eat. Content is determined by many things and is a reflection of other factors, such as cultural demands, environmental constraints, and present level of development. Content does not stand alone and does not determine the level of functioning, but only reflects it.

Function refers to those invariant (never-changing) processes that are characteristic of all levels of development, specifically the processes of adaptation (assimilation and accommodation) and organization. These functional invariants are universal occurrences that produce changes in content. Content changes with development, but function does not. These are the underlying, ever-present operating forces that guide development.

Finally, there is the concept of *structure*, which represents internal schemes and other patterns of behavior. In many ways, structures serve as an interpreter or mediator between function and content, and, as illustrated in Figure 9-5, both content and function are mutually affected by structural organization.

John Flavell (1963) presents an excellent comparison of how these three different components of the model differ from one another.

> To use a simple and somewhat imprecise capsule definition, function is concerned with the manner in which any organism makes cognitive progress; content refers to the external behavior which tells us that functioning has occurred; and structure refers to the inferred organizational properties which explain why this content rather than some other content has emerged (p. 18).

In effect, Flavell is explaining the how (function), what (content), and why (structure) of developmental change.

The most important element of the model, however, is the underlying assumption that development results from the child's active participation and interchange with the environment. Through this interaction, structure and content both undergo dramatic changes, and, in concert with forces such as adaptation and organization, produce what is a fascinating and rich perspective on growth and development.

HOW THEY STUDY DEVELOPMENT

One of the most popular of all the ideas put forth by Piaget is the concept of *egocentrism* and how preoperational children view themselves as the center of their activities.

To examine this concept, Piaget used the three-mountain task described earlier in this chapter. There is, however, some discussion that the three-mountain task might not be appropriate for very young children since they cannot understand the demands of the task. In the following study (Borke 1975), this hypothesis was tested and its implications for understanding cognitive development in young children are discussed.

The subjects in this study were eight three-year-old and fourteen four-year-old children who attended a day care center.

Each child was presented with a set of four three-dimensional displays that included a fire engine, and Grover, a character from "Sesame Street." The children were asked to tell the examiner to predict how the fire engine would look to Grover when he was placed in different positions relative to the fire engine. The four different displays consisted of a practice display, a Piaget mountain-like display, a small lake and a sail boat, a horse and cow, and a small house. The last display consisted of seven miniature animals and people in "natural settings."

An analysis of the children's responses revealed that there were differences in the accuracy of their responses to the different displays but not as a function of age. Although the children were most accurate while responding to the displays with toys, the error rate increased when the original mountain task was used.

Borke's conclusion is an interesting and important one. It appears that if children are presented with age appropriate role playing task, they can demonstrate what is called "perceptual role taking ability." There is at least some reason to believe that such young children are not always primarily egocentric in their thinking and actions.

JEROME BRUNER'S INFORMATION PROCESSING APPROACH

The work of Jean Piaget certainly provided a foundation for understanding the nature of intellectual development. His training in biology, combined with his strong application of philosophy, led to the major contributions in developmental psychology he continued to make up to his death in September 1980.

Other cognitive developmental theorists have used some of Piaget's work as a basis for the development of their own theory regarding how children learn to, and do, think. One such theorist is Oxford University psychologist Jerome Bruner. He is often referred to as a *cognitive structuralist* because, even more than Piaget, he believes that changes in intellectual development result from the modification of internal structures.

The outstanding contribution that Bruner has made is offering a better understanding of how the child's mind operates much like an "information processing system" and, in many ways, like a computer. We'll focus on this analogy again and again in our discussion, which begins with his theoretical outlook.

The Cognitive-Structuralist View

One of the major tenets of Piaget's theory of cognitive development was that development results from a combination of strong maturational forces that are subsequently acted on by environmental influences. The end result of this interaction is qualitative change, such that the young child views the world as being qualitatively different from the older child. We recognized this in an earlier discussion by the young child's lack of ability to conserve or reverse operations.

Bruner's cognitive-structuralist theory assumes somewhat the same approach, but there is one major difference. Bruner believes that cognitive growth "occurs as much from the outside in as from the inside out" (Bruner et al., 1966). Such a statement has some profound implications for the way we understand the growth of children's intellectual skills, as well as how we teach them (and they learn) in both informal and formal settings like the home and school.

Interestingly, some of Bruner's basic assumptions reflect some of the ethological approach we discussed in Chapter 4. He believes that the most unique thing about the developing human is the cultural context in which development takes place. Furthermore, in cultures like ours, that are sophisticated in many ways, the limits of growth depend on how well the culture can assist the process of development. For example, how well does the teaching process bring to the child the challenges and mysteries of the world? And in what way or mode does it present such material? Finally, what expectations for performance and intellectual growth are present? Given that our intellectual development is reflected in and by one culture, it's not a surprise that Bruner beleives we have not even begun to tap this potential.

Not only is some of his theory grounded in part in what ethologists discuss, but a great deal of his work is based on his observations and comparisons of children and animals playing in the same habitat, yet developing distinctly different skills.

He observed films of baboons and of children of the !Kung Bushmen of Kalahari. The baboons seemed to focus primarily on their peers for attention and the practice of certain skills, yet the children maintained an almost constant interaction with adults, and they would play and dance together. He observed how for the children the majority of culturally transmitted values, rituals, and customs are passed on indirectly, with little regard for intentional teaching.

Bruner believes that when such teaching is placed in a more formal context, such as the school system or classroom, it loses some of its effectiveness since the children are being asked to understand events outside of the context within which they occur. We'll see later on in this section how such thoughts about education characterize Bruner as one psychologist whose ideas about intellectual development have been extensively applied in the educational community.

The Child as a Computer. Bruner views the process of intellectual growth or development as one that sees a pattern or system of rules and strategies develop and be used when necessary. Consequently, it's not at all unreasonable within Bruner's theory to think of the child's mind operating in the same way that a sophisticated computer does.

Even the most basic computer requires *input*, does something with that input, and then has a mechanism to output the product such as a video screen. For example, if we program the computer to add two numbers together (input 4 + 5), the result or output is 9. The computer does this by using a set of several different functions that are "internal" or hard wired into the machine. These functions are already present. They come built into the system. They are patterns or systems that the computer uses to solve problems.

In much the same way, the child's mind operates like a computer. At birth, there is a series of adaptive and well-functioning innate behaviors that are hard wired just like the internal contents of a personal computer. Also, like the computer, the child's mind is at a state of readiness to function if the appropriate environment changes sufficiently interesting. We don't "turn on" the child's mind as we do a computer, but parents and teachers do provide certain environmental stimuli that encourage (or discourage) the child to exercise the patterns (or programs) of thinking that help expand the mind by introducing new challenges.

There are other parallels between the child's intellectual development and the operating computer.

Much like Piaget's notion of organization (the tendency for the parts of a system to function together), so Bruner sees the process of *integration* as being crucial to the development of cognitive skills. Integration reflects how thoughts and actions are organized into higher order categories, through the addition and modification of experiences. For example, the very young child becomes a more efficient processor of information when he or she groups objects by general attributes or characteristics (they are all animals) rather than by a singular descriptor ("it's a bear"). Through this process of integration, the mind begins to function in an increasingly efficient manner needing less and less information to make a decision or understand the relationship between objects or events.

This process of integration does not operate, however, in a vacuum. How experiences are represented by the child is influenced by what Bruner calls *conventions* or the social rules established by the child's culture. Part of cognitive development is being able to transmit these rules or conventions through the symbol systems adopted by the culture.

Why are these conventions so important? In order for us to effectively deal with our environment, we need to use a set of symbols that communicates what we want to others. For example, it is conventional in our society to speak English according to a certain set of rules we call grammar or syntax. Should we violate those conventions by speaking incorrectly, or in some cases by speaking a dialect that no one can understand, our speech is not very communicative, and the opportunity for increased cognitive growth is minimized. The necessary input from the environment for growth just will not materialize.

Conventions or social rules do not only apply to the development and use of language. There are many other classes of behavior, such as how we behave interpersonally, that also have a set of conventions attached to them as well. We don't turn our backs on people when they are talking, nor do we interrupt them. It's not only unsocial to do this, but also violates some of the unwritten social mores or conventions the general class of "interaction with other people" behaviors demands. It's Bruner's contention that we adjust our behavior to fit the mores and conventions of our culture and through this process "stretch" our minds to fit these new circumstances.

Although some of the other theorists we have discussed are interested in the *content* of the child's mind, Bruner's interest is in the rules found in a culture that help shape and develop the child's pattern of thinking and problem solving. In fact, Bruner sees the development of intellectual thinking as moving toward more efficient operation. As computer programmers try to write programs using as few statements as possible, so the child's mind changes with development to become more sophisticated and efficient in its problem-solving skills. As we will shortly discuss, this is accomplished by changes in the modes of operating that children use to represent their experiences.

The Child's Representation of the World. Piaget had a great deal to say about the different stages of development that all children pass through during the course of cognitive development.

Although Bruner believes that there are qualitative differences in the way that children view the world, he did not characterize these as stages of development, but rather as *modes of representation*. As such, they are somewhat less age bound than stages and more in line with his belief about the important influences that culture can and does have. As Bruner notes, however, each of these stages do occur in a fixed order, "each depending upon the previous one for its development, yet all remaining more or less intact throughout life" (Bruner, 1966, p. 2).

The first of these three forms of representation is called the *enactive* mode, where the child's intellectual growth is characterized by action. Here, the way the infant learns to experience the world is through direct contact with his or her surroundings.

We know from watching young infants that one way they gain knowledge about the world is by acting on it, whether this means putting things in their mouth or developing the kinds of motor skills it takes to explore their immediate surroundings.

During the second year of life, there is a dramatic change in the strategy that the child used to learn about the world. This new and more powerful way of representation is called *iconic* representation (or the iconic mode), where children use mental images of objects or pictures "in their mind" to represent the acquisition of knowledge and to foster understanding of the world.

This ability to formulate images is a major advance, yet it represents something even more important: the framework for the use of symbols characteristic of the third mode of representation, *symbolic* representation. Here the child formulates the most efficient symbolic system available, that of language. Language is a very flexible and adaptive tool that will now be used to help understand and organize patterns of thinking. Instead of simply imagining objects or experiences, the child can now manipulate these images to form new products. Many of these new products increase the child's control over the environment and facilitate further intellectual development.

We can see then a progression in the development of the child's operating system from one of experiencing the world through direct action such as playing (the enactive mode), to the imagination of new things to experiment with (the iconic mode), through to the most sophisticated level of representation where words and concepts are formed to describe what it is that happened (the symbolic mode).

The Application of Bruner's Theory to Education

The most widespread application of Bruner's work has been in the education of young children. Before we discuss what he considers some of the essential elements of this application, let's briefly discuss how he views the role of learning in cognitive development. You should keep in mind that, unlike Piaget, Bruner places a strong emphasis on the role of the environment and discusses the effects of learning within that context.

Like many other cognitive theorists, Bruner believes that we are genetically "wired" with certain basic capabilities, such as discriminating sounds, visually following a moving object, and responding to other changes in the environment as well.

A primary focus of the role that learning plays within Bruner's theory is that of *readiness*. We have already mentioned the concept of readiness when we discussed Arnold Gesell's notion of how children must be biologically ready before they can advance to the next stage of development. In the same sense, Bruner's idea of *readiness for learning* applies to both the learning and development of the young child. He extends the importance of readiness beyond Gesell's application to biological growth by including changes in cognitive functioning as well.

Bruner believes that at different stages along the developmental continuum from primarily enactive processing of the world to primarily symbolic processing, children are ready for different things at different times. This premise led Bruner to believe that the "tasks of teaching a subject to a child at any particular age is one of representing the structure of that child's way of viewing things" (Bruner, 1966, p. 33.).

This is especially strong language for an educational community that at one time (and to some extent still does) believed that learning certain subject matters can only take place when the child reaches a certain age, regardless of his or her level of development. In other words, the child needs to adapt to the instructional method, instead of the method being adapted to the child's needs.

The Role of Teaching. We have mentioned several times in our discussion of Bruner's view of cognitive development that culture plays a very significant role. For the child, a major part of his or her years from toddlerhood through young adulthood are spent in school. To understand how Bruner sees the relationship between intellectual growth and the role that schools and the teacher plays, let's examine six characteristics of growth detailed by Bruner (1966).

First, Bruner believes that *intellectual growth is accompanied by an increased ability to represent and understand the environment*. We mentioned several times that the highest form of representation, that of symbolic representation and the use of language, is essential for higher level intellectual functioning to take place. With more advanced modes of representation, there is more room for additional growth.

Second, *intellectual growth depends on the use of a "storage system" to remember objects, events, and experiences*. The nature of this storage system is in part formed by the demands of the environment. For example, if a child is trying to understand the relationship between a set of objects, the categories he or she uses to classify them will probably be determined by the set of objects itself rather than some outside criterion. At the least, this says that it is essential to provide children with extensive experiences in a variety of settings. The logic is that the

more experiences children have in different settings, the more adaptable and trans-
ferable across setting these developing storage systems will be.

Next, *the key to increased intellectual growth is the use of language.* For
Bruner, language represents the use of symbol system. Growth of the child's mind
can take place using other symbol systems as well, but above all, the system must
be logically organized so that the child can, if necessary, be aware of logical
inconsistencies in his or her thinking. For example, when the young toddler sees
a cow and calls it a dog because it has four legs and a tail, the correction from the
parent "no, that's a cow" needs to be understood in order for it to further the
child's intellectual growth. In the same sense, the parent needs to understand the
nature of the child's error of thinking.

Fourth, *the growth of the child's intellect is a reflection of the interaction
between the child and the teacher.* Here the child's role as the developing individual
should suggest to the teacher ways of organizing material to facilitate the child's
development as well as his or her learning. It's important to note that the word
teacher does not refer only to the school-based person, but to anyone who comes
in contact with the child as a socializing agent.

Five, *the use of symbol system (usually language) greatly enhances the effectiveness of teaching and subsequent learning.* Symbolic reasoning is the highest
form of representation discussed by Bruner, and one that is best characterized by
the use of a sophisticated symbol or language system. Bruner contends, however,
that it is not just the development of language that parallels cognitive growth, but
that the use of language enhances cognitive development.

Language is like the set of tools we use to build a house, with the final structure
representing another step in the development of intellectual competence. Like a
hammer, we can use language to build something new to us. For example, the
young child uses language to explore new relationships between things. The little
boy might want to know why leaves turn color in the fall, and then follow that up
with another question of the "what if" type. A more sophisticated use of language
tools to promote intellectual growth would be when the child uses an "if . . . then
. . . because" progression of statements. Such use encourages the child to adjust
his or her thought system to fit the content of the question that reflects conditions
in the environment.

In any case, the use of language as a tool for expanding the mind as well as
communicating to others is significant change in the child's cognitive development.

Finally, *the growing child learns to deal with several alternative events at the
same time.* To return for a moment to our analogy between the developing child's
mind and the computer, a more efficient way of processing information is accompanied by an ability to process more than one thing at a time. So the child who
can attend to more than one dimension of an event, choose those that have value,
and make some decision as to what alternative is most attractive, is functioning in

a much more efficient way than the younger child who can't keep track of simultaneous changes across more than one dimension.

Applying Theory to Instruction

Bruner's theory has some clear consequences for the design and implementation of instruction.

To begin with, we must remember that it is his belief that readiness for learning is crucial to the success of the developmental and learning process, but that the environment (represented by the culture, the classroom, and the teacher) must also be suited to the child's level of readiness.

The first task is to clearly identify what the concepts are that must be taught to the child. For example, the second grader might be expected to work in the area of adding and subtracting one- and two-digit numbers. Often problems in teaching arise because teachers themselves are unclear as to what they should be teaching, or what their substantive goals are as far as content is concerned.

Next, the teacher needs to consider the child's level of readiness, so that the material presented to the child will not be too difficult as to be beyond his or her ability (or level of readiness). At the same time the material must be different enough from previous work to hold the student's attention. Perhaps the appeal of computer-based instruction for young children is this element of difference combined with a finely tuned system for approximating a level where the child should begin.

The third step in the design of instructional materials in the presentation of the content is a "spiraling fashion" so that for every new step the child takes toward the teacher-defined goal, the child reviews previous skills. This redundancy helps assure that the groundwork is well established for all subsequent steps.

Finally, perhaps the most important element taken from Bruner's theory and applied to instructional strategies is for the child to go "beyond the information given." Here the child should be given the opportunity to advance beyond that which is offered by the teacher and explore on his or her own the next logical step in the sequence. The child should be encouraged to create his or her own challenges and through "discovery learning" seek out answers or solutions.

The late 1960s and early 1970s saw a great deal of interest generated in the application of both Piaget's and especially Bruner's theories of cognitive development.

The open classroom concept and that of "free education" appealed to such an extent that several programs began privately, and even now are still a part of a more traditional system. Yet, much of what theorists like Bruner would like to see for education has not come to pass. Budget restraints, traditional beliefs in instructional systems, and the lack of imaginative education of our teachers are all hindrances to such progress.

HOW THEY STUDY DEVELOPMENT

A good deal of our discussion about Piaget and Bruner focused on the active role that the growing child plays in the development of cognitive and intellectual abilities. In a set of experiments Jerome Kagan of Harvard University studies a variety of dimensions about infant's attention span, trying to understand those internal operations that occupy the infants change from a sensory oriented to a more operationally oriented thinker.

One of the topics we discussed in this past chapter is Piaget's use of the word "scheme" as the mental representation of events. For a young infant, the number and type of schema are relatively small, and through the processes of organization and adaption, schema change become integrated, modified, and refined.

Jerome Kagan (1971) indirectly examined the content of these schema by examining what environment events cause children to habituate or become bored, and what events attract them.

To accomplish this, he used a set of 180 first-born, white boys and girls and had them view a series of clay faces at 4, 8, 13, and 27 months of age. These four clay faces were very different from one another. Although one looked like a "normal" face with two eyes, a nose, and whatever else you'd expect, the other faces were in various stages of disarray. In fact one face had no features, just hair.

The primary question asked by this study is what kinds of faces will keep the child's attention, and which kinds will not. Kagan believed that the child will attend to those stimuli that are discrepant from what he or she already knows, but not so different as to be unrelated to anything the child has experienced before. On the other hand, if the faces are too familiar, the child is likely to ignore them completely.

What is most useful about the results of this experiment, which showed that moderately discrepant faces held the most interest, is that the young infant is capable of formulating and indirectly testing hypotheses. This is a major thesis of cognitive-developmental (and organismic) theorists since it demonstrates how even very young children actively try to understand their world as the result of an interaction between their own perceptions (or schema) and the reality of the world around them.

SUMMARY POINTS

1. Cognitive developmental theorists stress the role of the organism as an active, not a reactive one.

2. Development is a broad spontaneous process that results in the addition, modification, and reorganization of psychological structures.

3. A schema is a primary unit of mental organization that is a flexible structure that can change qualitatively and quantitatively.
4. Assimilation is the process through which the organism incorporates experiences into already existing schemes.
5. There are three types of assimilation: functional, generalizing, and recognitory.
6. Accommodation is the process of modifying already existing schemes to satisfy the demands of a changing environment.
7. Adaptation and organization are functional invariants that operate at all levels of development.
8. Egocentrism is a preoccupation with one's own point of view. It characterizes development at all stages.
9. Development occurs as a progression through a series of four interrelated yet independent qualitatively different stages.
10. The basic premise of Piaget's theory is the striving for a state of equilibrium.
11. Development is a discontinuous process characterized by abrupt changes from stage to stage.

FURTHER READINGS

Furth, H. *Piaget and knowledge: Theoretical foundations*. Englewood Cliffs, N.J.: Prentice-Hall, 1969.

Gardner, H. *The arts of human development*. New York: Wiley, 1973.

Gardner, H. *The shattered mind*. New York: Knopf, 1973.

Piaget, J. *Piaget's theory*. In P. Mussen (Ed.), *Handbook of child psychology*, Vol. 1. New York: Wiley, 1983.

Piaget, J. *The origins of intelligence in children*. New York: International Universities Press, 1952.

Siegler, R. S. *Information processing approaches to development*. In P. Mussen (Ed.), *Handbook of Child Psychology*, Vol. 1. New York: Wiley, 1983.

OTHER READINGS OF INTEREST

Elkind, D. *Children and adolescents*. Oxford: Oxford University Press, 1974.

10

The Organismic Model: Orthogenesis and Dialectics

You know children are growing up when they start asking questions that have answers.

John J. Plump

The more things change, the more they remain the same.

Alphonse Karr

THE ORGANISMIC PSYCHOLOGY OF HEINZ WERNER

Introduction: Definition of Development

Like the work of Jean Piaget, Heinz Werner's research and writings represent an approach to understanding development that is clearly different from the behavioral perspectives we have already discussed. For Werner (pronounced Verner) and his colleagues at Clark University, the concept of development had a unique and highly specialized meaning.

Just as Freud received direction from the field of physics (the dynamics of energy) and Piaget from biology (the emphasis on adaptation), Werner drew heavily from the disciplines of anthropology, aesthetics, and especially embryology to develop a comprehensive theory of developmental psychology.

In its most general terms, Werner believed that development represents a "systematic, orderly sequence: of events consisting of two general dimensions (Werner, 1957). The first is the *pattern of different developmental levels* (or stages) and how each of these is characterized. The second dimension is *what form development takes*. For example, is change in development a smooth process from one stage to the next or an abrupt transition between qualitatively distinct stages? Within this perspective, the process of development involves both the organism (the mechanisms that are involved in that change), as well as its developmental processes (the nature of the changes that occur through ontogenesis). Hence the term *organismic* is used to describe the theory.

The Principle of Orthogenesis

The *orthogenetic principle* distinguishes Werner's theory from other theories of human development. This principle transcends the physical, emotional, intellectual, and other dimensions of development and provides a foundation for *all* developmental processes.

The orthogenetic principle states that "wherever development occurs it proceeds from a state of relative globality and lack of differentiation to a state of increasing differentiation, articulation, and hierarchic integration" (Werner, 1957, p. 126). This definition of orthogenesis includes some terms you have seen before. "Differentiation" was a major element in Piaget's approach to understanding egocentrism. One of the characteristics distinguishing one stage of egocentrism from another is the degree of differentiation between children and objects in their world. Werner's work stressed the same basic principle but he added the process of integration of those separate elements after differentiation has occurred.

For example, the newborn infant cannot differentiate objects from the activity associated with those objects. This distinction becomes more clear with increasing developmental maturity. Werner proposed that development can be characterized by a general underlying trend of *increased differentiation* between the subject and the object as well as a decreased domination of the subject's cognitive abilities by basic concrete situations and experiences. In other words, differentiation and integration of the different psychological systems (perceptual, cognitive, and emotional, and physical) takes place, encouraging the individual to move away from a dependency on sensorimotor information. In Piagetian terms, the process is much like decentration. For Werner, "development" represents the degree to which a system is organized and the extent to which the separate components of that system are in communication with one another while still functioning interdependently.

The foundation for such ideas parallels the biological development of the individual from conception through gestation. The fertilized egg is essentially an undifferentiated structure with no specialized function. During maturation, the egg cleaves to form new structures. Eventually, these different parts of the embryo develop highly specialized structures and functions, such as a beating heart, buds where arms will form, and a central nervous system. Biological development is characterized by an increasing degree of differentiation and hierarchic integration or coordination between the systems.

Just as Piaget placed a great deal of importance on the innate forces of organization and adaptation, Werner believed in the inherent basis of the orthogenetic principle. The capacity for differentiation and integration is inherited. It is not learned and cannot be taught. Werner deemphasized experience and learning as parts of the developmental process and saw the primary operating force as a set of biologically controlled factors.

A Model of Orthogenesis

Figure 10-1 illustrates the process of orthogenesis. At first, perception (the beginning step in any mental operation) is global, and whole qualities of the experience (color or size, for example) are the most important factors. Following this global stage, perception becomes increasingly analytic and directed toward specific components and elements of the stimulus. Finally, the third step in this illustration shows a synthesis wherein the different dimensions of the stimulus situation become well organized and integrated. This movement from global to analytic to synthetic characterizes the parallel operations of increasing differentiation and integration. In the illustration, each circle represents a separate element or component. The initial step from global to analytic involves the breaking down of the larger whole into more discrete parts. Each of these units is then connected by lines that represent a degree of organization between the different units. After the analytic stage, in which differentiation is at a maximum, the process of synthesis or recombination begins. The separate discrete units are joined or grouped together to form individual clusters, all of which communicate either directly or indirectly with each other through another cluster.

The nature of this integration is hierarchical in that different levels of development subsume those that came before. This is another restatement of the major theme that underlies most organismic theories: that development occurs in qualitatively different stages wherein a later stage is based on the elements of an earlier one, yet is qualitatively different from that earlier stage.

With this definition of orthogenesis as a basis for defining development, simple quantitative additions to an already existing dimension of development (such as the acquisition of more words) are not truly developmental. Even though there is a degree of differentiation in that many new words are refinements of a larger class (beagles, greyhounds, and German shepherds are all dogs), there does not appear to be any hierarchic integration. There is no recombination of existing elements to produce a qualitatively different outcome.

The Role of Phylogeny and Ontogeny. Throughout this book, development has been defined in a variety of ways, and these definitions reflect the basic assumptions

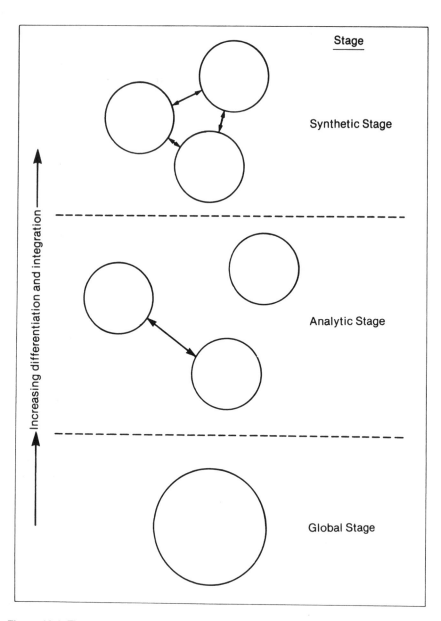

Figure 10-1. The process of orthogenesis.

of different developmental theories. We have also mentioned how cultural influences have affected the development of certain theories and their impact on the field of developmental psychology. For example, Freud's focus on the unconscious and explicit reference to sexual matters went against the cultural beliefs of his Victorian contemporaries. Likewise, the mechanistic approach characteristic of the early American behaviorists reflected an increasing cultural preoccupation with technology and efficiency.

Trained in part as an embryologist, Werner found himself in an interesting position regarding the relationship between developmental biology and developmental psychology. Even during the middle of the twentieth century, the "ontogeny recapitulates phylogeny" debate was still in full swing. Basically, the *law of recapitulation* (first discussed by Aristotle) states that "in its embryological development, an animal tends to repeat or recapitulate the sequence that its ancestors followed during their evolution" (Sagan, 1977, pp. 57–58). For example, humans have many vestigial (present but no longer functional) organs and appendages, such as a tail bone, an appendix, and gill slits, that during early embryological development were similar to those of their aquatic cousins.

Ernst Haeckel was the German scientist who popularized the thesis of recapitulation, and it has since undergone major revisions, critiques, and finally a good deal of empirical refutation. It is an historically important idea, and an excellent discussion of it can be found in Gould (1977).

When Werner was formulating his ideas, there was some discussion that a phenomenon parallel to what we just discussed in the field of developmental biology might exist in the field of developmental psychology; that developmentally less mature ways of processing information, adapting to the environment, and solving problems are natural and necessary precursors to later more sophisticated ways of accomplishing the same goals. In addition, one characteristic of a later stage is that it contains some of the elements of an earlier stage, although all those elements do not appear in equal intensity, nor are they recoverable once the later stage has been reached.

All this information and debate provided Werner with the realization that there are distinct parallels between the mental development of the species and the mental development of the organism. Most important, it was the basis for Werner's position that "primitive" means developmentally less mature, not developmentally inferior. Interestingly, in Chapter 4 we discussed how Darwin tried to make the very same point. Werner frequently pointed out how important it is that earlier forms of information-processing skills (on a very concrete level, for example) be utilized to solve certain problems that otherwise would be unsolvable. All the cognitive and intellectual equipment available should be used to differing degrees depending on the demands of the situation. This is why the human being is characterized as a tremendously adaptive organism and why a young child, who has fewer tools available and less experience in using them, is less adaptive than an adult.

BASIC ISSUES IN DEVELOPMENT

Werner's work followed a tradition characteristic of many European-trained psychologists. His major impetus was to formulate a theory, rather than to detail the specifics of child development, as, for example, Gesell did. His energy was invested in defining the general rules and principles that underlie the process of development. Werner himself states that "the orthogenetic law, being a formal regulative principle, is not designed to predict developmental courses in their specificity" (1957, p. 130). His work led to some important empirically derived findings, but Werner's lasting contribution (and that of his colleagues, such as Seymour Wapner and Bernard Kaplan) reflects a genuine concern for understanding the system of development through the application of general developmental laws. Although abstract in nature, the "polarities," as Werner called what are discussed here, provide a foundation for understanding development from the organismic perspective.

Uniformity versus Multiformity of Development

This first general polarity of development poses a question: Does behavior develop "through the progressive expansion of a perfectly integrated total pattern" or as "stereotyped reflexes subsequently combined into complex patterns?" (Werner, 1957, p. 130)? The two aspects of this question are illustrated in Figure 10-2. In Figure 10-2a, development is represented by the progression from an integrated yet global whole to more discrete elements (uniformity). Figure 10-2b represents development by the integration of discrete global units differentiated from one another at the beginning of the process (multiformity). Interestingly enough, both modes result in the formation of the same organized, integrated system of elements. Werner points out that both interpretations support the basic tenet of the orthogenetic prin-

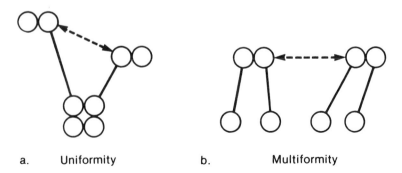

a.   Uniformity   b.   Multiformity

Figure 10-2. Uniformity versus multiformity.

ciple—that development results from the simultaneous processes of differentiation and hierarchic integration.

Continuity versus Discontinuity of Development

Another general underlying process of development that Werner examined was the continuity of development versus the discontinuity of development. For Werner, this issue occupied a place of special significance.

Developmental change can assume one of two qualities. First, it can be quantitative in nature, with change occurring along a dimension such as frequency of words spelled correctly or height. Second, it can be qualitative, with change occurring along a dimension that deals with substantive differences between levels such as the transition from babbling to one-word phrases. Werner viewed quantitative developmental changes as either gradual or abrupt. That is, does change take place abruptly and suddenly with little forewarning, or is it a gradual or continuous process that occurs smoothly without apparent shifts from one level to the next? Qualitative changes were described as having one of two different attributes: emergence (can later stages of development be reduced to earlier ones?) and intermediacy (what is the nature of the transition from one level to the next?).

Werner would never claim that developmental change was characterized by either continuity or discontinuity, or qualitativeness or quantitativeness. He believed that according to the orthogenetic principle, the best representation of development is that it is "the result of quantitative changes which are either gradual or abrupt, and qualitative changes which by their nature are discontinuous" (Werner, 1957, p. 137). In the most simple form, continuity refers to different levels of development being regulated by the same fundamental laws. Discontinuity of development stresses that the levels of development are different from one another and not based on the same general principles.

Table 10-1 shows the different ways of describing the developmental process in terms of the dimensions of continuity and discontinuity and qualitative and quantitative change. Quantitative continuity could be characterized as creeping or gradual change, while quantitative discontinuity is characterized by abrupt or steep, yet related, changes in the developmental process. Qualitative continuity involves the transition between different developmental levels (intermediacy), and qualitative

Table 10-1 Continuity versus Discontinuity

	Continuity	*Discontinuity*
Quantitative change	Gradual change	Steep change
Qualitative change	Intermediacy	Emergence

discontinuity focuses on the emergent quality of development and the irreducibility of later forms to earlier ones (emergence). Werner characterized any type of qualitative change as primarily discontinuous in nature.

Because these different categories overlap, any behavior observed as part of the developmental process might belong in any of the four cells, depending on how we define that particular behavior. For example, consider the development of language in the child. Discontinuous change takes place (an emergence of new forms of language that are different and not reducible to what came earlier), as well as a type of quantitative continuity (a gradual addition of new words and phrases that are used in a different context). In Table 10-1, the cells on the upper left and lower right are the easiest to recognize as clear developmental possibilities, because continuity is often associated with quantitative change and discontinuity is often associated with qualitative change. Werner saw development as a complex process that involved both types of change (qualitative and quantitative) within the format or structure of the change (continuous or discontinuous).

Unilinearity versus Multilinearity of Development

According to Werner, development can be a process based on a universal law (unilinearity), or the action of individual variation "viewed as a branching-out process of specialization or aberration" (multilinearity) (Werner, 1957, p. 137). It is difficult to imagine a compromise between these two. There might be some underlying mechanism that pervades all development (such as Piaget's notion of function), yet the development and diversity of individual formations would not necessarily be hampered by the existence of this process. In other words, the primary question is whether development is characterized by a unidirectional thrust or by a series of hierarchically arranged branches off a central shoot. The unilinear view envisions development as the result of a broadening of a major influence or force (such as maturation), and the multilinear perspective is best illustrated by a branching out from one (or more than one) general law.

Fixity versus Mobility of Development

Werner points out that the assumption that all organisms operate on a fixed developmental course ignores the fact that skills and abilities are often employed far below (as well as far above) present developmental status. For example, a reliance on basic sensory information is the first step in figuring out why the lawnmower doesn't work. Running out of gas comes to mind first, and checking this possibility (through sensory level information) is the first logical step in the process. If that is not the problem and more sophisticated steps are needed, another form or level of intellectual functioning would be employed. The adaptive organism can make those shifts to different levels through progression as well as regression.

The issue of fixity refers to the individual's directedness toward a certain end stage. An example of an end stage is reaching maximum stability or the optimal balance between one's intellectual skills and the demands placed on those skills (much like Piaget's notion of equilibrium). This is a rarely achieved state, because an end stage is so fixed and rigid that little reorganization (that is, further differentiation and integration) can take place.

Mobility, on the other hand, refers to the individual's capacity to utilize more than one operation to satisfy the demands of the situation. It provides the flexibility for adapting to an environment that is continually changing, such as in an increasingly technological world. Mobility is represented by both horizontal (the transference of an operation to a new setting) and vertical (the use of more than one type of operation) dimensions. The adaptive organism can and does move on both these dimensions as the degree of mobility is increased and the degree of fixity is decreased.

The concept of mobility plays another, crucial role in understanding the developmental process. Because the organism has this quality of mobility, Werner theorizes that to progress from one developmental level to the next, the organism must first *regress*. In other words, the organism must regress or return to a genetically more stable level of functioning in order to progress, as illustrated in Figure 10-3. This also illustrates how developmental change takes place only through a process of reorganization that involves reusing previous means and operations.

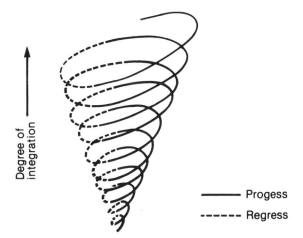

Figure 10-3. The progressive and regressive nature of development (adapted from Langer, 1969).

Summary of the Basic Issues

These polarities are not all-or-nothing phenomena. They are ongoing processes that characterize the dynamic, changing nature of the organism during development. These different processes are based on some inherent component that guides the organism along these dimensions. This does not mean that the course of the organism's development is determined at conception, but it does mean that the organism's basic structural equipment is a biological and not an environmental phenomenon. This strongly reflects Werner's background in embryology.

In sum, the developmental process can be characterized as progressing from a global whole to a discrete yet integrated system (uniformity versus multiformity), as smooth or discontinuous (continuity versus discontinuity) in its course of change, as the extension of a central thrust or a group of individual thrusts (unilinearity versus multilinearity), and as being fixed and stable or adaptive and mobile (fixity versus mobility).

MAJOR TRENDS IN DEVELOPMENT

Werner did not stop with the identification of these basic issues. He went on to identify four developmental trends that simultaneously occur during the life span.

Syncretic to Discrete

The organism progresses from a state where perceptions are fused together and cannot be distinguished from one another, to a point at which these separate elements are independent of each other. A good example of this is the lack of differentiation between the subject and object that characterizes the young child's egocentric thinking. Werner called this type of perception physiognomic, meaning a lack of differentiation or a fusion of these two elements of the child's world. Another example might be a child's reaction to something new that might be excitement, expressed as distress or delight. However, as this trend progresses, these two responses differentiate into anger and elation, instead of being fused as one emotion. Adults often fuse different sensations and thoughts; for example, an artist might say that he or she can "feel a color."

Rigid to Flexible

As development progresses, the organism tends to move from a state or rigidity, where the individual does the same thing regardless of the changing demands of the situation, toward a state of flexibility, where different operations and strategies are employed as needed. For example, overly stubborn adults will not change their minds regardless of the evidence that might contradict a given argument.

It is important for the organism to be flexible in order to be fully adaptive. It really does not matter if children approach various problems using the same criteria, because the sanctions against such behavior tend to be less the younger we are. For adults, however, it becomes more costly to be inflexible and not to adapt to the demands of the environment.

Diffuse to Articulated

This trend characterizes Werner's general orthogenetic principle and refers to the degree of coordination that exists between separate elements of a system. During the early stages of development, the system tends to be diffuse in that the different elements are generally unrelated to one another and function independently. As development progresses, the general pattern is toward articulation, where the separate elements are independent of one another, yet clearly function as parts of an overall system.

During the early stages of embryological development, different organs function on their own, with little communication with one another. With progress, these different organs form systems and the systems become interrelated. Language becomes more specific with age as well. More words, for example, are available to express the same sentiment (happy, joyous, merry, buoyant, playful). Another example of this is when the adult has many different emotions about the same experience and cannot organize them. At the beginning of any developmental process elements can be seen as diffuse and moving toward a state of higher articulation.

Labile to Stable

One of the outstanding characteristics of young children is the degree to which their behavior is labile, or fluctuating. Lability is characteristic of any new system that has not yet established the level of stability necessary to move on to the next level of development. Stability, on the other hand, lends strength to any level of functioning. If the theoretical assumption that an organism must regress in order to progress is accepted, then the stability of an earlier level or stage of development is essential for later successful development to occur. This is perhaps why developmental problems early in life often become harder to overcome as the years pass.

Summary of the Major Trends

What appears to happen during the process of development (see Table 10-2) is that the organism moves from a state of fusion, rigidity, lack of organization, and instability to a state of separateness, flexibility, organization, and stability. These four trends are present throughout development, although the tendency to move

Table 10-2 Major Trends in Development

From	*To*
Fusion of ideas and thoughts	Separation of operations
A rigid approach to similar situations	Flexible and open application of alternatives
Diffuse and unrelated elements of the system	Clearly articulated and related components
Lack of stability	Stable and well-established foundation
⟶	Biological processes, time, experience or developmental change ⟶

toward one end of each trend increases. The adaptive organism, however, is moving significantly faster than the nonadaptive one in the directions defined as more developmentally mature than earlier ones. Finally, all these trends are subsumed under the general orthogenetic principles that Werner postulated as the basis for all of development.

A Model of Perception: Sensory-Tonic Theory

Werner was dissatisfied with the attempts made by his contemporaries to define the general process called "perception." There seemed to be a movement toward quantifying perception to such a degree that little if any attention was paid to underlying psychological processes. Werner believed that to understand the process of perception one must not only consider the sensory component of the process, but the tonic or organismic component as well. In other words, no perceptual experience is purely sensory in nature. This combination of sensory and tonic dimensions of perception parallels the general organismic-developmental distinction discussed earlier. For Werner, it was clear that "perception and certain other aspects of cognition have to be conceived in terms of an interrelationship between sensory input and intraorganismic factors" (Werner, 1957, p. 194).

Within this framework, the organism becomes an active mediator between the demands of the environment and organic or cognitive capabilities and seeks a degree of equilibrium between the opposing forces of sensation and tonus (muscle tension). In doing so, the organism sometimes finds it necessary to alter or change some aspect of a certain experience or belief in order for the perceptual process to have meaning and be adaptive, much like the cognitive dissonance work of Leon Festinger (1957).

One of the primary methods Werner and his associates used to examine and test the different questions that were raised by sensory-tonic theory was the rod and frame apparatus originally invented by Herman Witkin (described in Witkin et al., 1962). In this task, the individual looks into an enclosed chamber and is asked to move a vertical line until it is perpendicular to an imaginary horizontal axis represented by the ground, or vertical axis represented by the walls. In order for the system to be in balance, individuals must change the degree of tilt of the line to match their perception of verticality. The organism adjusts to the situation by altering some organismic state (the definition of what is vertical), or changing the course of sensory input (adjusting the vertical).

In this case, a stimulus is a force, either internal or external, that alters the relationship between the environment and the organism. For example, if someone is very hungry, or accidentally gets stuck with a needle while sewing, both these events act as stimuli toward further action and reorganization of the relationship between the state of the organism (tonus) and the environment (sensation).

This notion of organism-environment interaction is what Werner meant when he called his approach to development an organismic-developmental one. It includes the mutual and multiplicative interaction between the organism and the environment.

Other theorists have criticized the sensory-tonic theory of perception as being too broad and general. In addition, critics feel that Wapner and Werner (1957) created a dichotomy (sensory-tonic) that does not reflect the complexity of the perceptual process. On the other hand, however, sensory-tonic theory was meant to be a very general theory of perception and was not the major thrust of Werner's theoretical work.

In a 1964 publication, Seymour Wapner presented the general theory, research objectives, and experimental methods of the organismic-developmental model (Wapner, 1964). The four-dimensional model of organismic-developmental theory (Figure 10-4) integrates the material that we have discussed in this section. The four di-

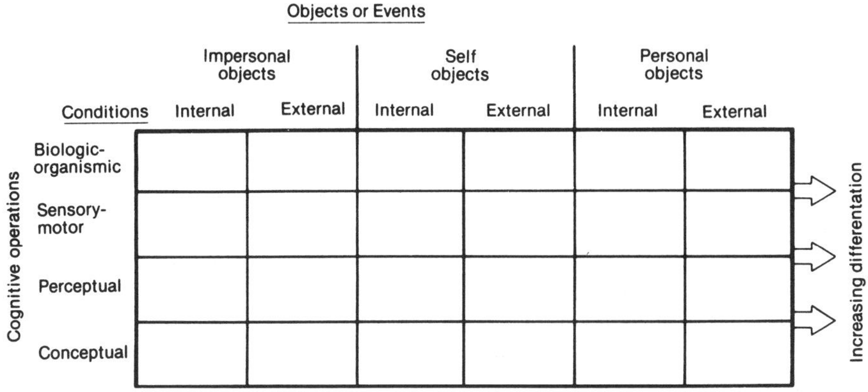

Figure 10-4. A model of organismic-developmental theory (adapted from Wapner, 1964).

mensions are cognitive operations, objects or events, conditions, and degree of differentiation.

Cognitive operations are the degree of differentiation between the organism and the environment. Biological-organismic operations occur on a level where the seperation between the environment (the object) and the organism (the self) is absolutely minimal, such as the purely sensory processes of sight and touch. These operations are the only available means open to the new infant of adapting to the world and are similar to the earlier substages detailed by Piaget that occur during the sensorimotor period. The second level of cognitive operations, sensory-motor operations, are more advanced in their separation of object and self in that the individual now focuses on the manipulation of objects and can effectively deal with concrete information as represented by the object. The third level, perceptual, shows an increasing degree of differentiation and the quality of intent, wherein the notion of cause and effect begins to be understood. Finally, the last and most sophisticated level of cognitive operations is conceptual, where the organism can represent objects through the use of symbols and manipulate them as well: hence the development of language. Again this is a progression of stages that is characteristic of organismic theory in general. Werner spent less time detailing the different behaviors that are characteristic of each of these stages than did Piaget, possibly because Werner had a greater concern for the process that was the foundation for development. The similarity between Werner's levels of cognitive operations and Piaget's four invariant stages is somewhat striking.

The second dimension of this matrix is the three basic classes of objects or events. Impersonal objects are objects or events that "deal with temporary changes in properties or relations between properties of impersonal objects" (Wapner, 1964, p. 197). For example, the setting of the sun or driving a car might be characterized as impersonal events. Self- or body-as-object are objects or events that "involve temporary changes in properties of body-as-object" (Wapner, 1964, p. 197). For example, such an event might be a change in one's perceptions or feelings. Finally, the third class of objects or events is the person-as-object event, which "deals with temporal changes in properties or relations between persons" (Wapner, 1964, p. 197). An example of this might be the interaction between a supervisor and an employee.

The third dimension deals with influences on the organism's development that are internal in nature (temperament, biological processes) or external (physical and social constraints that are placed on behavior).

Finally, the last dimension, degree of differentiation, is represented by a movement from less to more differentiation, represented by the arrows on the right-hand side of Figure 10-4. In effect, this movement represents the trend from lesser to greater differentiation and hierarchic integration.

Werner sees the developmental process as an analysis of the changes that take place in a dynamic, living system, defined as the "progressive changes in a system undergoing transition'' (Wapner, 1964, p. 200). The four different dimensions of the hypothetical model presented in Figure 10-4 can be combined in any way so that any one cell might be examined.

Werner's theory represents a unique approach to development, and one that is rooted in the general principle that increasing differentiation and hierarchic integration characterize the developmental process. His work, and that of his colleagues, has not been widely accepted in the United States. This may be in part because of some of the criticisms mentioned earlier (that his work is too general, for example), but also because psychologists have been increasingly drawn to more concrete and less philosophical explanations of behavior. The work of people like Werner and his colleagues is important but insufficiently developed and applied to the everyday concerns of many developmentalists, such as child rearing or early intervention.

DIALECTICS: AN IDEA GROWS

Introduction and Historical Perspective

One underlying assumption encompasses all the organismic theories that have been discussed: that development is a function of an interaction between the organism and the environment, and that the organism is an active participant in that process. Of all the developmental perspectives that are presented in this book, dialectics best represents this interactionist approach. The most interesting characteristic of this perspective is that it does not dictate a method of studying development (such as the psychodynamic model), nor does it attempt to identify specific developmental outcomes or processes (such as Piaget's model). The most significant attribute of dialectics as it relates to human development is that it is more a philosophy than a highly detailed theory. Its unique value as a tool for developmental psychologists is in the identification and organization of new ideas. In other words, dialectics helps define what might be the important questions to be asked, but not necessarily how they should be answered. As Baltes and Cornelius note: ''Advancements in dialectical psychology will be less likely to come from the efforts to use dialectics as a specific methodology than from efforts to employ dialectics as a general theoretical orientation'' (1977, p. 121).

Dialectics consequently appears to be a highly useful organizational tool for framing the focus of our studies. For example, within this perspective it is irrelevant whether one wants to view the interactional nature of the mother or the child in behavioral or psychoanalytic terms. Within the dialectical theory, both views are acceptable, because they both engender some type of interaction between opposing forces. Hayne Reese, in his paper on discriminative learning (Reese, 1977), comments that dialectics as an approach resolves some of the major problems of the behaviorist perspective. In another paper (Reese, 1982) he stresses how the term "dialectics" has several meanings, all of which are useful for understanding development. Most other theories of development have their own methods or techniques but dialectics does not. It is seen as "a key to understanding not only separate spheres of reality, but literally all fields of nature, society and thought: it is the key to the cognition of the world as a whole" (Afanasyen, 1968, p. 14). The theme of the Fifth West Virginia University LifeSpan Developmental Psychology Conference was dialectical perspectives and experimental research. A review of the papers presented at that conference (Datan & Reese, 1977) shows a broad range of topic areas, including "Dialectics and Operant Conditioning," "The Status of Dialectics in Developmental Psychology: Theoretical Orientation versus Scientific Method," and "The Dialectics of Time." These, which are only a few of the titles, show how widespread the impact of dialectics has been over a relatively short span of time.

Hegelian Philosophy

Dialectics has evolved from the penetrating philosophy of Georg Wilhelm Frederich Hegel (1770–1831), developed throughout his productive career as a philosopher and professor. In a series of books such as **Phenomenology of Mind** (1807) and **Philosophy of Right** (1821), he presented a highly integrated view of the world that circumscribed theories of ethics, history, politics, aesthetics, and religion. His basic writings became a primary source for the works of Karl Marx and Mao Tse-Tung.

The two basic notions that Hegel presented are that (1) reality consists of ideas and not necessarily of corporeal things, and (2) these different ideas are always in a state of change (Eastman, 1940). Hegel's basic belief is that human life (and all of nature) is based on a principle of dialectical change. The dialectic consists of a concept, or thesis, which by the nature of change will precipitate the formation of another concept, called an antithesis. Through the dialectical process, these two elements interact to produce a synthesis, which is actually a new thesis. As a result of this process the world is a dynamism undergoing constant change. Furthermore, no force within this world can ever be static, because the different elements of nature are so intertwined that few changes if any can occur without having some impact on another element. As in a closed system, an alteration in one dimension of the system results in the alteration of another dimension.

Figure 10-5 illustrates Hegel's concept of dialectics. In the box at the bottom of the figure are the thesis, the antithesis, and their mutual interaction, which leads to a synthesis of these ideas or concepts. But the progression does not stop here.

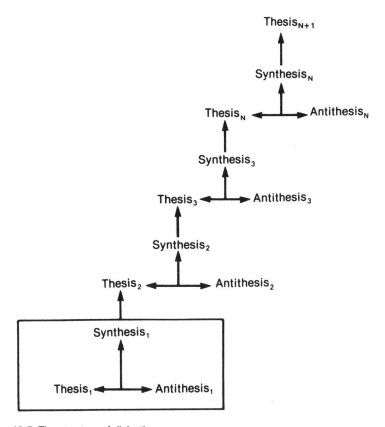

Figure 10-5. The structure of dialectics.

The previous level of synthesis (Synthesis₁) leads to a subsequent thesis (Thesis₂) that in turn creates another antithesis, and the cycle then starts again. Development thus can be seen as a series of hierarchically ordered progressions from one level of synthesis to another. An example of this is the process through which we might try to make a point in a debate or discussion. For example, if a point of view is presented (which is a thesis), the logical next step (for the debate to continue) is for some antithesis resolution to be presented. Finally, there is a resolution of the conflict in the form of a synthesis. In the developmental process, however, there is invariably unfinished business, and the process itself must continue. Some of the conclusions from the earlier debate could be used as a foundation for a later exercise of the same form, and a new synthesis is formed based on a developmentally prior one.

General Laws of Dialectics

In an excellent summary of the role that dialectics has played in the development of Soviet psychology, Wozniak (1975) describes the three basic laws of dialectics.

Law 1: The Unity and Struggle of Opposites. This is the primary principle of dialectics, which states that contradiciton is present in all actions, operations, and things. The law of contradiction (Hook, 1957) states that all the elements that occur in nature have as a function of their existence a counterpart that works in opposition to them. For example, the positive and negative subatomic particles such as protons and electrons operate in tandem to produce different levels of atomic organization. Likewise, physical maturation is characterized not only by an increase in size or weight, but also by an accompanying degeneration of cells through aging. Finally, in Piaget's focus on the mutually complementary yet often oppostional forces of assimilation and accommodation, we see a unity as well as struggle as part of these processes.

Law 2: Transformation of Quantitative into Qualitative Change. The second general law of dialectics is that after a certain threshold of quantitative change has occurred, a qualitative or structural change occurs as well. In other words, sufficient quantitative change produces qualitative or structural transformations. A good illustration of this is that the perception of color (red versus blue) is a function of wavelength of light (short versus long). Once the length of the wave (which is quantitative in nature) reaches a certain size, the qualitative character of the experience of viewing the light changes as well. The dialectical approach thus removes some of the difficulty in seeing development both as a quantitative as well as a qualitative process. This issue can be found in the discussion of Piaget's theory of intellectual development, where quantitative change occurs within stages.

Law 3: The Negation of the Negation. The third and final general law of dialectics reflects the idea that "things change in time" but that "every opposition in time loses its defining character and assumes the traits of its converse" (Hook, 1957, p. 15). This law, or "negation of a negation," is analogous to subtracting a negative number from a negative quantity, which results in a positive value. In much the same way, negation of the negation implies "a replacement of the old by the new (negation), and the re-replacement of the new by the newer still" (Wozniak, 1975, p. 34). This re-replacement process can be seen in Figure 10-5, where later levels of development (if each resolution or synthesis is viewed as a level) replace former ones. The old is eventually incorporated by the new and the new by the newer yet.

The brevity of this discussion on dialectics does not reflect its importance as a model for developmental psychologists. Since it is new in its application to the field, many questions are yet unanswered about its role as a source of new direction.

Klaus Riegel, who did more to popularize and meaningfully interpret much of what is important about Hegelian philosophy for developmental psychologists, wrote a very important article in the *American Psychologist* that deals with the fundamental nature of dialectics (Riegel, 1976).

In this article, he presents a fourfold table of factors that can dialectically interact with one another (as well as with themselves) to form the content of these interactions (Table 10-3). The four categories are the inner-biological, individual-psychological, cultural-sociological, and outer-physical. These different categories interact with one another and result in either positive or negative outcomes. In Riegel's presentation, the upper word in any one cell represents a negative outcome, and the lower word represents a positive outcome.

These four categories are referred to by Riegel as "planes of developmental progression" (p. 693). That is, they are the dimensions across which change and transition can take place. Inner-biological refers to changes that are biological or physical in occurrence, such as pain, respiration, and other biological processes. Individual-psychological refers to those interactions between individuals such as those between a husband and a wife or between an employer and the work force. Cultural-sociological interactions represent abstract forces such as the family, a tribe, the federal government, mores and rules; the last developmental plane, outer-physical, represents "large scale external interventions" such as natural disasters (earthquakes, forest fires, etc.), and corresponding internal events, "the organismic, cellular, molecular, atomic, and quantum levels" (Riegel, 1977, p. 23).

The matrix in Table 10-3 illustrates the way in which these interactions can have differential effects on the development of the organism. For example, individual reactions on a psychological level (individual-psychological) to interactions with local and federal governments (cultural-sociological) can be characterized by dissidence (protests, strikes, and recall referendums) or by passive acceptance of

Table 10-3 The Four Dimensions of Developmental Change

Dimension	Inner-Biological	Individual-Psychological	Cultural-Sociological	Outer-Physical
Inner-Biological	Infection Fertilization	Illness Maturation	Epidemic Cultivation	Deterioration Vitalization
Individual-Psychological	Disorder Control	Discordance Concordance	Dissidence Organization	Destruction Creation
Cultural-Sociological	Distortion Adaptation	Exploitation Acculturation	Competition Cooperation	Devastation Conservation
Outer-Physical	Annihilation Nutrition	Catastrophy Welfare	Disaster Enrichment	Chaos Harmony

Note: Upper lines of entries denote negative outcome of crises; lower lines of entries denote positive outcome of crises. Entering from the rows indicates generative changes; entering from the column indicates reactive changes.
Source: Klaus Riegel, The dialectics of human development, *American Psychologist*, 1976, *10*, 689–701.

laws. Using this conceptual organization, the dialectical approach can help developmental psychologists identify the important ways in which an issue or an area should be studied (as an interaction), but at the same time not dictate what the content of or methods used in that study should be.

The future of dialectics as a theory will not be in the detailing of specific hypotheses to examine development. Its power and utility can be found in its simple and elegant approach to development, which in turn will lead to investigations of many different phenomena.

UNDERSTANDING THE COGNITIVE-DEVELOPMENTAL AND ORGANISMIC APPROACHES

1. *What is the major force that influences the course of development?*

Piaget's and Werner's theories of development are rooted in the discipline of biology, and they both stress the role that genetic or hereditary processes play in setting the stage for development. As a biologist, Piaget stressed the adaptiveness of biological structures in lower animals, and this model was in part transferred to his extensive work on the development of the child's mind. Likewise, Werner's principle of orthogenesis has an organic basis and presupposes a genetic structure that controls the timing and sequence of developmental levels.

In spite of this strong emphasis on genetic or hereditary factors, the organismic model also emphasizes the role of the environment. The organismic perspective is sometimes referred to as an interactional model because it places importance on both environmental influences and genetic factors. This is especially true for Piaget, who repeatedly states that experience, one of the four defining elements of development, plays a critical role in the process, and that without input from the environment little successful growth could be expected. Werner too placed a special importance on the role of factors originating in the environment, especially as feedback that the individual uses to alter his or her perceptions of the world.

2. *What is the underlying process responsible for changes in development?*

For all the organismic theorists, it is clear that biological or maturational mechanisms are responsible for the invariant sequence of developmental stages. Along with equilibration, social transmission, and experience, Piaget listed maturation as one of the four factors that define development. Similarly, Werner's early work in embryology served as a foundation for the emphasis on a maturational component to development.

For Piaget and Werner, learning provides much of the content or the specific repertoire of behaviors that result from varied experience. Practical applications of Piaget's work place children in a child-centered curriculum and provide them with many options for exploring the environment. Many of the experiences we have and the things we learn are crucial to the developmental process, but learning is constrained by the biological or maturational structures of the individual. Without the presence of structural equipment that has its origin in maturational processes, the individual can make little sense out of the varied stimuli in the environment.

3. *What roles does age play as a general marker of changes in development?*

Because maturation and biological forces do play an important role in development in the cognitive-developmental and organismic model, we should not ignore the fact that there are relatively consistent ages at which the transitions between different stages of development take place. Organismic theorists, however, do not place a great deal of importance on age other than as a general guideline for when an individual should be capable of completing a task.

The use of age as a marker helps to systematize the sequential component of any theory. It allows the researcher to assign approximate periods of time in a sequence of development from the primitive to advanced levels. This notion is sometimes placed in the "ages and stages" category, but this oversimplifies the meaning and importance of the construct of a stage.

4. *Are there certain sensitive or critical periods during development, and how are they related to rate of change?*

In order for development to be successful (in that the individual progresses through each stage without suffering any delays), the individual must be maturationally ready and exposed to the appropriate experiences. This sounds a bit like Gesell's idea of readiness and in some ways it is similar, except that the organismic theorist places much greater emphasis on the role of the environment than Gesell did. What is sensitive or critical is the timing of when the child is presented with the necessary and best-fitting experiences to maximize growth. Because the nature of the organismic approach is interactional, in one sense the developing individual is always in a critical or sensitive period, because the environment and biological factors are always interacting.

5. *Is development smooth and continuous, or do changes occur in abrupt stages?*

The theories of Piaget and Werner clearly exemplify the discontinuous shape of development. Although the stages are related to one another, they are qualitatively distinct. The transitions between stages from one qualitative level to the next indicate a shift or a change in the structures that are reflected in behavior.

For Piaget, this progression of stages from sensory-motor through formal operational consists of abrupt transitions that parallel the shift from a period of equilibrium to one of disequilibrium. Likewise, Werner proposed a progression from a sensory-motor to conceptual stage of development and stressed the unique quality of each stage. Werner also proposed a very complex and elaborate account of how the issue of continuity can involve quantitative and qualitative change. Werner stressed that the qualitative changes of development are discontinuous in nature and are not based on the same general principles.

The "schema" as a structure of behavior in Piaget's organismic model is the building block of development. Through the modification of these different schemes or addition to the existing schemes, the individual learns how to adapt to the environment. The presence of these underlying structures provides the fabric of development. When a change in a problem-solving strategy takes place, it is reflected not in the behavior of the individual, but in the underlying structure that provides a new set of capacities through which the individual can function.

The maxim that function follows structure is not new to the field of psychology, nor is it applied only in this area. For biologists, architects, and others, the notion that what something does depends on how it is designed is critically important. For Piaget and Werner, structural change is the critical element that sets their perspective apart from others.

> 6. *How does the theory explain differences in development between individuals of the same chronological age?*

Whether we are discussing the theoretical approaches of Piaget, Bruner, Werner, or that of dialectics, each one views development as an interaction between the organism and its environment. Individual differences are a function of how biological events set the foundation for whatever environmental influences are available to have some impact. Yet, more specifically, it seems that many of these approaches do present a set of antithetical forces in opposition to each other. The dominance of one force over another at a specific point in time might lead to differences in susceptibility to one or another potentially powerful influence. Another consideration as far as individual differences are concerned is the effectiveness with which the individual might resolve or deal with these various conflicts. For example, while one individual might not find it essential to consolidate skills and abilities, another might need to regress to an earlier developmental point in order to consolidate sufficient resources to move on. It's the very nature of cognitive and organismic approaches in that they are so "open" to change through both biological and environmental influences, and hence contribute strongly to the wide diversity we see in individuals of the same age.

SUMMARY POINTS

1. Development involves both the organism as well as its ontogenesis; hence the term organismic-developmental.
2. The orthogenetic principle states that development progresses from a state of relative globality and lack of differentiation to a state of increasing differentiation and hierarchic integration.
3. Perception as an example of the orthogenetic principle proceeds through the global to the analytic to the synthetic stage.

4. Werner believed that more developmentally mature levels of problem solving incorporate earlier, more primitive ones.

5. Behavior develops as a basic innate pattern expands (uniformity) or as a series of independent thrusts are combined (multiformity).

6. Development can be continuous or discontinuous, and change can be qualitative or quantitative.

7. Development is based on one general law (unilinearity) or several different simultaneous but distinct forces (multilinearity).

8. An individual has high mobility if he or she uses a variety of operations in any one situation.

9. According to Werner, the major trends in development are synthetic to discrete, rigid to flexible, diffuse to articulated, and labile to stable.

10. A four-dimensional model of organismic-developmental theory includes interactions among cognitive operations, objects or events, conditions, and degree of differentiation.

11. Dialectics is more a tool that helps us to ask the right questions than a theory of development.

12. Dialectics is based on the philosophy of Georg Hegel.

13. Dialectical change consists of a thesis, an antithesis, and a synthesis.

14. The three general laws of dialectics are the law of contradiction, the transformation of quantitative into qualitative change, and the negation of the negation.

15. The four factors that dialectically interact to produce change are inner-biological, individual-psychological, cultural-sociological, and outer-physical.

FURTHER READINGS

Baltes, P., and Nesselroade, J. R. Cultural change and adolescent personality: An application of longitudinal sequences. *Developmental Psychology*, 1972, 7, 244–56.

Cohen, S. Another look at the issue of continuity versus change in models of human development. In N. Datan and H. Reese (Eds.), *Life-span developmental psychology: Dialectical perspectives on experimental research*. New York: Academic Press, 1977.

Werner, H. The concept of development from a comparative and organismic point of view. In D. B. Harris (Ed.), *The concept of development*. Minneapolis: The University of Minnesota Press, 1957.

OTHER READINGS OF INTEREST

Riegel, K. The dialectics of human development. *American Psychologist*, 1976, *10*, 689–701.

Kozinski, J. *The devil tree*. New York: Harcourt Brace Jovanovich, 1973.

Wapner, S., and Werner, H. (Eds.). *Perceptual development*. Worcester, MA: Clark University Press, 1957.

11

A Discussion and Comparison of Developmental Theories

In every child who is born, under no matter what circumstances, and of no matter what parents, the potentiality of the human race is born again.

James Agee

In the past 10 chapters, we have introduced you to the major theories of human development and to some of those theorists who represent these perspectives. This diversity of ideas and approaches is as varied as human behavior itself.

This closing chapter has three purposes. The first is to present some statements that summarize the status of developmental theory. Here we focus on such areas as the comparability of theories to one another, how effectively they explain or predict future outcomes, how similarities in language between theories do or do not represent similar theoretical assumptions, and whether any one theory is "superior" to any other.

The second purpose is to review each of the general approaches to understanding development using Sidman's six criteria (Sidman, 1960) that were mentioned in Chapter 1: inclusiveness, consistency, accuracy, relevancy, fruitfulness, and simplicity.

Finally, each of the seven questions that we asked in Chapter 2 and used throughout the book to "understand" the different approaches will also be used to compare perspectives to one another.

SUMMARY STATEMENTS

Comparability of Theories

Regardless of one's theoretical orientation, behavior is the subject matter from which different theories of development are advanced. However, even though different theories of development describe similar phenomena (such as the development of language), these perspectives are not necessarily comparable to one another.

The most fundamental reason why this is true is that each of the theories that we have discussed (and the more general models from which they are derived) is based on radically different "world views" or sets of basic assumptions. For example, the behavioral model views the individual as a passive participant who reacts to changes in the environment. The organismic model, on the other hand, views the individual as an active participant in the developmental process. The same fundamental differences are present across other issues, such as heredity/ environment, or whether the shape or form of behavior is continuous or discontinuous.

Each different developmental theory has a unique focus as well. For many people, Freud and his psychoanalytic model represent the most valid approach toward understanding the development of personality and abnormal behavior. For these same people, Piaget may represent a bold and innovative analysis of the way cognitive development takes place. Clearly, these two views of development are quite different from one another not only in the central focus of the theory but also in philosophical assumptions.

Frequently an attempt is made at combining the best qualities of different theories to produce an eclectic model, one that draws from other theories but has little philosophical or theoretical rationale of its own. This appeared to be the case when Sears and his colleagues combined both the assumptions and methods of some of the psychoanalytic and behavioral models.

An eclectic model (wherein ideas and concepts from different theories are selectively used to explain the developmental process) is acceptable for understanding a behavior in isolation, but may not be effective for deriving a theoretical account of how development occurs. As we discussed in Chapter 1, at least one purpose of a theory is to interrelate different facts or ideas. The lack of any underlying rationale may prevent eclecticism from being successful. Simply put, practitioners use what works best. For example, the pediatrician who is treating an eneuretic child (a bed-wetter) is probably more interested in how techniques from operant psychology can be used to change this behavior than in the philosophical foundations of behaviorism.

It's questionable whether comparing different theories of human development is worthwhile because the substantive focus of each seems to be so different. The one good reason for doing such a comparison, however, is that seeing how one theory operates, and how its focus, might suggest directions worth pursuing within the guidelines of another.

Explanation and Prediction

The effectiveness with which different theories explain past outcomes—and predict future ones—depends on the specificity of the behavior being predicted and the mechanisms the theory has for explaining past outcomes.

Two important purposes of any theory are to explain past events and to predict future outcomes. This is one element most theoretical descriptions of behavior have in common: a mechanism for understanding what has happened as well as what will happen. For example, a great deal of Freud's developmental theory was based on the importance of past experiences and how these experiences form the foundation for later behavior. Freud called these early predictors of behavior ''prototypes,'' defined as ''the original mode of adjusting to a painful or disturbing state'' (Hall, 1954, p. 104). In other words, a prototype serves as a model for later adaptations. The individual who sought satisfaction and a reduction in tension by aggressive acts when very young is likely to use a similar strategy later on in life when placed in a similar set of circumstances. This notion of a prototype may be an effective conceptual tool for understanding the relationship between early and later behaviors or continuity as we discussed earlier. Within the psychoanalytic model, the only mechanism for predicting future outcomes is past behavior. Historically, detailed case studies have been used and their rich, yet highly subjective quality do not lend themselves to reliable replication over an extended time period.

The behavioral perspective focuses on the past history of the individual as well as on the current set of environment influences that are now operating. For example, we know that to understand the fears a child might have about the dark, we should examine the experiences the child has had and is having during the night as well as at bedtime. We might also operate on the assumption that if the conditions are similar from one point in time to another, then the same set of responses might be expected to occur. This is an extreme interpretation of the individual's passivity, since people do bring different sets of experiences to the same environmental setting at different times. This might be one reason why those behavioral approaches that stress intervening or mediating variables (such as that of Sears and Bandura) have been met with some degree of acceptance by a large number of developmentalists.

Similarities in Language

All theories of development tend to use different terms to describe very similar phenomena. These different phenomena, however, assume different positions of importance within the particular theory.

One of the hallmarks of science, as we discussed in Chapter 2, is that it is a process of building on the work of others. Even though different theorists might not have worked during the same time period, they were, in general, familiar with the work that was being done by others in their own and different fields. Just as Freud "borrowed" the principle of the conservation of energy from physics, so other theorists found that axioms and contributions from other theorists could serve them well.

Chapter 2 listed some general similarities that developing humans share. There are unquestionably some universals to development, but they are often couched within a language frame that best fits the assumptions of a specific theory. The phenomenon might be similar, but the language used to describe the behavior might be very different.

For example, certain theories of development describe forces that oppose each other (a "push and pull") and are always seeking some kind of balance (equilibrium, homeostasis, synthesis). Freud wrote about such conflicts (the Oedipal and Electra complexes, for example), and Piaget posits a similar kind of mechanism through the functional invariants of organization and adaptation. Within both these theoretical perspectives, the individual is continually reorganizing structural mechanisms in response to changes in the environment. Although there is always some pressure to remain at a level that conserves energy and does not demand additional output, the motivation to reach out and explore is often very strong. Gesell viewed "reciprocal interweaving" as the process through which oppositional forces reach some level of physical equilibrium or balance. Another example is how the essence of the dialectic perspective is a product that ends in a synthesis of oppositional forces.

These terms are conceptually similar but do not represent equally important constructs within the different theories. This illustrates that the same general construct can be described in language that best fits the basic assumptions of a particular theory. One cannot assume that because the different phenomena are comparable to one another the language used to describe them is purely ornamental. These differences in language are real, and they reflect fundamentally different world views.

Superiority of Theories

In general, because theories of human development are based on different assumptions and historically assume different roles in the study of human behavior, none is superior to any other.

However, one theory might do a better job than another in explaining certain kinds of outcomes. For example, Gesell's detailed descriptions of child growth and development have been useful to millions of parents, but little in his writings provide a detailed analysis of unacceptable behavior and how to handle it. Similarly, ethological approaches give us valuable insight into formation of parenting behaviors early in the infant's development.

Bijou and Baer's functional analysis approach and Piaget's genetic episte-mology have similar advantages and disadvantages for understanding human be-havior. The most significant contribution that Bijou and Baer made to the study of developmental psychology is their detailed and systematic analysis of the environ-ment and of the way in which stimulus events establish and maintain control over the developmental process. But because of the behavioral philosophy that their theory follows, there is the possibility that by ignoring certain internal changes in the individual (''How I feel'') they have excluded an important source of infor-mation.

Piaget's theory of cognitive development is best recognized for its detailed description of the different stages of cognitive development and for its theoretical explanation of how the transition from one stage of development to the next takes place. Many people have called Piaget an interactionist, because he places great importance on the biological and environmental influences that surround the de-velopmental process. One critical comment concerning Piaget's thesis focuses on his preoccupation with structural changes represented by overt behavior, rather than with description of the experiences that might be necessary to better understand different behavioral outcomes. This criticism has encouraged developmental psy-chologists to look more and more into the role of the ecology of human development: the events surrounding developmental change.

EVALUATIVE CRITERIA

In the beginning of the book, we discussed six criteria that could be used to evaluate any developmental theory: inclusiveness, consistency, accuracy, relevancy, fruit-fulness, and simplicity. If we assume that these are all qualities we would like a theory to have, it would be useful to discuss how the different theoretical viewpoints we have covered measure up to these arbitrary, but important, standards.

Inclusiveness

When we ask a question about the inclusiveness of a theory, we are interested in how comprehensive the theory is. In other words, how many and what kinds of events can the theory explain? Does it represent a narrow view of the world, or does it cover a broad, far-reaching arena of possible outcomes?

First, it is important to recognize that there are two different types of inclu-siveness. The first deal with how many different kinds of events are explained and is a quantitative dimension. Some theories simply explain more events than others. The second is how content-free the theory is, or how well the theory can stand independent of any specific content. That is, what kinds of events does the theory attempt to explain? For example, the theory of relativity is almost content-free, because its assumptions and hypotheses can be tested regardless of the nature of the content.

The behavioral model is probably the most comprehensive of any that has been discussed in this book, because it addresses the process of development and has little concern for the type or content of behavior that characterizes that process. The fact that so many of the principles of operant psychology are applicable to animals as well as to humans demonstrates this lack of emphasis on the content of behavior. One criticism directed at this approach, however, is that if the behavioral model is all process, then additional theorizing cannot lead to anything more than reinventing something that already exists. In other words, if we understand how reinforcement works, the future use of the technique is not likely to generate new knowledge or new questions. This is not entirely the case, however, since recent years have seen efforts by behaviorists at extending the model, especially in such areas as cognitive behavior modification and social learning theory, where these viewpoints generate new questions.

The cognitive-developmental and organismic theories share some of the same characteristics as the behavioral model in terms of inclusiveness. They are relatively content-free (they do deal with such areas such as cognition and moral development), but they are best represented by the dual processes of organization and adaptation.

In contrast to these two models, the psychoanalytic and maturational models tend to be highly content specific. For example, the psychoanalytic model is a very comprehensive theory of human development, yet it is also the most highly content specific. It leaves little room for a distinction between the process of development and the outcomes that result from that process. For example, conflicts such as those that occur during the phallic stage of development (Oedipal and Electra) are clearly defined on the basis of content. For Gesell, the case seems to be similar. The maturational model is highly content specific and more comprehensive than either the behavioral or organismic models. Gesell's description of development was less inclusive than that offered by the psychoanalytic model, because he concentrated primarily on physical development and only peripherally on such issues as emotional and social development. Gesell's five principles of development were never applied to other dimensions of development, although the potential for such application exists. Those theories that are highly inclusive are not tied to specific content, but make statements about the general nature of behavior.

Consistency

The consistency of a theory addresses whether it explains new phenomena without changing its basic assumptions. In other words, how effectively can a theory explain a new event without altering its basic framework? For example, if a developmental psychologist discovered that infant girls can recognize the sound of their mothers' voices during the first six hours after birth while infant boys cannot, how much alteration in the basic assumptions of a theory would be necessary to explain this?

This is an important question. As we discussed in Chapter 1, a crucial part of theory development is the reassessment of ideas and hypotheses—a continual questioning of how consistent a theory is. A "good" theory should be able to incorporate new events with minimal alteration of the theory.

The psychoanalytic model is probably the most consistent of all the models we have examined. It can be applied to aspects of behavior outside of those that the model was originally based on in an easy and efficient way. This does not assume that psychoanalytic theory describes all these events with the same degree of "validity." Indeed, many critics of the psychoanalytic model believe that because the assumptions of the model are basically untestable (for example, there is no operational definition of the id), the issue of consistency may not be relevant. The theory may explain a lot of events, but the explanations may be questionable. Because the basic assumptions of the theory are not open to examination, whether the model is consistent or not depends on the user's own view.

The contrast between the consistency of the behavioral and psychoanalytic models is very interesting. The psychoanalytic model is consistent because it is so inclusive, while the behavioral model is consistent because it is so content free. Both attempt to explain and can explain many different things.

The cognitive-developmental and maturational or biologically based models, however, seem to be somewhat less consistent. For example, the maturational model focuses on biological change, and few attempts (beyond writings in the mass literature) were made to apply it to social, emotional, and psychological development. Historically, it has been very important, but it has not been successful at explaining other behaviors outside of its basic formulation without a change in the model itself. The cognitive-developmental and organismic models are more consistent than the maturational model, but are also somewhat limited. They focus generally on the areas of cognitive and moral development, with little application to other areas of development. Currently, some work is being done within these models as they apply to imitation and other variables, but up to now this work has been centered in a few specific areas.

This lack of consistency is not necessarily a serious fault. If a theory is largely content specific, then perhaps it should not be judged as a theory of human development, but instead a theory of personality, maturation, or sex differences. Perhaps one of the reasons some theories are so vulnerable to criticism is that they have been applied to too many settings or to inappropriate ones.

Accuracy

A theory of development is accurate if it can predict outcomes with a relatively high degree of success. In other words, with what degree of confidence can certain relationships between variables be predicted?

The least predictive of all the models that have been discussed is probably the psychoanalytic model. This is true only because no real criterion for accuracy is defined. In effect, most of the predictions are done on an ex post facto (after the fact) basis. Within Freud's theory, little if any emphasis was placed on manipulation of variables in a true experimental sense, and it is very difficult to conclude exactly what influences in the individual's life are responsible for what kinds of changes. Similarly, the cognitive-developmental model is not highly accurate. It does do a good job of predicting the sequence and content of stages (a global prediction), but it is limited by its lack of operationality in definitions of crucial terms such as scheme or structure. In other words, it is often difficult to predict or evaluate an outcome when the criteria are not clearly operationalized and in some cases are artificial.

On the other hand, both the maturational and behavioral perspectives provide a high degree of accuracy. Gesell's primary focus was on normative behavior, and the large body of norms he assembled has high predictive validity in terms of what behaviors can be expected at what age (as far as biological growth is concerned). The behavioral model also has a high degree of accuracy. Under controlled conditions it can accurately predict certain outcomes. In fact, the behaviorist would say the only reason that all of behavior cannot be predicted is that a sufficiently sensitive technology has not yet been developed to study all the dimensions of development, such as emotion and cognition and the complete consequences of our actions.

Relevancy

Whether a theory is relevant depends on how well the theory represents the data on which it is based. This is a difficult criterion to apply, since it is like a chicken-and-egg problem in trying to determine what comes first, theory or data. As discussed in Chapter 1, the development of a theory is an ongoing process between confirmation (or disconfirmation) of hypotheses and a reevaluation of the theoretical assumptions that generated the hypotheses in the first place.

For example, it is difficult to see how the psychoanalytic model has great relevancy, since it is unclear (given the vague definitions that accompany the model) what variables are of importance. If the hypothesis concerns conflicts that occur during the Oedipal period, they should be tied as logically as possible to the underlying structure of the theory. For psychoanalytic theory, this is often very difficult. The same may be true for the cognitive-developmental model, which dictates that the data collected represent some underlying operation. Some critics of the organismic and psychoanalytic models raise the question of whether it is reasonable to proceed based on the assumption that the data you collect represents the phenomenon you are interested in studying.

The behavioral and maturational models, however, seem to have a degree of relevancy. The foci of both models (and the behaviors of interest) are explicitly defined, in part because the behaviors almost directly represent the theory. For example, Gesell's principle of developmental direction was based on head-to-tail (cephalocaudal) and near-to-far (promimodistal) trends that were seen in all the infants he studied. In the behavioral approach, the behavior is defined in a highly operational way, and those definitions give development an almost one-to-one relationship with behavior.

Fruitfulness

As far as the value of a theory to the overall goal of understanding the developmental process, this may be the most important criterion to apply. When a theory generates new questions for future research, it is a fruitful theory. Another way of saying this is to ask how *heuristic* or generative a theory is.

The least accurate and least relevant theories appear to be the more fruitful. The psychoanalytic theory left a rich legacy of future questions that could be asked about human development, and in part this is due to the complexity of the theory. Often, the more multifaceted the theory, the more potential it has for providing new direction. Many of the popular theories of psychological development that are offered through the press and mass media ("I'm O.K., You're O.K.") are heuristic in the sense that additional questions are generated.

On the other extreme, the maturational view does not seem very fruitful at all. It had widespread influence on child-rearing and parenting practices, but it did not generate many new directions for further study.

Finally, the behavioral and cognitive-developmental and organismic models seem comparatively fruitful. Both have recently been surrounded by a great deal of controversy, especially because they have been applied in educational settings. The social importance and implications of extending these theories into applied settings acts as a catalyst for generating new ideas and future directions. Perhaps these two viewpoints are the most fruitful in their usefulness to applied settings.

Simplicity

The simplicity of a theory is synonymous with how parsimonious that theory is. In other words, how complex must the theory be to explain behavior? For example, the germ theory of disease is quite simple because only one or two postulates were needed to refute the idea of the spontaneous generation of disease.

In contrast, the psychoanalytic model is very cumbersome. It does not make many basic assumptions about human development, but a great deal of detail must accompany these assumptions for the theory to be workable.

The maturational and cognitive-developmental models are somewhat simple but still require more elaboration than the behavioral view to be effective according to this criterion. Although Gesell proposed only five principles, the theory is limited in its applicability. The organismic theory also presents relatively few principles (organization and adaptation) but still includes a detailed group of laws and axioms. It seems that the more content-free a theory is, the more simple it is as well.

At various points throughout this book we have tried to summarize each of the theoretical viewpoints we have presented through a discussion of questions that focus on such areas as heredity and environment, the role of age, and so on. A major portion of Chapter 2 focused on the nature of these differences and why it is important to understand them in order to fully appreciate the different theoretical orientations that have been presented.

A SUMMARY

These questions were first presented in Table 2-1, and are now reproduced in Table 11-1. The purpose of this final section is to help you better understand substantive difference between theories, using these seven questions as a set of guidelines.

Question 1: What is the major force that influences the course of development?

The primary focus of this question is whether genetic or hereditary influences guide development or are those forces located in the environment the primary influences behind developmental change.

As a result of our discussion of different theories of development, it should be clear by now that although there is no "black and white" to the issue of whether heredity or environment "controls" development, there certainly are certain theoretical views that are aligned with one or the other side of this very narrow fence.

For the biologically based views of development such as that offered by Gesell and ethological and sociobiological views, heredity influences seem paramount.

Table 11-1 Important Issues in Development

The Issue	The Question We Ask
The nature of development	What is the major force that influences the course of development?
The process that guides development	What is the underlying process primarily responsible for changes in development?
The importance of age	What roles does age play as a general marker of changes in development?
The rate of development	Are there certain sensitive or critical periods during development, and how are they related to the rate of change?
The shape of development	Is development smooth and continuous or do changes occur in abrupt stages?
Individual differences	How does the theory explain differences in development between individuals of the same chronological age?
How development is studied	What methods are used to study development, and how do they affect the content of the theory?

Even though the "recapitulation" argument made in the early 1900s was disclaimed, the notion of our ancestors contributing a set of genes that controls major dimensions of our behavior has had a profound influence on the formulation of developmental theory.

Yet, for a variety of theorists, especially those with strong behavioral orientations, heredity only contributes the basic building blocks of behavior, to be later acted on and shaped by the environment. To different degrees, behaviorists endorse the importance of the environment, but all attribute a primary role to it as an influence.

Question 2: What is the underlying process responsible for changes in development?

There are two distinct, yet overlapping processes that combine to produce those developmental outcomes that psychologists study. These are the processes of maturation and learning. Although the preceding question focused on what influences development, this question asks about the mechanism or the "how" of development.

The strongest proponent of maturation being a guiding force is Gesell and his maturational theory. The sociobiologists could argue just as strongly, yet the lack of information on humans within a sociobiological context prevents this from happening.

As you might expect, the process of learning is characteristic of and paramount for understanding development as viewed by behavioral approaches such as those offered by Skinner and Bijou and Baer.

What is most interesting about the maturation/learning question is how theorists who fall somewhat between these two "extremes" incorporate some of each into their theoretical formulations. For example, Piaget is often viewed as an "interactionist," that is, a theorist who viewed both the action of the organism and the role of the environment as being important. He did, however, stress that maturational processes set the stage for structural change to take place in the developing child. In Werner's discussion maturation is also a major feature, but the organismic process of adjusting to changes in the environment receives more emphasis.

Question 3: What role does age play as a general marker of changes in development?

If you look back on the discussions that we have had in the last 10 chapters, it seems that the variable of age can assume a pre-eminent position or one of no importance (or even some danger in its use) to none at all.

As to the first extreme, Gesell clearly used age as an organizing variable. What is interesting, however, is that age probably did not take on the "predictive" powers of the "terrible twos" and so forth, until Gesell's work was made popular through its direct application to child-rearing problems. It's difficult to know, but perhaps Gesell himself did not mean for the notion of age to take any kind of causal roles some proponents of this theory would have you believe.

At the other extreme, age becomes relatively unimportant for the cognitive-development and organismic theorists, as well as for the psychoanalytic model. Although each of these approaches does mention the notion of stages, which occur within general age ranges, they occur concurrently with changes in age, and not necessarily as a direct result. The fact that these different stages can occur over a great range of ages helps support this argument.

Finally, there are times where a consideration of age can be a significant distraction, especially from the point of view of certain behaviorists. We might even say that, from the functional analysis perspective, age might confuse the issue of what kind of behaviors occur when, simply because it is an irrelevant factor.

Question 4: Are there certain sensitive or critical periods during development?

Perhaps more than any of the other questions we are posing here, the answer to this one has particularly significant implications for the application of what we know about human development to development itself.

For example, one of the major questions that developmental psychologists often ask is What are the effects of early experience upon later behavior? This becomes particularly important in its application to programs that try to assist developmentally disadvantaged children. Yet the critical question of when such interventions should be offered is very difficult to answer.

From the point of view of those theoretical approaches that emphasize the importance of heredity and biological operations, there may be particular times when the organism is most receptive to factors that can influence development. For example, the absence of one parent might have little impact on a newborn, but a great deal of impact on a three-year-old.

On the other hand, theorists like Bruner believe that any subject can be taught in an ''intellectually'' honest way, to any child at any age, thereby deemphasizing the importance of critical or sensitive periods. Such a viewpoint, also endorsed by many behaviorists, sees the developing organism as being untied to the constraints of nature in terms of potential for change.

Question 5: Is development smooth and continuous, or do changes occur in abrupt stages?

If we were to meet a child when he was one month old, and then see him again at six months, one of our reactions would undoubtedly be, ''What a change!'' If we met a similar child at one month, and observed him every day, we would much less likely be impressed by the degree of change, although both children changed the same amount.

Development also takes place much like the comparison of these two boys. On one hand, it can be very smooth, where changes are barely noticeable. On the other hand, changes can be so abrupt that we can't really see how one level of development relates to the next. In the past, developmental theorists who saw developmental change as being of the smooth kind, where what comes later is more of that which was there before, tended to be more behavioral in their orientation. This is because they believe that the changes that occur are not structural in nature and, hence, not qualitative.

On the other hand, the abrupt quality associated with qualitative change characterizes many psychoanalytic and cognitive-development theorists that we have discussed. The "stage" quality of their approaches lends itself to abrupt transition, and the very nature of the transition often provides the most important and provocative information about development.

Keep in mind, however, that the process of development itself might be discontinuous (or jagged) or continuous (or smooth) in shape because of the way we look at it, and not because of the nature of the phenomenon itself.

Question 6: How does the theory explain differences in development between individuals?

It's almost startling to think that of the 60,000 people in a stadium watching a football game, they all look very different from one another. Their physical appearance is different, but so are their patterns of behavior, their likes and dislikes, and their attitudes.

Most theoretical viewpoints would dismiss the hypothesis that we are born with certain attitudes, beliefs, or abilities. Although this might be a philosophical premise on which certain views are based, it is not a major assumption of any perspective.

To understand individual differences, we mostly focus on past and present histories, as they interact with some biological givens. Perhaps most interesting about this question, is that there is more heredity/environment and maturation/learning overlap than for any of the other questions we have put forth.

Although a behavioral view would no doubt stress the importance of past histories of reinforcement while a psychoanalytic approach would focus on the important young years, both can't ignore the importance of all potential factors as they relate to individual differences. The primary reason for this is that psychologists are still not very good at understanding the degree of correspondence between the cause of a behavior (whether it is the resolution of a conflict or the frequency with which a reinforcer is delivered) and the behavior itself. Even if we view behavior as being independent of any underlying structure, we are still somewhat ambivalent as to what we might call overt behaviors. It's easy enough to recognize hitting a baseball for what it is, but what about more complex interactions between people, or personal feelings?

Individual differences are the essence of what makes the study of behavior so fascinating. Understanding different developmental theories can help us understand these differences. In turn, understanding these differences can give us insight into people's behaviors that will be helpful no matter what course we choose to follow.

SUMMARY POINTS

1. Different theories are rarely comparable to one another, because they are based on such different world views.

2. Most theoretical perspectives posit a mechanism for explaining present as well as predicting future behavior.

3. Theories of development often use different language to describe similar phenomena.

4. No one theory of human development is clearly superior to the others, but each tends to focus on certain select areas of behavior.

5. Theories that stress the process of development are the most inclusive, because they are content-free.

6. The psychoanalytic model is the most consistent of all the models we have examined, because it has wide applicability with little change in underlying assumptions.

7. Theories of development that are accurate, such as the maturational and behavioral perspectives, can help us predict outcomes with a high degree of confidence.

8. The behavioral and maturational models are highly relevant because they represent the data on which the model is based.

9. A theory of development is fruitful when it generates new directions for study, as the psychoanalytic approach does.

10. Theories that are simple, such as the behavioral approach, minimize the number of underlying assumptions.

11. All the models of development that we have discussed can be compared on the set of differences presented in Chapter 2.

References

Achenbach, T. (1978). *Research in developmental psychology: concepts, strategies, methods.* Riverside, N.J.: The Free Press.

Ainsworth, M. (1973). The development of infant-mother attachment. In B. Caldwell and H. Ricciuti (Eds.), *Review of child development research* (Vol. 3). Chicago: University of Chicago Press.

Ainsworth, M. (1979). *Patterns of attachment.* New York: Halsted Press.

Allen, K., Hart, B., Buell, J. S., Harris, F. R., and Wolff, M. M. (1962). Effects of social reinforcement on isolate behavior of a nursery school child. *Child Development, 35,* 511–18.

Ames, L. B., and Ilg, F. L. (1964). Gesell behavior tests as predictive of later grade placement, *Perceptual and Motor Skills, 19,* 719–22.

Anastasi, A. (1958). Heredity, environment, and the question "how?" *Psychological Review, 65,* 197–208.

Applebaum, M., and McCall, R. B. (1983). Design and analysis in developmental psychology. In P. Mussen (Ed.), *Handbook of child psychology.* New York: Wiley.

Ausubel, D., and Sullivan, E. (1970). *Theory and problems of child development.* New York: Grune & Stratton.

Baer, D. (1970). An age-irrelevant concept of development. *Merrill Palmer Quarterly, 16,* 238–45.

Baer, D. (1976). The organism as host. *Human Development, 19,* 87–98.

Baltes, P. B., and Cornelius, S. W. (1977). The status of dialectics in developmental psychology: theoretical orientation versus scientific method. In N. Datan and H. W. Reese (Eds.), *Life span developmental psychology: dialectical perspectives on experimental research.* New York: Academic Press.

Baltes, P. B., and Nesselroade, J. (1974). Adolescent personality development and historical change: 1970–1972. *Society for Research in Child Development Monographs*, serial no. 154, 39, no. 1.

Bandura, A. (1971). Vicarious and self-reinforcement. In R. Glaser (Ed.), *The nature of reinforcement*. New York: Academic Press.

Bandura, A. (1977). *Social learning theory*. Englewood Cliffs, N.J.: Prentice-Hall.

Bandura, A. (1979). *Principles of behavior modification*. New York: Holt, Rinehart, & Winston.

Bandura, A., Ross, D., and Ross, S. (1961). Transmission of aggression through imitation of aggressive models. *Journal of Abnormal and Social Psychology, 65*, 575–82.

Barash, D. P. (1977). *Sociobiology and behavior*. New York: Elsevier.

Beard, R. (1969). *An outline of Piaget's developmental psychology*. New York: Basic Books.

Bettelheim, B. (1977). *The uses of enchantment*. New York: Random House.

Bijou, S. (1968). Ages, stages, and the naturalization of human development. *American Psychologist, 23*, 419–27.

Bijou, S., and Baer, D. (1961). *Child development I: a systematic and empirical theory*. Englewood Cliffs, N.J.: Prentice-Hall.

Bijou, S., and Baer, D. (1976). *Behavior analysis of child development*. Englewood Cliffs, N.J.: Prentice-Hall.

Bloom, B. S. (1964). *Stability and change in human characteristics*. New York: Wiley.

Borke, H. (1975). Piaget's mountain revisited: Changes in the egocentric landscape. *Developmental Psychology, 11*, 24–43.

Bowlby, J. (1958). The nature of the child's tie to his mother. *International Journal of Psycho-Analyses, 39*, 350–73.

Bowlby, J. (1969). *Attachment and loss*, Vol. 1. New York: Basic Books.

Bronfenbrenner, U. (1977). Toward an experimental psychology of human development. *American Psychologist, 32*, 513–31.

Bronfenbrenner, U., and Crouter, A. C. (1982). Work and family through time and space. In S. Kammerman and C. D. Hayes (Eds.), *Families that work*. Washington, D.C.: National Academy Press.

Bronowski, J. (1977). *A sense of the future: essays on natural philosophy*. In P. Ariotti and R. Bronowski (Eds.), Cambridge, Mass.: MIT Press.

Bruner, J. S. (1966). Growth of the mind. *American Psychologist, 21*, 1007–17.

Bruner, J. S., Goodnow, J. J., and Austin, G. A. (1956). *A study of thinking*. New York: Wiley.

Bruner, J. S., and Kennedy, H. (1966). The development of the concepts of order and proportion in children. In J. S. Bruner, R. R. Oliver, and P. M. Greenfield (Eds.), *Studies in cognitive growth*. New York: Wiley.

Byck, R. (1974). *The cocaine papers*. New York: Stonehill Publishing Co.

Carmichael, L. (Ed.). (1954). *Manual of child psychology*. New York: Wiley.

Chess, S., and Thomas, A. (1977). *Annual progress in child psychiatry and child development*. Vol. 10. New York: Brunner-Mazel.

Coghill, G. E. (1929). *Anatomy and the problem of behavior*. New York: Macmillan.

Dalrymple, A. T. (1971). The role of modeling contingencies in the learning of pre-operational concepts by disadvantaged children. *Dissertation Abstracts, 32* (6-B), 3616–17.

Datan, N., and Reese, H. W. (Eds.). (1977). *Life span developmental psychology: dialectical perspectives on experimental research.* New York: Academic Press.

Dennenberg, V. H. (1964). Critical periods, stimulus input and emotional reactivity: a theory of infantile stimulation. *Psychological Review, 71,* 335–51.

Dewey, J. (1899). *The school and society.* Chicago: University of Chicago Press.

Dollard, J., and Miller, N. E. (1950). *Personality and psychotherapy.* New York: McGraw-Hill.

Dusek, J. B., and Flaherty, J. F. (1981). The development of the self-concept during the adolescent years. *Monographs of the Society for Research in Child Development, 4,* serial no. 191.

Eastman, M. (1940). *Marxism: is it science?* New York: Norton.

Elkind, D. (1974). *Children and adolescents.* New York: Oxford University Press.

Erikson, E. (1950a). *Childhood and society.* New York: Norton.

Erikson, E. (1950b). Growth and crises of the healthy personality. In M. Senn (Ed.), *Symposium on the healthy personality.* New York: Josiah Macy, Jr. Foundation, 91–146.

Erikson, E. (1968). *Identity, youth and crisis.* New York: Norton.

Escalona, S. K. (1968). *The roots of individuality.* Chicago: Aldine.

Ferster, C., and Skinner, B. F. (1957). *Schedules of reinforcement.* New York: Appleton-Century-Crofts.

Festinger, L. (1957). *A theory of cognitive dissonance.* Stanford, Cal.: Stanford University Press.

Fisher, S., and Greenberg, R. P. (1977). *The scientific credibility of Freud's theories and therapy.* New York: Basic Books.

Flavell, J. (1963). *The developmental psychology of Jean Piaget.* New York: D. Van Nostrand.

Freud, S. (1933). *New introductory lectures on psychoanalysis.* New York: Norton.

Freud, S. (1955). Beyond the pleasure principle (1920). In J. Strachey (Ed.), *The standard edition of the complete psychological works of Sigmund Freud.* Vol. 18. London: Hogarth, pp. 3–64.

Freud, S. (1957). Character and anal eroticism (1908). In J. Strachey (Ed.), *The standard edition of the complete psychological works of Sigmund Freud.* Vol. 11. London: Hogarth, pp. 21–28.

Freud, S. (1959). Three essays on sexuality (1950). In J. Strachey (Ed.), *The standard edition of the complete psychological works of Sigmund Freud.* Vol. 9. London: Hogarth, pp. 169–75.

Freud, S. (1961). The ego and the id (1923). In J. Strachey (Ed.), *The standard edition of the complete psychological works of Sigmund Freud.* Vol. 19. London: Hogarth, pp. 3–66.

Freud, S. (1964). New introductory lectures on psychoanalysis (1933). In J. Strachey (Ed.), *The standard edition of the complete psychological works of Sigmund Freud.* Vol. 22. London: Hogarth, pp. 3–182.

Gagne, R. (1968). Contributions of learning to human development. *Psychological Review, 75,* 177–91.

Gesell, A. (1928). *Infancy and human growth.* New York: Macmillan.

Gesell, A. (1954). The ontogenesis of infant behavior. In L. Carmichael (Ed.), *Manual of child psychology.* New York: Wiley.

Gesell, A. (1956). *Youth: Years from ten to sixteen.* New York: Harper & Row.

Gesell, A., and Amatruda, C. S. (1947). *Developmental diagnosis: normal and abnormal child development: clinical methods and pediatric evaluations* (2nd ed.) New York: Hoeber.

Gesell, A., Ames, L. B., and Bullis, G. E. (1946). *The child from five to ten.* New York: Harper & Row.

Gesell, A., Ilg, F. L., and Ames, L. B. (1940). *The first five years of life.* New York: Harper & Brothers.

Gesell, A., and Thompson, H. (1929). Learning and growth in identical infant twins: an experimental study of individual differences by the method of co-twin control. *Genetic Psychology Monographs, 6,* 1–124.

Gesell, A., and Thompson, H. (1941). Twins T and C from infancy to adolescence: a biogenetic study of individual differences by the method of co-twin control. *Genetic Psychology Monographs, 24,* 3–121.

Gould, S. J. (1977). *Ever since Darwin.* New York: Norton.

Gould, S. J. (1979). *Transformations.* New York: Simon and Schuster.

Gould, S. J. (1980). *The panda's thumb.* New York: Norton.

Hall, C. (1954). *Primer of Freudian psychology.* New York: Mentor Books.

Havighurst, R. (1952). *Developmental tasks and education.* New York: Longmans, Green & Co.

Hebb, D. O. (1947). The effects of early experience on problem solving at maturity. *American Psychologist, 2,* 306–7.

Hebb, D.O. (1949). *Organization of behavior.* New York: Wiley.

Hess, E. H. and Polt, J. M. (1960). Pupil size as related to interest value of visual stimuli. *Science, 132,* 349–50.

Hook, S. (1957). *Dialectical materialism and scientific method.* Manchester, England: Special supplement to the Bulletin of the Committee on Science and Freedom.

Hunt, J. McV. (1961). *Intelligence and experience.* New York: Ronald Press.

Ilg, F. L., and Ames, L. B. (1955). *Child behavior: from birth to ten.* New York: Harper & Row.

Jones, E. (1953–1957). *The life and work of Sigmund Freud.* 3 vols. New York: Basic Books.

Kagan, J. (1970). The determinants of attention in the infant. *American Scientist,* 89–95.

Kagan, J. (1971). *Continuity and change in infancy.* New York: Wiley.

Kagan, J., and Moss, H. (1962). *Birth to maturity: a study in psychological development.* New York: Wiley.

Kerlinger, F. (1973). *Foundations of behavioral research: educational, psychological, and sociological inquiry.* New York: Holt, Rienhart, & Winston.

Kitchener, R. F. (1978). Epigenesis: The role of biological models in developmental psychology. *Human Development, 21,* 141–60.

Lane, H. (1976). *The wild boy of Aveyron.* Cambridge: Harvard University Press.

Langer, J. (1969). *Theories of development.* New York: Holt, Rinehart, & Winston.

Lennenberg, E. H. (1967). *Biological foundations of language.* New York: Wiley.

Levine, S. (1957). Infantile experience and resistance to physiological stress. *Science, 126*, 405.

Lorenz, K. Z. (1958). The evolution of behavior. *Scientific American, 199*, 67–78.

Lorenz, K. (1965). *Evolution and modification of behavior.* Chicago: University of Chicago Press.

McGraw, M. B. (1935). *Growth: A study of Johnny and Jimmy.* New York: Appleton-Century.

Mallick, S. D., and McCandless, B. R. (1966). A study of catharsis of aggression. *Journal of Personality and Social Psychology, 4*, 591–96.

Maslow, A. (1968). *Toward a psychology of being.* New York: D. Van Nostrand.

Miller, N. (1944). Experimental studies in conflict. In J. M. Hunt (Ed.), *Personality and the behavior disorders.* New York: Ronald Press, pp. 431–65.

Miller, N. (1971). Liberalization of basic S-R concepts: extensions to conflict behavior, motivation and social learning. In N. Miller (Ed.), *Neal E. Miller; selected papers.* Chicago: Aldine & Atherton, p. 314.

Money, J., and Ehrhardt, A. A. (1973). *Man and woman, boy and girl.* Baltimore and London: Johns Hopkins Press.

Montessori, M. (1936). *The secret of childhood.* New York: Longmans & Co.

Munroe, R. (1955). *Schools of psychoanalytic thought.* New York: Holt, Rinehart, & Winston.

Murphy, L., and Moriarty, A. (1976). *Vulnerability, coping and growth: from infancy to adolescence.* New Haven, Conn.: Yale University Press.

Pavlov, I. (1927). *Conditioned reflexes.* London: Oxford University Press.

Piaget, J. (1950a). *Introduction to genetic epistemology.* Paris: University Presses.

Piaget, J. (1950b). *The Psychology of intelligence.* New York: Harcourt, Brace, & Co.

Piaget, J. (1952). *The origins of intelligence in children.* New York: International Universities Press.

Piaget, J. (1957). *Logic and psychology.* New York: Basic Books.

Piaget, J. (1970). *Science and education and the psychology of the child.* New York: Orion.

Piaget, J., and Inhelder, B. (1956). *The child's conception of space.* London: Routledge & Kegan Paul.

Reese, H. W. (1977). Discriminative learning and transfer: dialectical perspectives. In N. Datan and H. W. Reese (Eds.), *Life span developmental psychology: dialectical perspectives on experimental research.* New York: Academic Press.

Reese, H. W. (1982). A comment on the meanings of "dialectics." *Human Development, 25*, 423–29.

Riegel, K. (1976). The dialectics of human development. *American Psychologist, 10*, 689–701.

Riegel, K. (1979). The dialectics of time. In N. Datan and H. W. Reese (Eds.), *Life span developmental psychology: dialectical perspectives on experimental research.* New York: Academic Press, pp. 4–46.

Roeder, K. D. (1963). Ethology and neurophysiology. *Z. Tierpsychol., 20*, 434–40.

Rousseau, J. J. (1979). *Emile.* New York: Basic Books.

Sagan, C. (1977). *The dragons of Eden.* New York: Random House.

Sameroff, A. J. (1965). Early influences on development: fact or fancy? *Merill-Palmer Quarterly, 21*, 267–94.

Schaie, K. W. (1965). A general model for the study of developmental problems. *Psychological Bulletin, 64*, 92–107.

Sears, E. R., Maccoby, E. E., and Levin, H. (1957). *Patterns of child rearing*. Stanford: Stanford University Press.

Senn, M. J. E. (1975). Insights on the child development movement in the United States. *Monographs of the Society for Research in Child Development, 40*, serial no. 161.

Sheehy, G. (1976). *Passages*. New York: Bantam.

Sherrington, C. S. (1906). *The integrative action of the nervous system*. New York: Schribner's.

Sidman, M. (1960). *Tactics of scientific research*. New York: Basic Books.

Skeels, H. (1938). *A study of environmental stimulation: An orphanage preschool project*. The University of Iowa.

Skeels, H., and Dye, H. (1939). A study of the effects of differential stimulation on mentally retarded children. *Proceedings of the American Association on Mental Deficiency, 44*, 114–36.

Skinner, B. F. (1938). *The behavior of organisms: an experimental analysis*. New York: Appleton-Century-Crofts.

Skinner, B. F. (1948, 1976). *Walden two*. New York: Macmillan.

Skinner, B. F. (1957). *Verbal behavior*. New York: Appleton-Century-Crofts.

Skinner, B. F. (1976). *Particulars of my life*. New York: Knopf.

Stevenson, H. (1983). How children learn—the quest for a theory. In P. Mussen (Ed.), *Handbook of Child Psychology*, Vol. 1. New York: Wiley.

Thorndike, E. L. (1898). Animal intelligence: an experimental study of the associative processes in animals. *Psychological Review Monographs Supplement, 2*(8).

Thorndike, E. L. (1903). *Educational psychology*. New York: Lenicke & Buechner.

Waber, D. B. (1976). Sex differences in cognition: a function of maturation rate. *Science, 192*, 572–74.

Wapner, S. (1964). Some aspects of a research program based on an organismic-developmental approach to cognition: experiments and theory. *Journal of the American Academy of Child Psychology, 3*, 193–230.

Wapner, S., and Werner, H. (Eds.), (1957). *Perceptual development*. Worcester, Mass.: Clark University Press.

Watson, J. B. (1925). *Behaviorism*. New York: Norton.

Werner, H. (1948). *Comparative psychology of mental development*. New York: International Universities Press.

Werner, H. (1957). The concept of development from a comparative and organismic point of view. In D. B. Harris (Ed.), *The concept of development*. Minneapolis: University of Minnesota Press, pp. 125–48.

Wilson, E. D. (1975). *Sociobiology*. Cambridge: Harvard University Press.

Witkin, H., Dye, R. B., Faterson, H. F., Goodenough, D. R., and Karp, S. A. (1962). *Psychological differentiation*. New York: Wiley.

Wozniak, R. H. (1975). A dialectical paradigm for psychological research: implications drawn from the history of psychology in the Soviet Union. *Human Development, 18*, 18–34.

Index

Questions   Related to Measuring:

1) When basic needs are not met — What happens to child's development?

2) When schooling is not appropriate dev. for child — Overlay?

3) What motivates child to learn?

4) How does this child learn?
   socially —
   cognitively —
   behaviorly (not mentally) —
   Theory of Learning

5) What happens when children have to grow up fast? Are treated like adults at young age?